Learning Through Life

Inquiry into the Future for Lifelong Learning

Tom Schuller and David Watson

IFLL
Inquiry into the Future
for Lifelong Learning

promoting adult learning

Company registration no. 2603322
Charity registration no. 1002775

NIACE has a broad remit to promote lifelong learning opportunities for adults. NIACE works to develop increased participation in education and training, particularly for those who do not have easy access because of class, gender, age, race, language and culture, learning difficulties or disabilities, or insufficient financial resources.

You can find NIACE online at
www.niace.org.uk

Cataloguing in Publication Data
A CIP record of this title is available from the British Library

Designed and typeset by Creative by Design

Cover design by Book Production Services

Printed and bound in the UK by Page Bros (Norwich) Limited

ISBN: 978 1 86201 433 6

The authors

Tom Schuller is Director of the Inquiry into the Future for Lifelong Learning in the UK. From 2003–2008 he was Head of the Centre for Educational Research and Innovation (CERI) at OECD, the international thinktank based in Paris. Dean of the Faculty of Continuing Education and Professor of Lifelong Learning at Birkbeck, University of London from 1999 to 2003, he was also Co-Director of the Centre for Research on the Wider Benefits of Learning. Previous positions were at the Universities of Edinburgh, Glasgow and Warwick, at the Institute for Community Studies in London, and for four years at OECD in the 1970s. His most recent books are *Understanding the Social Outcomes of Learning* (with Richard Desjardins, 2007) and *The Benefits of Learning* (with John Preston *et al,* 2004). He chairs the Governing Board of the Working Men's College in London.

David Watson is an historian and Professor of Higher Education Management at the Institute of Education, University of London, and chairs the Inquiry into the Future for Lifelong Learning. He was Vice-Chancellor of the University of Brighton between 1990 and 2005. He has contributed widely to developments in UK education. He was a member of the Paul Hamlyn Foundation's National Commission on Education and the National Committee of Inquiry into Higher Education chaired by Sir Ron Dearing. He was the elected chair of the Universities Association for Continuing Education between 1994 and 1998, and chaired the Longer Term Strategy Group of Universities UK between 1999 and 2005. He is a Trustee of the Nuffield Foundation, a Companion of the Institute of Management and a National Teaching Fellow (2008). His most recent books are *Managing Civic and Community Engagement* (2007), *The Dearing Report: Ten Years On* (2007), and *The Question of Morale: Managing Happiness and Unhappiness in University Life* (2009). He was knighted in 1998 for services to higher education.

Contents

List of tables and figures

Tables

Figures

The following material is included by permission of the publishers:

Tables 1, 3, 5, 8; Figs 8, 9, 15, 16, 17, 20. Crown copyright material is reproduced with the permission of the Controller of HMSO and the Queen's Printer for Scotland.

Table 13. National Skills Forum: Mind the Gap (2008) and Fletcher M. (2008) *Funding Adult Learners in FE and HE*, National Skills Forum

Table 14. UK Online Centres, 2009

Table 15. Copyright: The Data Service, 2008

Fig 2. OECD (2008), *Highlights from Education at a Glance 2008*, p. 25, www.oecd.org/edu/eag2008

Fig 3. Copyright: The Equality Trust, published in Wilkinson, R. and Pickett, K. (2009) *The Spirit Level: Why More Equal Societies Almost Always Do Better*. London: Penguin

Figs 4, 5. Boateng, S.K. (2009) *Population and social conditions (Eurostat Statistics in Focus 44.2009)*. Copyright: European Communities, 1995–2009

Fig 6. Copyright: The Learning and Skills Council

Fig 12. UK Government Actuary's Department

Fig 13. Furlong, A., Cartmel, F., Biggart, A., Sweeting, H. and West, P. (2003) *Youth transitions: Patterns of vulnerability and processes of social inclusion*, Scottish Executive, Edinburgh

Fig 14. Oswald, A. and Powdthavee, N. (authors' calculations using the British Household Panel Study)

List of acronyms and abbreviations

ALP	Association of Learning Providers
AoC	Association of Colleges
BIS	Business, Innovation and Skills (Department for)
CIF	Congé individuel formation
CIPD	Chartered Institute for Personnel Development
CLI	Composite Learning Index
DBMLWG	Digital Britain Media Literacy Working Group
DCMS	Department for Culture, Media and Sport
DIF	Droit individuel à la formation
DIUS	Department for Innovation, Universities and Skills
DWP	Department for Work and Pensions
EAL	EMTA Awards Ltd
ELC	Enhanced Learning Credit
ELLI	European Lifelong Learning Index
EMA	Education Maintenance Allowance
EPPE	Effective provision of pre-school education
ESOL	English for Speakers of Other Languages
EU	European Union
FAB	Federation of Awarding Bodies
FE	Further education
FSA	Financial Services Authority
GCS	Graduate Contribution Scheme
HE	Higher education
HEPI	Higher Education Policy Institute
IfL	Institute for Learning
IFLL	Inquiry into the Future for Lifelong Learning
IiP	Investors in People
ILA	Individual Learning Account
ILO	International Labour Organisation
JCQ	Joint Council for Qualifications
LEIA	Lift and Escalator Industry Association
LLE	Local Learning Exchange
LLUK	Lifelong Learning UK
LSC	Learning and Skills Council
LSIS	Learning and Skills Improvement Service
NALS	National Adult Learning Survey
NES	National Employer Service
NESS	National Employer Skills Survey
NUS	National Union of Students
OECD	Organisation for Economic Cooperation and Development
ONS	Office for National Statistics
OU	Open University
PEL	Paid educational leave
PIAAC	Programme of International Assessment on Adult Competences
PSA	Public Service Agreement
QCA	Qualifications and Curriculum Authority
QCF	Qualifications and Credit Framework
SLC	Student Loan Company
SLC	Standard Learning Credit
SME	Small and medium-sized enterprises
TASSC	The Alliance of Sector Skills Councils
U3A	University of the Third Age
UKCES	UK Commission for Employment and Skills
ULR	Union learning representative
VCS	Voluntary and Community Sector
WEA	Workers' Educational Association
WI	Women's Institute

Foreword

Roger was a highly successful tunneller working on the then new Victoria Line, making a good living, in the prime of his life. A serious accident to the man working next to him, who broke his back in a rock fall, led Roger to re-appraise his circumstances. He recognised that his ability to provide for his family relied entirely on his physical health, since poor reading skills had left him with little formal education. As a result, he signed on to the first adult literacy programme offered at Brighton's Friends Centre where I was working. He followed this with full-time literacy study, followed by the City Lit's Fresh Horizons access programme, and higher education study. After a period as a qualified social worker, Roger became landlord for accommodation for single homeless people. Adult learning opportunities played a key role in Roger's life – helping him negotiate career change. By contrast, Mary, a 94-year-old woman who buttonholed me recently to protest at the end of public subsidy for the art class she had attended for the last decade, saw learning as a key mechanism for social engagement, and a continuing challenge. 'It's not a matter of learning a skill and moving on', she explained to me. 'It keeps me going. The challenges are fresh every day, whether you are 19 or 95'. Adults use learning for very different reasons – as a step to secure or change work, but also to sustain and improve their quality of life.

Public policy affecting learning through the life course has been on something of a roller coaster over the last 15 years. In 2007, the National Institute of Adult Continuing Education (NIACE) recognised that in addition to its day-to-day work in responding to changes affecting opportunities for adult learning, there was a need for a clear-eyed and authoritative view on the components of a medium-term strategy for lifelong learning. The Board of NIACE persuaded Sir David Watson, professor of higher education policy at the Institute of Education, and former vice-chancellor of the University of Brighton, to chair an independent inquiry, alongside a team of ten other commissioners. We recruited Tom Schuller, then head of the Centre for Educational Research and Innovation at the OECD, to direct the Inquiry into the Future for Lifelong Learning (IFLL), which the Board agreed to fund from NIACE's reserves with a budget of £1 million.

The task facing the Inquiry was daunting – in order to advise on a strategy for lifelong learning for the next ten or 15 years, the Inquiry needed to explore demographic change and the impact of migration; changes in technology and their impact on how we work and learn at work; the way information and communication technologies are changing our lives; how learning can contribute to a revitalised and active citizenship; how learning can contribute to health and well-being; the role of learning in reducing offending behaviour; and, not least, how it should be paid for.

The result of the work is this main report, together with over 30 other publications on detailed aspects of the system. The work drew on extensive consultation with people in and beyond the field of adult learning. It is no small achievement that the authors have produced such a powerful, lucid and persuasive account of the complex and untidy territory, and I am delighted to welcome *Learning Through Life*. It is more than we could have hoped for.

Just how NIACE arrived at the decision to sponsor an independent inquiry is worth some attention. In the 1990s, throughout the European area there was a shared dynamic for thinking afresh about adult learning, leading to the adoption of the Lisbon strategy by the Council of Ministers in 2000. UNESCO engaged in a parallel development, leading to the Delors report, *The Treasure Within*, with its elegant capture of the four pillars of lifelong learning – learning to know, learning to do, learning to live together, and learning to be. NIACE was active in supporting both processes.[1] The optimism of the era was captured in the fifth world conference on the education of adults, CONFINTEA V, in 1997. However, since the millennium, European initiatives in lifelong learning have focused more and more on learning at and for work, whilst in the wider global context adult learning is not explicitly reflected in the Millennium Development Goals.

Developments in the UK, but especially in England, have been even bumpier. The enthusiasm for lifelong learning as a tool for economic development and social inclusion emerged in the later years of the last Conservative government, and were given a major stimulus by David Blunkett's vision in the Green Paper, *The Learning Age*,[2] and by the legislative changes that flowed from it. For a while, it seemed that a thousand flowers bloomed, with initiatives appearing in quick succession in neighbourhood renewal, union learning, online and distance education, to name just three. There was a *Skills for Life* Strategy, and an Adult and Community Learning Fund. From 2003, however, with the first government Skills Strategy, and especially following the Treasury-commissioned Leitch report,[3] resources shifted sharply from courses open to all and offered mainly in public institutions towards provision secured through employers, at or for workplace learning, and providing

---

[1] International Commission on Education for the Twenty-first Century (1996).
[2] Department for Education and Employment (DfEE) (1998).
[3] Leitch Review of Skills (2006).

opportunities to train and certificate the adult workforce. Again, NIACE played an active role, as a critical friend of government, in responding to these changes.

There was widespread agreement that for a lifelong learning society everyone needed to invest more: government, employers and individuals alike. But at the same time there was a recognition that for many adults whose experiences of initial education were negative, fees were often just one more barrier to taking the step to seek a second chance. From the work of the Wider Benefits of Learning research centre at the Institute of Education, University of London, it was clear that there were quantifiable, if sometimes modest, benefits to better health, crime reduction, and other social policy goals, from engagement in adult learning. Adult learning has a set of clear and measurable outcomes, relating to the acquisition of knowledge and skills, but also acts as a catalyst in securing improved mental health, and an active and engaged civic society. It has an impact on our tolerance of difference; it makes us more likely to volunteer. But what weight should be given to these catalytic effects, and who should pay for the provision that secures them? These and other thorny questions were examined in the Big Conversation, a wide-ranging set of discussions hosted by NIACE through 2006, involving policy-makers, practitioners and civil society agencies in education and the broader social policy area. The discussions took place at a time when the number of adults engaged in publicly funded adult learning opportunities had dropped sharply, and many of its conclusions addressed the concerns of people who had lost, or were at risk of losing, their classes. However, a key recommendation made by the participants was for a strategy for lifelong learning that looked beyond the arguments of the moment. My colleagues and I took their proposal to the Board of NIACE, who agreed that there was a need to re-examine the vision articulated in *The Learning Age* in the changing circumstances facing Britain. As a result, the Inquiry was established.

Its work began in the late stages of the economic boom, and is being completed in the middle of the sharpest recession we have seen for 30 years. Inevitably, the changed economic climate has thrown into relief quite different questions about the social and economic dimensions of lifelong learning, about priorities for public investment, and about what it is possible to do through publicly and privately secured education and training.

In my view *Learning Through Life* more than meets the challenges put to the Inquiry. In particular, its radical reworking of the learning lifespan, divided into four stages, provides a powerful tool for exploring the different balance of need and benefit at different stages in life, and helps make clear that responsibility for lifelong learning stretches far beyond the remit of a single government department. I think, too, that the work reported here on the total investment made in lifelong learning by public, private and individual sources provides the groundwork for future discussions on how investment should be shared at different stages in life.

The report provides an inspiring vision and practical steps towards its achievement. NIACE is grateful for all the work undertaken by Sir David and his fellow commissioners, and Tom Schuller and his team of researchers. The report is, of course, the independent view of the commissioners, but NIACE will be happy to help secure debate on its findings, to work towards their adoption and implementation, and as a platform for future research and advocacy, in our pursuit of a society where the chance to learn throughout life is taken for granted as a universal right.

Alan Tuckett, OBE
Chief Executive, NIACE

Preface: the process of Inquiry

The independent Inquiry into the Future for Lifelong Learning was set up in 2007, sponsored by the National Institute of Adult Continuing Education (NIACE). The Inquiry's terms of reference are to offer an **authoritative and coherent strategic framework for lifelong learning in the UK**. This involves:

- articulating a broad rationale for public and private investment in lifelong learning;
- a re-appraisal of the social and cultural value attached to it by policy-makers and the public; and
- developing new perspectives on policy and practice.

The time horizon for the Inquiry is 10–15 years – a deliberate attempt to lengthen the usual timeframe. Although we provide an analysis of the major gaps in the current system, we refrain from critiquing specific current policy, except in cases where it has a particular consequence for longer-term systemic thinking.

In the middle of the Inquiry came the credit crunch and the recession. The implications of this for the Inquiry's work have been threefold. First, there has been a tension between maintaining a longer-term horizon and yet not ignoring these events as if we assumed there would sooner or later be a reversion to the status quo ante. Secondly, the economic crisis, and the huge increase in government debt, has set obvious constraints on what it is realistic to propose. It confirmed what had already been the Inquiry's position in respect of public spending, namely that we were not setting out to make a case for massive increases in public spending, but to maintain a focus on the strategic framework. Thirdly, though, the recession has paradoxically done much to open up thinking about future possibilities, and to allow broader options – we think notably of future mixes of learning time and paid and unpaid work.

The Inquiry covers the UK, with its four constituent nations. We have gathered evidence from across the UK, and held seminars in Wales, Scotland and Northern Ireland, with very different points of focus. We have attempted to cover the variations, and in particular to signal where one or more nations have distinctive policies which are worth noting for the future.

The constituent elements of the Inquiry's work have been as follows.

Themes

The core of the Inquiry's work has been a set of nine themes:

- Prosperity, Employment and Work;
- Demography and Social Structure;
- Well-being and Happiness;
- Migration and Communities;
- Technological Change;
- Poverty Reduction;
- Citizenship and Belonging;
- Crime and Social Exclusion; and
- Sustainable Development.

The list indicates the breadth and ambition of the Inquiry. For each theme, a Call for Evidence was issued. This resulted in over 250 submissions, from a wide range of sources: researchers, professionals in the field and individuals. A day-long seminar was organised around each theme, with a set of papers from different experts. In each case, the results of the seminar have been brought together with the evidence submitted and synthesised into a Thematic Paper, written by a member of the Inquiry Secretariat or a Commissioner, and circulated to a reference group for critique and comment. The Thematic Papers are published; they are available electronically and in hard copy. The key conclusions from the Thematic Papers have been selectively woven into this report. However, there is too full a set for them all to be included here, so readers are encouraged to go to the individual papers for further detail.

Context: participation, expenditure and equality

A second strand of the Inquiry's work has been the gathering of a comprehensive set of information on who takes part in lifelong learning, with trend data over the last decade; and of how much is spent, from public, private, third sector and individual sources. It covers a range of government departments. It includes a detailed examination of spending by employers in and beyond the workplace, and by voluntary organisations and individuals. This presents what is, in our understanding, a uniquely broad picture of lifelong learning across the board. It makes an original contribution to how we might strengthen our knowledge base in respect of the different categories of lifelong learning. An overview of these analyses is given in *Chapter 4*.

This work is complemented by a legal analysis of age discrimination and education in the light of the recent Equality Bill (introduced in April 2009) which informs our proposals for greater intergenerational equity in *Chapter 5*.

Sectoral reflections

The breadth of the Inquiry includes the full range of provision of learning opportunities. This runs from early childhood through schools to further and higher education, including the role of local authorities. It extends beyond the formal system; and it covers private training providers. We commissioned a set of reflections on the implications for each sector of a move to a more systematic approach to lifelong learning. The authors of these papers were given a free rein to think about the possible implications. We ran a set of seminars to consider their reflections, and help them to revise their initial drafts.

Public value

A fourth strand of work deals with the links between lifelong learning and areas of social concern, in order to explore how we can best estimate the public value of lifelong learning. These include analyses of the areas of crime, poverty, health and well-being. The public value strand of the work overlaps with the thematic work; the specific aim in this strand is to illustrate different approaches to valuing the social outcomes of learning.

Learning infrastructures

An initial round of consultations revealed a strong concern that the notion of 'infrastructure' was being interpreted too narrowly. Too often, infrastructure is equated with buildings. To broaden the debate, we needed to link the physical environment with the virtual, i.e. with technological developments which enable learning independent of place, and with the skills needed to make best use of both types of environment. The project to explore this was designed to include two rounds of electronic discussion, with around 170 people drawn from a range of different professional backgrounds. The results have been processed into a set of key signals and scenarios.

Learner involvement

We have involved learners in our consultations. A selection of evidence received from learners at an early stage of the Inquiry is available from the Inquiry website.

We ran three seminars for learners on the draft conclusions, and extended the consultation via a questionnaire to NIACE's Learners Network.

This outline indicates the range of the work on which this report draws. We want to emphasise not only the breadth but the process of the Inquiry. The process is not over. This report is the 'main report' from the Inquiry, but it is nested in a whole range of other publications, listed in full in *Annexe C*. Other publications are still in the pipeline, and we are already planning a review of the debate that should follow this, which we shall publish in spring 2010. In short, the Inquiry is launching what should be a rolling debate on the future for lifelong learning; we aim only to have provided a secure but springy platform for it.

All of the Inquiry's supplementary papers are available to download from the Inquiry website (www.lifelonglearninginquiry.org.uk).

Acknowledgements

Our first debt is to the Inquiry's Commissioners: John Field, Bob Fryer, Leisha Fullick, Helen Gilchrist, Clare Hannah, Teresa Rees, David Sherlock, Nick Stuart and Tom Wilson.[4]

The Commissioners have given very generously of their time. They met on ten occasions between September 2007 and June 2009, including one 24-hour residential meeting. In between these meetings they have responded repeatedly to our requests for thoughts and comments, and to chair or participate in the Inquiry seminars. This report represents a distillation of the discussions at these meetings and of numerous iterations with the Commissioners individually and collectively. We are very grateful to them for their time, expertise and unfailing good humour. The Commissioners have all approved the shape and the recommendations of this report, but the final text has been our responsibility as Chair and Director of the Inquiry.

The Inquiry has been underpinned by evidence from existing research, as well as evidence from professional practitioners. We have benefited from the experience of very many people in different fields, from policy-makers to field-workers. Without this enormous spread of contributors, we would not have been able to attempt the coverage we have. We are grateful to all those who contributed, as individuals or organisations. We are particularly grateful for the support provided by Professors Andrew Pollard and Miriam David, Director and Associate Director of the ESRC's Teaching and Learning Research Programme (TLRP).

---

[4] See *Annexe B* for details of the Commissioners. Murziline Parchment was a Commissioner until June 2008.

We have been helped by many NIACE staff, too many to list here. Despite the independence of the Inquiry from its sponsor, we drew heavily on their expertise, time and patience during a period when the organisation was going through particular change, and invariably received a positive response to requests for help.

Useful comments on successive drafts of particular chapters have been supplied by a number of other individuals: Jarl Bengtsson, Natalie Champion, Claire Callender, Tom Cook, Kate Gavron, Fay Lomax Cook, Mel Muchnik, Andrew Sich, Lindsey Simpson, Mark Spilsbury, Carole Stott and Michel Thery. We should also like to acknowledge the authors of the many IFLL papers referred to above (see *Annexe C*), and the reference groups who commented on them. These have provided a rich source of ideas and information for us.

Jim Gallagher, Richard Spear and Paul Nolan read the draft and identified for us many points where we had not sufficiently taken into account the specific features of lifelong learning in Scotland, Wales and Northern Ireland. We thank them, and absolve them of any responsibility if we have not nuanced the discussion sufficiently.

The Inquiry Secretariat consisted of the following: Fiona Aldridge, Hanya Gordon, Emily Jones, Stephen McNair, Helen Plant, and Jenny Williams. They worked throughout as an excellent team, juggling the Inquiry's various activities enthusiastically and skilfully, fuelled at team meetings by large quantities of bonbons and unacceptably strong coffee. Fiona, Stephen and Jenny contributed very significantly to the quality of this report, both with substantive inputs and with careful reading of repeated drafts. We owe a particular debt to them. Jenny has been a superb project manager for the Inquiry as a whole. Sarah Bennett was an excellent copy-editor, under considerable pressure.

We conclude by thanking the NIACE Board, and Alan Tuckett as NIACE's Chief Executive, for having the vision and the courage to invest so heavily in this Inquiry. It represents a major commitment of scarce resources. We are grateful to the Board and its Chair, Nick Stuart, for their sustained support, and to Alan for his unflagging enthusiasm and persistence. We learnt much from them.

Summary of principal recommendations

Our vision is of a society in which learning plays its full role in personal growth and emancipation, prosperity, solidarity and global responsibility. We believe that learning is intimately connected with the achievement of freedom of choice, control over individual and group destinies, health and well-being, cultural identity and democratic tolerance. As a consequence, we begin from the premise that the *right to learn throughout life is a human right*.

1. Basing lifelong learning policy on a new four-stage model

The United Kingdom's current approach to lifelong learning is not responding adequately to two major trends: an ageing society and changing patterns of paid and unpaid activity.

a) A genuinely lifelong view means that a *four-stage model* – up to 25, 25–50, 50–75, 75+ – should be used as the basis for a *coherent systemic approach to lifelong learning*.

b) People in the first stage (up to 25, but starting for our purposes at 18) should be looked at as a whole, with all of its members having claims to *learning and development as young people*.

c) Learning in the second stage (25–50) should aim at sustaining productivity and prosperity, but also at building strong family lives and personal identity. This is part of a *new mosaic of time* with different mixes of paid and unpaid work and learning time.

d) For those in the third stage (those aged between 50 and 75), *training and education opportunities* should be greatly enhanced. We should recognise the desire of most people in this phase to remain active and engaged. Policy, including learning policy, should treat 75 as the normal upper age limit for economic activity (not linked to state pension age).

e) The emergence of the fourth stage (those aged 75 and over) means that we urgently need to develop a more appropriate approach to the *curriculum offer in later life*.

f) 25, 50 and 75 should be identified and used as *key transition points*, each requiring access to advice and guidance about life planning.

2. Rebalancing resources fairly and sensibly across the life course

Public and private resources invested in lifelong learning amount to over £50 billion; their distribution should relate to our changing economic and social context.

a) We need public agreement on the *criteria for fair and effective allocation of resources for learning across the life course.*

b) As a start, we propose a very broad goal: to shift from the current allocated ratios of *86: 11: 2.5: 0.5* across the four stages to *80: 15: 4: 1* by 2020, approximately doubling the proportional support for learning in the third and fourth stages.

c) As a counter to any sense that we favour age segregation, we recommend sustained efforts to support *family and intergenerational learning.*

3. Building a set of learning entitlements

A clear framework of entitlements to learning will be a key factor in strengthening choice and motivation to learn.

We need a clear overall framework of entitlements, with two key categories: *general entitlements* and *specific 'transition' entitlements.*

a) *General entitlements*
   - A *legal* entitlement of free access for all who need it to learning to acquire basic skills, i.e. literacy and numeracy, up to Level 1.
   - A *financial* entitlement to a minimum level of qualification needed to be able to play a full contributing part in society; this is currently Level 2, but will rise and change over time.
   - Both these entitlements should extend to all, regardless of age.
   - A *'good practice'* entitlement to learning leave as an occupational benefit to be developed flexibly and over time as part of mainstream employment conditions.

b) *Specific 'transition' entitlements*
   These should be designed to help people use learning to make potentially difficult transitions; for example, guaranteeing access to learning for those leaving prison or institutional care, moving between areas or countries, or becoming 50. The transition entitlements can be developed flexibly over time.

c) These entitlements should be *underpinned by infrastructure guarantees*: to universal access to advice and guidance (currently being developed in the adult advancement and careers service), and to a minimal level of digital technology (currently broadband at 2Mbps, but this will rise and change).

d) Funding of entitlements should be channelled through a *national system of Learning Accounts*, giving individuals the maximum control over how they are used. The Learning Accounts should be set up by the State for people reaching their twenty-fifth birthday. Fifty per cent of the public contribution to the Child Trust Fund should be allocated to this.

4. Engineering flexibility: a system of credit and encouraging part-timers

Faster progress is needed to implement a credit-based system, and to support people to combine study with other activities.

a) We should *move quickly to implement fully a coherent system of credits* as the basis for organising post-compulsory learning.
b) The *funding for learning (both fees and student support) should be credit-based* and should not discriminate against part-time provision or part-time students.
c) There should be *greater fairness and consistency in funding for further and higher education*.

5. Improving the quality of work

The debate on skills has been too dominated by an emphasis on increasing the volume of skills. There should be a stronger focus on how skills are actually used.

a) We need *increased understanding of the kinds of work environment which encourage formal and informal learning* as a means of raising performance and productivity.
b) There should be *a clearer set of standards for gauging employer engagement with learning*. Claims to corporation tax relief for training should be linked to these standards.
c) There should be *greater transparency in training performance and expenditure*. Data on training performance and expenditure, including on learning leave, should be published in organisations' annual accounts.
d) *Licence to practice* requirements should be used more widely to promote the raising of the level and use of skills.
e) *Procurement policy should be used* to drive up levels of training along the supply chain.

6. Constructing a framework for a citizens' curriculum

A common framework should be created of learning opportunities, aimed at enhancing people's control over their own lives.

a) An agreed *framework for a citizens' curriculum* should be developed, built initially around a set of four capabilities: digital, health, financial and civic, together with employability.

b) In every area there should be a *minimum local offer* which guarantees access to the citizens' curriculum, locally interpreted to meet diverse needs.

7. Broadening and strengthening the capacity of the lifelong learning workforce

Stronger support should be available for *all* those involved in delivering education and training.

a) There should be *a broad definition of who makes up the lifelong learning workforce*, including school teachers and early years practitioners, and learning support staff.

b) The work of *union learning representatives and community learning champions* should be further promoted and supported.

c) Other people who play, or could play, roles as learning 'intermediaries' in 'non-educational' fields such as health, probation or citizens advice should be identified and supported.

8. Reviving local responsibility…

The current system in England has become over-centralised, and insufficiently linked to local and regional needs. We should restore life and power to local levels.

a) *Local authorities*, as the key democratic agencies responsible for the welfare of local communities, should lead the development of lifelong learning strategy at local level. They should develop the local infrastructure, including links to non-educational services such as health.

b) *FE colleges* should be seen as an institutional backbone for local lifelong learning, with a *predominantly local focus*.

c) *Local strategies should embrace cultural institutions* – including voluntary organisations, libraries, museums, theatres and galleries.

d) *Local employer networks should be promoted* as part of strengthening a culture of learning in and out of work.

e) The idea of *Local Learning Exchanges (LLEs)* should be developed to connect people as socially networked learners, and to provide spaces for local groups to engage in learning.

f) *Higher education institutions* should commit themselves to joining in local strategies for lifelong learning; and to disseminating their research knowledge to the community.

9. ...within national frameworks

There should be effective machinery for creating a coherent national strategy across the UK, and within the UK's four nations.

a) *A single department should have the lead responsibility for promoting lifelong learning*, with cross-government targets for lifelong learning.

b) There should be a *cross-departmental expenditure study* as part of the next Comprehensive Spending Review, identifying cost efficiencies from a coordinated approach to lifelong learning.

c) An *authoritative body should be established to oversee and scrutinise* the national system of lifelong learning, with suitable arrangements in the devolved administrations.

10. Making the system intelligent

The system will only flourish with consistent information and evaluation, and open debate about the implications.

a) A three-yearly *State of Learning* report should be published, covering major trends and issues, including evidence collected by and submitted to international bodies.

b) Routine use should be made of *external comparators*, including a benchmark group of countries, with a one-off OECD review of the UK's lifelong learning strategy.

c) We need stronger and broader *analysis of the benefits and costs* of lifelong learning over time, and systematic experimentation on what works.

d) There should be regular use of *peer review and of inspections*, and of 'learner voices'.

'This report sets out a *framework of opportunity*, structured around investment, incentives and capabilities. Our goal is to set an agenda for lifelong learning that will make sense for the next quarter-century.'

'If we were to sum up the goals of lifelong learning in a single phrase, it would be that it should enable people to take control of their lives.'

1 Opening up to learning
Our vision and values

Learning: a fundamental human attribute

Learning is arguably what humans do best. We are writing this report in the anniversary year of Charles Darwin's birth. His genius was to show how our evolving brains enabled us to advance in leaps and bounds, exploring, innovating and reflecting. Using tools and inventing abstractions, the human race has pressed forward at an extraordinary rate.

Individuals cannot survive without learning, nor can societies. Not all the learning is good. There are many habits and practices which are repeatedly learned – even systematically taught – that are unpleasant or even evil. But without learning in almost all its diversity we would literally not be human.

Yet we do not organise our learning as well as we might. In fact, in many respects the way we organise our learning reflects unfavourably on our collective intelligence. This is especially true of organised education and training: the formal types of learning as distinct from the incidental learning which just happens as part of day-to-day life. We do not think effectively about how we might improve how we learn: the systems, the institutions and environments within which learning and teaching take place. Not only do we not use our knowledge, we neglect that other fundamental human attribute, imagination, so that there is too little thinking about how things might be done otherwise. Of course, our system produces some excellent results; inspiring stories of path-breaking achievements at the highest level, and impressive accounts at all levels of progress against the odds. But the system as such continues to look like an adolescent crammed gawkily into an inappropriate school uniform: bits sticking out all over the place, a body full of potential but not knowing quite how to move coherently. Mature it is not.

We shouldn't press this analogy too far, so let's switch to another to illuminate the fundamental imbalance of our current system. Consider if the health service catered only for the needs of the elderly (since they suffer most from ill-health) and other types of service were designed primarily to prevent too painful or dependent an old age. The preventive provision might be very good, so younger people would not be totally ignored, but we would think it a strangely skewed health system if it subordinated to a large extent the needs of younger age groups to those at the end of their lives. Yet this is, broadly, a mirror image of how we organise our education and training, concentrating hugely on the initial phase and neglecting the subsequent ones.

The vision we set out is of a system that has recognisably evolved from the current one, but which is significantly different. We argue for incremental change, not a redesign from scratch. But here is where our adolescent analogy partly breaks down: the system will not evolve of its own accord – at least not effectively. It needs some strong pushes to help it on its way.

The Inquiry's vision

We recognise that learning is a complex and sometimes paradoxical phenomenon. Some of it takes place in institutional settings: in schools of all levels and types; in colleges and universities; in places of worship; in clubs and societies. A lot of it does not; for example, the workplace is both a significant site for learning, and a platform for learning elsewhere.

Sometimes learning has to be collective; sometimes it is profoundly individual. 'Personalisation' (framing the educational experience so that it is just right and just in time for the individual learner) can work well, but there is a danger of suppressing the shared understanding that comes from learning together.

Some learning requires formal recognition (as in accreditation) before it is of value; other learning will remain not only personal but also private.

Often learning is joyful; sometimes it requires pain, and especially endurance. You sometimes have to frighten yourself into learning what it is you have to learn.

Above all, learning is about an attitude of mind, a propensity, or a curiosity. Learning isn't just about subject knowledge; nor is it just about practical skills. It is also about developing the judgement needed to put these two together. Many people refer to this as 'learning how to learn'.

A final paradox: some learning is instrumental or routine; other learning is liberating or transformative. We learn to earn, but we also learn to live.

Our vision is of a society in which learning plays its full role in personal growth and emancipation, prosperity, solidarity and global responsibility. We believe that it is intimately connected with the achievement of freedom of choice, health and well-being, dignity, cultural identity and democratic tolerance. As a consequence, we begin from the premise that the right to learn throughout life is a human right.

We know that learning alone cannot bring about these personal and social goods. They depend also on social justice and the absence of poverty, principles in both personal and social life, and security. However, we see a further role for learning in supporting such aspects of a modern, inclusive, self-critical and harmonious society. We believe in the possibilities of learning *through* life, in both senses of the word.

The Inquiry's task has been to formulate a robust, longer-term strategy on how to move towards the achievement of this vision. What are the problems that we have to work together to solve in order to have a genuinely *learning society*; in which learning is natural as well as functional; is a source of personal and collective satisfaction, as well as of productivity and prosperity; and is self-motivated and voluntary rather than simply prescribed or even punitive?

What we have not done is to propose a rigid blueprint. Our instincts are against compulsion and fixed formulae. Above all, we do not want learning to be used as a weapon to impose uniformity, or a narrow view of individual, social or economic development. In so far as this report sets out a framework, it is a *framework of opportunity*, structured around investment, incentives and capabilities. Our goal is to set an agenda for lifelong learning that will make sense for the next quarter-century.

'Lifelong learning': its range

Lifelong learning has a range of meanings. As a term it generates a surprising amount of confusion and blank looks – which is surprising, since 'learning' is a common word and 'lifelong' is fairly self-explanatory. It is an untidy field, which is hard to delimit and define neatly without doing injustice to the reality of how people learn.

Any definition of lifelong learning is problematic. A contributor to *Wikipedia* captures the spirit rather well: 'Lifelong learning is the concept that "it's never too soon or too late for learning"'. We use the term literally, but with particular emphases that we need to make clear. Throughout the Inquiry we have used an interpretation which balances breadth with manageability.

By 'lifelong' in this report we mean from cradle to grave, and the Inquiry's thinking has included the implications for early childhood education and for schooling. However, our primary focus is on adult learning, and on adults returning to learn. The learning can occur in educational or training institutions, the workplace (on or off the job), the family, or cultural and community settings. We use 'learning' to refer to all forms of organised education and training (whether or not they carry certification); but we also include informal modes of learning to some extent, provided these have a degree of organisation and intention. Therefore, our broad definition is:

> Lifelong learning includes people of all ages learning in a variety of contexts – in educational institutions, at work, at home and through leisure activities. It focuses mainly on adults returning to organised learning rather than on the initial period of education or on incidental learning.[1]

Bearing these nuances in mind, we switch throughout this report between the terms 'education', 'training', 'learning' and 'lifelong learning'. They are not interchangeable, but we select them as appropriate to the context, recognising that this is sometimes inevitably a little arbitrary.

One further definitional note… We are concerned here with developing a *strategic framework* for lifelong learning. So sometimes we refer to learning as an *activity*, and sometimes as a *system*. Again, this should be clear from the context.

'Lifelong learning': its values

A lifelong learning system has values, whether we like it or not. The values are not just about a balance between different goals – say, between learning instrumentally to improve earnings on the one hand and learning for personal development or for meaning on the other – though this is certainly one significant dimension. The values cannot be read off directly from where money is spent, though this will provide a clue. Education is not short of rhetoric, but there are a lot of unbuttered parsnips lying around educational kitchens. We aim here to provide a brief statement of the value propositions which underpin the vision we have just described, and to do this in a way which has a clear link to the proposals that follow. These propositions overlap with and reinforce each other.

1. People are natural learners, but need different kinds of services at different points in their lives

This is a statement of fact, but it embodies a basic value: a belief in people's capacity to carry on learning. Too many people are written off as learners. This can happen, tragically, early on in their education, as so many biographical narratives testify.

---

[1] The term 'lifewide' is now acquiring some currency, to indicate that learning covers all the fields of human experience, and is not only a recurrence of formal education or training. We now even have the term 'lifedeep', to signal the existential meaningfulness of learning!

Children are judged unintelligent at school because their ears are full of wax or they have dyslexia or are distracted by trouble at home. The process of exclusion continues throughout life, though usually for different reasons. In many respects, we do not have a bad system by international standards, but it is not adequately underpinned by a constant belief in people's continuing capacity to learn.

This view – that we are all by nature learners, given the chance – may seem banal. Taking it seriously, though, is anything but banal. It means, for example, that whilst dreary jobs still have to be done, the people doing them should not be condemned to a lifetime of work without opportunity for development. It means too that we do not give up on older people whose cognitive capacities are in evident decline; they can still be learners, benefiting from suitable opportunities. No one is shut out. It means above all that we take seriously the notion of opportunity for all, at whatever age. This is a fundamental commitment, with practical implications.

2. Inefficiency means that human potential is wasted

Efficiency talk raises hackles. We are not Frederick Taylors – time-and-motion merchants itching to get out there with the stopwatch and improve output. But we do want the debate to focus on how the resources – time, effort and money – we all put in, as taxpayers, employees, employers and individual consumers, can be used best, for both social and economic purposes. Are they used at the right time, in the best way, and for the biggest effect? Our proposition is that anyone who steps backwards and takes an honest view would conclude that we don't do as much as we could with what we already invest. The relevant thought experiment is to imagine how we would justify our current arrangements as the best for learning throughout life; for example, why do we not put the same effort into training staff for early years learning as we do for teachers in schools, or give them the same status as college staff? Why does the system in England discriminate against part-time study, making it harder rather than easier for people to combine employment with study? Why do university philosophy students get a loan, but not bricklaying students in further education? Why do our training arrangements discourage older workers from carrying on learning, when it is public policy for them to continue working later in life?

There is a long list of similar questions to be posed which reveal anomalies in the way we do things. We know that people learn best when they are motivated, and when the learning offer matches how, when and what they need to learn. The closer we can get to that for everyone, the better; at present we are still far away.

3. Equality and fairness are fundamental

This is the counterpart of the preceding proposition. Our analysis of expenditure and participation in *Chapter 4* shows very clearly how some of us do infinitely better than others out of the system, and how the advantages some of us gain early on tend to be accentuated over time. The converse is necessarily the case: if you fail at first you are much more likely to fail later – or you will not even be given the chance to fail. Short-term efficiency arguments can reinforce this process. It can look more efficient to invest in someone who has already done well in education. They are more likely to learn quickly, and so they will look like a better investment to a public funder or private employer. This is one reason why they get better access to learning opportunities throughout life. The resulting pattern is one of cumulative advantage and disadvantage.

However, lifelong learning should be an essential and fundamental component of fairness in society, precisely because it is lifelong. Some inequalities will always be with us, however much effort is put into equalising opportunities at school. So opportunities always need to be there to redress these initial, and recurring, disadvantages. Likewise, they need to be there to cater for diversity, as people from different social contexts and backgrounds express their learning needs at different stages in life. Learning cannot guarantee fairness, in society or in the economy; but its availability to all is a recurrent essential condition. We discuss this more in *Chapter 6*.

We choose to talk about 'fairness' as well as equality. Measures of inequality are crucial to expose the weaknesses of the current system, but equality is an elusive notion, open to misrepresentation. Fairness is not. Everybody intuitively grasps fairness; it calls on people to make normative judgements and hard choices. Of course, people disagree about what fairness means when applied to education or to employment or any other field, but it raises central questions with a directness which cannot be matched.

4. Learning has to do with power, for better and worse

If we were to sum up the goals of lifelong learning in a single phrase, it would be that it should enable people to take control of their lives. This is as individuals, alone or with families; and as communities and collections of citizens, of whatever size and make-up. The point about learning is that it should enable them to understand the choices they have, and to influence those choices in the first place. Some of these choices will be about the learning needed to earn a good living. But at a more general level we cannot better Raymond Williams' formulation of the functions of education broadly understood:

- understanding change;
- adapting to change; and
- shaping change.[2]

This trio gives us a strong grip on how education applies to different spheres: civil society, the workplace, the home. In the face of massive economic change, people need to be able to adapt, not just through acquiring new professional skills, but by having the resilience to search out job opportunities and to face the uncertainties that recession brings. They need to have some grasp of the direction change is taking in a globalised economy. They also need to be able to make their voices heard as to how their society should deal with the tremors which rock the foundations, for instance in the extent of welfare support which those most affected can expect. Similarly, in respect of social change: if intergenerational solidarity is to hold, people of all ages need to gain some understanding of how other generations perceive change, to modify their own attitudes to the behaviour and values of other generations, and to join in fashioning policies which can hold an increasingly multigenerational society together.

All these are to do with power. The relationship between learning and power is pervasive. However, we also need to be clear about the limits of learning. The equation of knowledge with power is an attractive slogan, but too simple. Women now outdo men in almost every aspect of education: at every level up to and including PhD, and in every subject except perhaps mathematics and engineering.[3] Has this brought them equal pay? Not yet, by a long chalk. Has it brought them equal access to power? Scarcely. Our point (which we reiterate later) is that learning cannot solve problems on its own; its effect may be overridden and nullified by other factors.

5. Learning should help to bind us together

Education fosters social capital – the glue that binds societies together. This does not come from being taught directly about the humanity of others, still less from some common ideological curriculum content. Solidarity with others can be taught directly only to a very limited extent. But the enterprise of learning is one that involves others, as fellow students, or as our teachers or trainees. It brings people together, with a common goal. In some measure, educational venues are the main surviving public spaces where people from different backgrounds come together as active participants in a common venture. This is an enormously important function, in schools but also for adults. Learning (and teaching)

---

[2] Williams (1990).
[3] Higher Education Policy Institute (HEPI) (2009).

alongside others increases our understanding of their difference from us, whether this derives from their age or generation, their social class, their ethnicity or any other social variable. Understanding the difference is not the same as feeling empathy or solidarity, but it raises the chances of it.

Secondly, we subscribe to the basic Enlightenment belief that knowledge shapes behaviour. The more ignorance about others is dispelled, the better we are likely to get along. This does not have to be direct knowledge about particular groups. We do not for the most part attend classes to learn about the other people who are there. This is something we learn anyway; more education means greater tolerance, because it improves awareness of the possibility of other viewpoints – those of fellow learners. In today's world of mobility and perceived threat, this is a precious advantage.

Learning together is a social act. It is also efficient; on the whole, people who learn together do better (a possible reason why girls now do better than boys). We share the view of the Children's Society report, *A Good Childhood*,[4] that there is excessive individualism in today's society. This damages adults as well as children. Since we are, on average, more highly educated than before, it is clear that more learning by itself has not generated better behaviour. However, a values-based system of lifelong learning which has as one of its goals 'learning to live together' (one of the famous pillars of the Delors report[5]) can make a big contribution.

6. To survive and thrive, the world needs us to learn

How many of us are reasonably convinced of the seriousness of climate change, but could not give a coherent account of the main arguments around it – in spite of hours of media time and acres of print coverage? How many of us can link our understanding of the challenge closely to our own behaviour? This is arguably the most important issue where we need to learn for our collective safety and survival, but there are many others, at all levels. An ignorant world is a more dangerous world, partly because it is so open to manipulation.

Levels of fear and insecurity are growing. This is not surprising, and in one sense quite rational, given the serious prospects of climate catastrophe or economic meltdown. But – and here again our propositions run into one another – we should all be better off if our judgements on what is risky and what is not are reasonably well-founded. Once again, more education is no guarantee of success

---

[4] Layard and Dunn (2009).
[5] International Commission on Education for the Twenty-first Century (1996).

or happiness: depression is perhaps just a reasonable response to being more aware of how bad things are. But being aware is the lesser of the 'worst' scenarios; we cannot invoke ignorance as a kind of umbrella to shelter us from the consequences of what we do to our environment.

Three capitals: a framework for understanding

Having set out a vision and a set of value propositions, we propose here a framework for bringing together thinking about the purposes and benefits of lifelong learning. It consists of three 'capitals': that is, forms of assets which have value for individuals and for society. These are human capital, social capital and identity capital.

- *Human capital* refers to the skills and qualifications held by individuals. It is built up mainly through formal education and training, but informal learning also plays an important part. People deploy their human capital in the workplace as a factor of production, but they also put it to use in social and community contexts.

- *Social capital* refers to participation in networks where values are shared, so that the people contribute to common goals. The networks may be local (including family) or global. It is less of a personal attribute than human and identity capital. Social capital supports learning and is in turn strengthened by it. Although social capital is not acquired directly through education in the same way as skills and qualifications are, getting more education is a powerful way of increasing access to networks.

Figure 1: The triangle of three 'capitals'

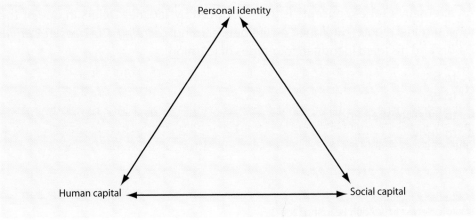

- *Identity capital* is the ability to maintain healthy self-esteem, and a sense of meaning and purpose in life. As a Nordic thinktank discussing *Future Competencies* put it, adult education should enable people 'to deepen their self-knowledge and reinforce their self-image, as this is the basis for effective competence development in other fields.'[6]

There is a long-running debate about these terms: how they should be defined, and how they should and should not be used. We do not propose to enter into that debate here. We use them as a way of insisting upon the interdependence of different kinds of learning. This is not just a conceptual matter. It affects policy and practice in very basic ways. Without the formal and informal networks which make up social capital, people will find it hard both to build up the skills and qualifications which make up human capital, and to apply them productively. Conversely, without skills, they will find it harder to gain access to networks. Without the self-esteem which makes up identity capital, it is difficult both to learn and to apply that learning. And so on.

Take one simple but significant illustration. Depression is now a major form of ill-health, across most industrial nations, with one in five adults in the UK thought to be affected by depression at some point in their lives. It affects adults and children of all classes. Depression has a major impact on productivity, reducing the value of people's contribution at enormous cost to organisations and societies, as well as individuals. It is linked to the extent to which people are part of thriving social networks: being a part of a network will help prevent or cure depression, and this includes work-related collegiality, as well as social relations outside the workplace. In turn, work that is unhealthy will have an impact on family and social relationships. The arrows go in all directions, linking each of the three capitals in both directions. This is common sense, but too often our approach to learning is based on splitting these different forms off from each other.

An alternative set of concepts is that produced by Jacques Delors in one of the most seminal reports published on lifelong learning: *Learning: The Treasure Within*. Delors and his team identified four types of learning:

- to be;
- to do;
- to live together; and
- to know.[7]

---

[6] Nordic Network for Adult Learning (2007).
[7] International Commission on Education for the Twenty-first Century (1996).

The parallels with the capitals are obvious. The language is possibly more elegant. We have chosen the triangle of capitals because we feel it gives us a firmer analytical grip, but salute the Delors pillars as a fine statement of purpose. The seeds of many of the ideas here can also be found in many other places beyond the Delors report, stretching back decades. Particularly influential on our thinking have been, at the international level, the 1973 OECD report on *Recurrent Education: A Strategy for Lifelong Learning*,[8] and in the UK, *The Learning Age: Renaissance for a new Britain* (1999).[9] We follow in a long tradition.

Overview of the book

In this chapter we have set out the basic principles which underlie the report. We follow this with a more evidence-based account of the rationale for lifelong learning: broadly speaking, what is the significance of it for our individual and collective lives? It pays particular attention to arguments about equality and fairness, as a fundamental part of the rationale. *Chapter 3* turns to a more critical perspective, setting out what we believe is wrong with the current system and needs fixing. This includes our failure to respond to major demographic, social and economic trends; a flawed approach to training and workforce development; the inequitable provision of opportunities generally; the unsystematic way in which we go about organising provision; and the weak state of our knowledge base. *Chapter 4* begins the process of strengthening the knowledge base, by presenting the results of our surveys of participation and expenditure. The expenditure analysis in particular breaks new ground, drawing together all sources of public and private investment in lifelong learning.

In the next set of chapters, we turn to the key areas of action that we are recommending. *Chapter 5* sets out the rationale for a new model of the educational life course. Our basic approach divides the life course into four stages, each of roughly 25 years (though open-ended for the fourth quarter). This will enable us to respond to demographic, social and labour market changes far better than the current confused and outmoded series of age-based dividing lines. We make it very clear this does not mean age segregation as the primary basis for organising actual provision. Mixed-age, family and intergenerational learning are wholly compatible with our model. We apply the four-stage model immediately to the results from the previous chapter, and this enables us to propose a gradual but significant rebalancing of the system. We see this as part of an emerging contract between the generations.

---

[8] OECD (1973).
[9] Department for Education and Employment (DfEE) (1998).

Chapter 6 sets out a framework for entitlements to learning. 'Entitlement' can mean very different things, from legally enforceable rights to broad aspiration. We review current learning entitlements, and propose a set of general and specific entitlements to enable and encourage effective participation in learning throughout the life course. We suggest that the notion of 'learning leave' be promoted as part of new patterns of working and other time. The entitlements should be underpinned by universal access to advice, and to appropriate technological infrastructure; they should be channelled through a national system of Learning Accounts.

Chapter 7 complements this with support for a universal system of credit – not financial credit, but the kind you acquire for successfully completing learning. This is not an original proposal, but it is an essential component of a shift to a coherent system of lifelong learning, and therefore requires reiteration here. We urge that funding systems should stop discriminating, as they currently do, against part-time study.

Chapter 8 puts forward an outline for a 'citizens' curriculum'. We phrase this in terms of four capabilities: civic, financial, health and digital. These 'capabilities' are broader than literacies; they are based on Amartya Sen's notion of capability, which suggests action as well as competence.[10] We are not suggesting a national curriculum from the top-down, but a framework which should be locally interpreted. We address the criticism that this shows our thinking in a very instrumental light.

Chapter 9 sets out what we see as the mechanisms for change, in order to get from where we are to where we want to be. This focuses on governance, especially at local level. We put forward the idea of Local Learning Exchanges, to bring together learners and those who have something to teach.

Chapter 10 brings together our recommendations, and restates the arguments around them. For readers who want only to get the essence of the report, this is it.

A reality check

One of the Inquiry Commissioners, Bob Fryer, in his IFLL discussion paper on contemporary citizenship,[11] has set us a number of tests about the path along this road.

---

[10] Sen (1985, 1992 and 2009, especially Part 3).
[11] Fryer (2009).

- Are our proposed solutions 'lifelong' and 'lifewide'?
- Have we covered the full range of learning (formal and informal)?
- Will we increase the autonomy of learners and citizens?
- Are our proposals based on the principles and practices of social justice?
- Have we sufficiently acknowledged difference?
- Have we set out a necessary infrastructure for lifelong learning?

We suggest that these tests can be used as a guide to critical reading of our report.

'High levels of inequality affect educational performance; in other words, the significant causal direction is from inequality to educational performance, rather than the other way round. This is a sobering result for educationalists.'

2 The case for lifelong learning

Building the case for lifelong learning

We set out here the case for recognising the value of lifelong learning. First, we list the areas in which we can reasonably assume that lifelong learning improves our economic and social well-being, as individuals and as members of families and of wider society. This is based on a mix of fact and logic. In some fields there is strong evidence that learning improves outcomes; in others, the argument may be persuasive though not backed up by substantial evidence or analysis as other results are. We emphasise the validity of evidence drawn from the accumulated experience of those working in the field, in addition to systematic professional research.

Overall, the case is compelling. We have no doubt that lifelong learning already makes a major contribution to sustaining economic and social well-being, to enabling people to understand, adapt to and shape change, and to promoting social justice; and that it could do more if the proposals in this report are pursued. But we are not Pollyannas. We do not wish to overstate the case. Some of the effects most commonly cited for education are not quite as firmly based as might be supposed, and we cannot cheerily attribute all the good things in life to a dose of learning. This is one reason why we spend some time on the issue of equality – stressing the significance of learning in addressing equality issues, but also emphasising its limitations, and the fact that to make an impact it needs to be linked with other, structural measures.

We place the discussion of equality in this chapter because it is such a fundamental part of the rationale. Lifelong learning can help achieve greater equality, however that is defined; but we need a clearer understanding of what we mean by it, and the issues that accompany it. Our society is 'superdiverse', and amongst other things this means there will be very different views of what learning is for – and about what constitutes disadvantage. We aim to illustrate that diversity with the individual stories which are interspersed through the book, but it also means that our generalisations here need regular qualification.

We deal, albeit briefly, with the issues of social mobility and meritocracy as examples of how complex the relationship is between education and equality.

The discussion shows how apparently unambiguous 'goods' can conceal tensions between different goals.

Finally, we offer some simple hypothetical calculations on how further investment in education might be justified, economically and socially. The investment pays off in areas beyond education – notably health, which should justify strong inputs from those sectors. We emphasise, here and elsewhere, that investment is not a matter for the public purse alone, and that our concern is with rebalancing the investment as much as increasing it.

The effects of learning

Irene's story[1]

Irene plucked up the courage to come into a family literacy group because she wanted to know how best to support her daughter who was just beginning to show signs of falling behind. A single parent with three children, Irene was living on a poor estate, with a lot to think about as well as the education of her children. Although she felt safer at the school than other places, she was still terrified about going 'back to school'. The course was publicised as 'help your child, help yourself', so she ignored the 'herself' bit, and went to help her daughter. She talks of the courage it took just to walk in through the door.

Irene finished the course and found she had learnt things too – she improved her spelling, found out a bit about how her daughter learns, visited the library, got into the habit of doing things at home with her daughter and was feeling OK with things.

What next? The group stuck together to do something for themselves. They did another course at the school, then, following a chat with a worker who wanted to know what they wanted to do next, they moved out of the school, but stayed on the estate, doing IT at the working men's club. Then, feeling brave, Irene left the group of friends and joined an English course at the adult centre, which was located on the other side of town (the 'posh side'). Then her husband left her; shortly afterwards her youngest started having epileptic fits – up to ten a day. Irene disappeared from all learning for two years, as she sought to get her life together, find a new house, earn money and deal with her son.

---

[1] We use a selection of learners' stories throughout to connect our recommendations with learners' lived experiences.

Eventually, she re-appeared and went on to an access course at the college; she set up a group for other parents with children with disabilities – this gave her the courage and the skills to decide she wanted to do something for her community – she joined the school governors, became chair of the tenants group, and got a job on the estate.

It took five years for Irene to get from that first course to becoming a school governor, learning a whole lot of skills on the way, and helping herself, her family, friends and community.

Although it may seem obvious that learning produces beneficial results, the way it does this, and the possible side-effects, are still not well understood. There are some important distinctions to be drawn about the way these links work – important because they should make us pause for thought before claiming too much for education, but also because they can point to different directions for policy. We do not assume that more means better. Our purpose is not a simple forensic one. In other words, we do not set out to make the strongest case for learning as the royal road to improved well-being. Sometimes it has little or no effect; sometimes it can even have negative effects, overall or for some groups.

Even where there is a strong logical case for greater investment, it does not follow that we should be investing in the same kinds of learning as currently occur. It could be that we should stop doing some things, and concentrate instead on different ways of tackling a problem. However, one of the trickiest issues, for both analysis and policy, is how far we can separate out specific effects and attribute them precisely to specific types of learning. Different types of learning interact with each other. Notably, getting involved in very informal settings can help people with little record of success to progress to formal education and training. A lifelong learning system is an interconnected web, and although we need to separate out as far as possible its different parts for the purposes of analysis, the process should not be taken too far. They cannot be treated in isolation from each other, as if the categories held entirely different populations, or all motivations to learn were clear and simple. Targeting is fine, but cannot be done with sniper's accuracy. As has been well said, lifelong learning is inherently untidy. This makes the job of assessing benefits awkward.

For all these qualifications, it should be clear that we are committed believers in the value and potential of lifelong learning. Whatever the formal research evidence can or cannot tell us, there is a mountain of compelling evidence from the field. Importantly, we do not consider this 'anecdotal', the label often given disparagingly to evidence which is not produced by systematic research. Anecdotal evidence is just happenstance; it's something you stumble across. In contrast, evidence from the field on the value of lifelong learning is built up from literally millions of hours of experience, from teachers[2] and learners, and from family members, who testify to the power that learning has to shape people's lives. The messages from this mountain are consistent and repeated. Many of the submissions in response to the Inquiry's Calls for Evidence were of this kind.

A brief comment is in order on some of the terms we regularly use. 'Investment' and 'returns' have obvious economic connotations. They suggest calculated economic decisions, with economic benefits in mind. We build our argument partly around the triangle of three capitals: human, social and identity capital (see *Chapter 1*). To some, this may be distasteful as applied to education. When the concept of 'human capital' was first used in the 1960s to analyse education,[3] there were many objections to it as an approach which inappropriately commodified a basic human process. Extending this vocabulary in the way we do may seem to represent a further subordination of educational to economic goals; on the contrary, we think it is an important way of shifting the balance of debate. Our intention in using these terms is to recognise the interpenetration between the social, the economic and the personal. All are legitimate as learning goals; bringing them together into a single framework encourages us to understand their mutual dependence, but at the same time allows people to approach the issues from their particular angle. We would therefore expect those primarily interested in training at the workplace to recognise that the potential human capital can only be realised if due attention is paid also to social and identity capital; conversely, community educators may think primarily of the social aspects, but recognise that their learners are also acquiring skills which could be put to use in the labour market. The goal is always to achieve an appropriate balance, whatever the context.

The boundaries between these dimensions are increasingly porous, and rightly so. Proposals such as that by the economist Richard Layard and others that national progress should no longer be measured by crude economic indices such as Gross National Product (GNP), but instead by indicators of well-being,[4] are no longer laughed out of court, but are taken seriously in both policy circles and more widely. Bhutan, which has actually taken the step of measuring its national progress by reference to happiness not material income, may yet be hailed as a

---

[2] We include here all those associated with teaching, training, tutoring and mentoring, including those playing often important intermediary roles.

[3] But perhaps earlier: 'Ay, ay, a cool hundred a year – that's all,' said Mr Tulliver, with some pride at his own spirited course. 'But then, you know, it's an investment, like; Tom's eddication 'ull be so much capital to him.' (George Eliot, *Mill on the Floss*, 1880, with thanks to John Vorhaus).

[4] Layard (2005).

true pioneer. English local authorities have a duty to promote the well-being of their populations, and expect to be made accountable on this.

One strand of the Inquiry's work has revolved around the notion of social productivity. This too was intended to fuse the social and the economic: appropriating an apparently economic term for use in a wider context. We wanted to provide a bridge between perspectives, a common language which could be used by participants from different disciplines and fields. We have been urged in the course of our consultations to seek out a new vocabulary to describe what we are doing, and although we cannot claim to have got far with this, these are part of our efforts to generate a debate which is both broad and coherent. Using terms and concepts which seem to be wedded to a particular perspective or discipline but giving them a broader application does something to stretch the debate. However, values are there, unapologetically so. Our terminology is a mix of the normative, the instrumental and the mildly subversive.

Alan's story

Having spent 18 years rising through the ranks in the army, Alan Taylor was forced to retire due to arthritis. He tried his hand at various jobs, from sales to working as a postman, but was never satisfied, so he decided about ten years ago to return to learning and now has a raft of qualifications which have enabled him to embark on a whole new career.

Alan began his learning journey at Loughborough College with an Access to Higher Education course alongside GCSEs in English and Maths, and achieved both with excellent results. These led to Alan achieving a BA (Honours) degree in Archaeology and Ancient History at Leicester University.

Alan has now become a lecturer at Loughborough College, and thoroughly enjoys inspiring his students to 'learn to love learning' in the way that he did. 'I help them to find a sense of self-worth as well as embark on a lifelong learning approach to their careers. I regularly work with students who need a gentle push in the right direction to help them reach their potential, and this is so worthwhile.'

Probably wealthier, usually healthier: at individual level...

Almost every advantage is positively associated to some degree with better levels of education. For individuals it tends to go along with:

- higher earnings;
- less unemployment;
- better health;
- better access to technology;
- lower crime rates;
- higher civic participation;
- longer lives; and
- other such advantages.

The relationships are not simple linear ones; it does not hold that the more education you get, the more you will benefit, in direct proportion, and it doesn't hold for all types of education in respect of all the different outcomes. However, by and large, it's a good bet that people who do well in education will do well in most or all of those other respects. The evidence on this is voluminous, for the UK and elsewhere.[5]

We need to make it clear that lifelong learning is not only an instrument to achieve these outcomes, however desirable they may be. Learning is a goal in its own right. When students achieve greater self-understanding and meaning in their lives (i.e. successfully build their identity capital, see *Chapter 1*), this makes the learning worthwhile, whether or not any of the other effects occur. Responses to the Inquiry's extensive consultations made it clear how strongly and widely that position is held. Moreover, learning is often a source of pure joy. But once again, these outcomes can rarely be separated out from one another.

This links to the proposals we put forward in *Chapter 8* for a citizens' curriculum built around four main capabilities: civic, health, financial and digital. So, for example, is it crudely instrumental to propose health capability as a core component of a universal curriculum framework? Does it suggest that lifelong learning is merely a way of raising the country's health levels and saving public money? We see things differently. Giving people the ability to manage their own health better, to exercise more control over how they live their lives, is an intrinsic not an instrumental justification. Similar arguments apply to the other capabilities. The intrinsic and the instrumental feed into each other.

---

[5] Feinstein *et al* (2008a); Feinstein *et al* (2008b).

...and for families and other social units: spill-over effects

A key component of our argument throughout this report is that learning is not just to do with individuals. Of course, it is individuals that do the learning, as trainees at work, students in college or learners in a community context or online. But learning involves interaction with others, and the case for learning involves effects which go beyond the benefits to learners themselves.

The strongest example of this is the family. The case here is very strong. There is a very close link between parental education levels and the performance of the child in school. Schools do their best to counter the disadvantage which may arise from this. However, if the parents have a poor experience of education themselves, the children are very likely to receive less support in their schooling, and are effectively running a race with one shoe off. This is not to demonise parents with low educational levels, but to recognise a basic inequality. The most effective way of changing this is to involve the parents themselves in learning. This does not necessarily mean learning related to that of their children (though it could). The evidence shows that if parents are involved in almost any form of learning, for their own pleasure or advancement, they will take a more active interest in their children. Therefore, investment in parental learning is a classic win-win.

This line of thinking has led to the development of family learning initiatives, which seek to involve parents and children in learning together. The pay-offs are evident (which is not to say that every family learning scheme is a success – just that the principle is clearly established). They include better learning, but also better family relationships generally. This certainly spills over into the wider community, so that everyone gains.

The effects are not all rosy, or not for all those affected. The film *Educating Rita* reminds us that finding new identities through adult learning can be associated with marital breakdown – even if it's not clear which leads to which. People can get hurt learning, and hurt others. Just as seriously, they may have their aspirations raised – and then dashed; there is some quite substantial evidence for its negative effects, on the learner and on those around them.

Families are, of course, not comprised only of parents and children. 'Reconstituted' families are on the increase as adults separate and remarry; we have same-sex couples, with or without children; and many families are now extended upwards, with several generations, as grandparents and great-grandparents survive longer. The extended family's internal social capital is important in the values it exhibits: the more of its members are involved in learning, the easier it is for others to be motivated to learn also. There might come a point when too many family members are busy learning, so the cat never gets fed or other sad consequences ensue, but the overall benefits are clear.

…at the workplace

The association between learning and economic success for an organisation is a complex one. At the company level, studies identify a positive association between a highly skilled workforce and the performance of a company, most commonly measured in terms of labour productivity. High value-added companies on average are better equipped with stocks of skills than other companies in the same sector. Companies with higher levels of skills and training are more likely to survive in tough times, and to thrive in better times. Those that spend more on training have a better return per employee, and higher levels of capacity utilisation. Again, the list of positive associations is long.[6]

The benefits of training for companies go beyond the straight acquisition of higher skills. Training has positive effects on job satisfaction, which in turn has been associated with lower absenteeism and quit rates,[7] However, training has little impact on job satisfaction and performance unless workers are given the opportunity to apply the skills they have acquired. This highlights the importance of job design and matching.[8]

There are significant sectoral, occupational and geographical variations in labour market patterns. A centrally driven system that seeks to apply a single set of targets to each sector, occupation or area of the country will not work. Moreover, the wider economy has a far greater impact on the structure of the labour market than do education and training interventions, which raises significant questions about the structural incentives and disincentives to engagement in learning that are embedded within UK labour markets.

The picture, therefore, is not straightforward. However, there can be no doubt that skills, and learning more generally, have a major role to play in raising levels of employment and productivity.

---

[6] Dearden et al (2000); Felstead et al (2007); Tamkin (2005); UKCES (forthcoming).
[7] Sloane et al (2007).
[8] According to a study by The Work Foundation (see Coats and Lehki, 2008), the UK has the lowest level of job matching in the EU – that is, where employee skills and abilities are matched to the demands of their job.

…and nationally

At country level, the pattern is broadly the same, though the comparative evidence is much stronger on the economic than the social effects. International organisations such as the OECD continually point to the advantages which highly educated countries have in a competitive global economy.[9] This is the case historically: countries that broke through industrially were the ones which had a relatively well-educated population – although by today's standards this was not high. It was true in the post-war wave, as the example of Japan shows, with its impressive economic recovery to a position of technological excellence. It is also the case for modern times, as new economies challenge the existing hierarchy: countries such as Korea, China and India have educational profiles which show steeply increasing levels of qualification, including at tertiary levels, as their national wealth drives upwards.

However, most of this basic picture refers to schooling and initial education (including higher education taken as end-on to school, not as adults returning). The picture on adult learning is much thinner. Nevertheless, there are strong associations at organisational level between investment in training and good economic performance, and the same is broadly true at national level. On the non-economic front, there are similar sets of relationships: broadly speaking, healthier countries are more educated ones, and ones which invest more in lifelong learning. However, many other factors, notably wealth and its distribution, intervene in this relationship, and it is not certain whether the causal relationship goes from learning to health or the other way around. (In fact, it almost certainly operates in both directions, but this is hard for conventional models to take on board.)

> Given my experience in learning and development, both within the public and private sectors, a key challenge for employers is to recognise the importance of lifelong learning outside of work as a vehicle to encouraging individual learning within it. Often 'recreational' or non-vocational courses are considered irrelevant to skills development at work, yet they often give the individual a sense of achievement and increased confidence. This feeling, if channelled in a supportive way, will encourage individuals to seek and adopt new ways of working and acquire new vocational skills. In the current economic climate the ability of a workforce to be confident enough to be flexible and take on new challenges should not be overlooked. Simultaneously the role that lifelong learning can have in achieving a good work/life balance should not be underestimated. The challenge and enjoyment of learning for pleasure is

[9] OECD (2009).

> a good way to counterbalance the mental demands of many of today's jobs. Employers should look for ways to enable and encourage recreational and non-vocational learning outside the core working hours as a means to engender a culture of continuous learning and therefore adaptability within it.
>
> *Clare Hannah, IFLL Commissioner and*
> *Head of Organisational Development, EWS Railways*

Measurement of learning's outcomes – beware simple solutions

The research evidence shows – fairly consistently, though to different degrees – that learning has positive economic and social effects, in some cases significantly so. For our purposes, though, this beguiling general conclusion – that higher educational achievement is the key to prosperity and well-being – is insufficient. First, the analysis nearly always refers to the effect of qualifications gained during the initial phase of education. How well you did at school, and then maybe at college or university, shapes your future career, your future health and so on. That's where the evidence lies. The data on schooling and on qualifications is very comprehensive, but on adult learning it is very fragmented. Research naturally focuses on where the data is, especially data which is reasonably tidy and computable. Drunks look for keys under lampposts; researchers naturally select the areas where data is available, or where it is relatively easy to gather. The analogy is not meant to be insulting to researchers. It is simply the case that we know a lot more about some types of effect than others because of what we can do with evidence that exists in forms more readily amenable to analysis.

Adult learning that does not lead to qualifications is particularly difficult to measure, and statistical relationships are correspondingly hard to discern. Some excellent work on this has been done, but it has nothing like the volume and weight of more conventional educational analysis.[10]

In addition, when adults learn, there are usually many other things happening in their lives. This makes it even more difficult to isolate the effects of the learning, even in detailed biographical analysis. Young people's lives are also highly complex, but because education plays such a relatively greater role it is easier to identify its effects.

---

[10] Feinstein and Duckworth (2006); Hammond and Feinstein (2006); Sabates *et al* (2006).

There are two major consequences of this set of problems. They point in rather different directions. First, even large-scale analyses may not find any effect of adult learning. However, this is not the same as demonstrating that there is no effect; it could mean that the techniques are just not able to capture the effects. Remember, we are not out to demonstrate that learning throughout life is always the *summum bonum*. We are just making the point that even very sophisticated techniques find it hard to identify all the interactions which occur.[11]

The second, very different consequence, is a naïve belief that upgrading qualifications for the population as a whole will produce all the benefits which are only accrued by the subset of people who currently have these qualifications. The fact that graduates generally earn significantly more than non-graduates (as they do in the UK, where the average graduate premium is still higher than in most countries) does not mean that all those who join the graduate club will necessarily scoop the same dividend. More generally, upgrading the skill levels of the population (as with the Leitch targets), does not necessarily mean that productivity will soar, and everyone will be better off.[12] Many other factors will shape the eventual outcome, notably the nature of the jobs on offer, the extent to which skills are actually used, capital investment and the managerial approach. Canada, Scotland and Northern Ireland are examples of countries where qualification levels are high, but productivity relatively low. There is likely to be some 'push factor': the more educated the workforce, the more jobs will tend to be adapted in response to these higher levels of competence. However, this is an uncertain process, to put it mildly. In particular, there are huge geographical variations in the relationship between the supply of qualified people and the demand for them.[13]

We can draw some preliminary conclusions from this overview of the knowledge base. First, we should beware of simplistic arguments for pushing up education or qualification levels. Secondly, we need a better understanding of the relationship between supply and demand, especially in relation to training. Thirdly, we should extend the range of methods used to analyse the relationships between learning and outcomes, social and economic.

If we ignore these, we get policy prescriptions that tend to the simplistic: drive up your levels of qualification, and you will move up the prosperity league table. One of the most influential of recent reports, the Leitch report on skills, followed this line assiduously (see box). It exposed, forcefully, though to no one's great surprise, the UK's poor performance on skills. However, despite recognising in its interim report the limitations of a qualifications-based analysis, it geared its

---

[11] Biesta *et al* (2008). See also Ziliak and McCloskey (2008).
[12] Keep, Mayhew and Payne (2006).
[13] Felstead *et al* (2007).

recommendations strenuously to an upgrading of skills, denominated rigorously in terms of qualification targets at different levels.

The Leitch Review of Skills[14] recommends that the UK commit to becoming a world leader in skills by 2020, benchmarked against the upper quartile of the OECD. This means doubling attainment at most levels. Stretching objectives for 2020 include:

- ninety-five per cent of adults[15] to achieve basic skills of functional literacy and numeracy, an increase from levels of 85 per cent and 79 per cent numeracy in 2005;
- exceeding 90 per cent of adults qualified to at least Level 2, an increase from 69 per cent in 2005. A commitment to go further and achieve 95 per cent as soon as possible;
- shifting the balance of intermediate skills from Level 2 to Level 3. Improving the esteem, quantity and quality of intermediate skills. This means 1.9 million additional Level 3 attainments over the period and boosting the number of apprentices to 500,000 a year; and
- exceeding 40 per cent of adults qualified to Level 4 and above, up from 29 per cent in 2005, with a commitment to continue progression.

Responses to the Leitch Review in the devolved administrations have been mixed. The Scottish Government Skills Strategy distances itself from Leitch and the concept of 'skills utilisation' has become central in Scotland. The Welsh Assembly Government has acknowledged some of the findings of the Leitch Review but favours an integrated approach, linking skill initiatives with employment services and business support – rather than just focusing on skills supply. Finally, we need a better balance in the distribution of our research, so that learning across the life course is better understood. We have some understanding of how adults learn in different contexts. Neuroscientific research confirms the plasticity of the brain – that is, its capacity to continue to change across the life course.[16] But the intellectual and financial resources devoted to later learning – from adulthood onwards – are extraordinarily limited, given the potential implications for the effectiveness of learning interventions. Most shocking – to the point of collective stupidity – is the tiny amount devoted to finding out more about how

---

[14] Leitch Review of Skills (2006).
[15] Adult here means age 19 to State Pension age. Basic means everyday literacy and numeracy skills; Level 2 equates to five good GCSEs; Level 3 equates to two A-levels; Level 4 equates to a degree (or their vocational equivalents).
[16] Blackmore and Frith (2005).

learning might help us deal with the impending growth of dementia: preventing it, slowing it down and catering for the needs of those afflicted.

> **Well-being**
>
> Adult learning matters. Everyone who works with adults knows that learning can change their lives. Recent research has confirmed that this is not a matter of a few isolated examples, and that taking part in organised learning can help people exercise more control over their lives, contribute to their communities more effectively, and develop the confidence and skills that help us survive and thrive in tough times. These are important messages, and we need to make much more of them if we are to build the sustainable learning society that so many of us would like to see. That means placing well-being at the centre of our educational goals, and rather than focusing narrowly on one specific set of skills or type of qualification, we should value a broad and generous range of adult learning.
>
> *Professor John Field, IFLL Commissioner and Director,*
> *Division of Academic Innovation and Continuing Education, University of Stirling*

Equality and diversity

The bleak truth is that the UK exhibits levels of inequality which place it close to one end of the international spectrum. We are considerably more unequal than almost all European countries (see Figure 2). Whilst measuring equality and inequality is complex, inequalities have increased rather than decreased in recent years on most measures.[17] This matters, not only for those who find themselves at the bottom of the pile; it affects us all – our health, our well-being and our prosperity.[18] Reducing inequality is a constant, recurring challenge.

Education has always been seen as a major channel for promoting equal opportunities. This is a highly contentious area, with several different dimensions: what do we mean by equality – opportunity or outcome? How is it to be measured? What are the limits on what the State should do to ensure equality? These issues will go on being debated. Our argument can be summed up as follows.

---

[17] Very significant work on this is being carried out by the National Equality Panel, covering several different dimensions of inequality (http://equalities.gov.uk/national_equality_panel.aspx).
[18] Wilkinson and Pickett (2009).

Figure 2: Gini coefficients of income inequality in OECD countries, mid-2000s

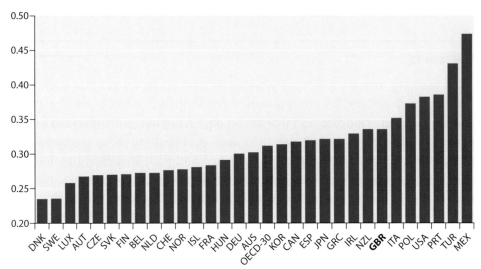

Source: OECD (2008)

- Efforts to ensure equality of initial opportunity are crucial. From early years, through schools, to widening access to further and higher education: the gaps between social class, between rich and poor, between lucky and unlucky, are unfair and not to be tolerated. The evidence on the scale of the inequality is massive.

- But however successful these efforts are, action in the initial phase will not suffice. In some cases, the disadvantage is just too big: material poverty, cultural disadvantage, or personal circumstances such as a disturbed or chaotic domestic set-up, mean that some people will always be left behind, gaining little from their initial education. This is realism, not fatalism. We therefore need recurrent opportunity, with a system designed to ensure that those who missed out initially have a fair chance later on – and this is a constant process, not just a one-off second chance.

- More fundamentally, however good and fair the initial spread of educational opportunity is, education in itself cannot resolve the wider question of inequalities. This is the biggest challenge – to be both realistic and assertive about what education can achieve in addressing inequality.

We therefore need to be clear about how strong, and broad, the link is between education and inequality. We can illustrate this directly from several of our Inquiry's themes. In each case, we argue that lifelong learning has a significant part to play in addressing the theme's challenge. However, we also need to recognise that the education system has to some extent been part of the problem rather than the solution.

Poverty

The issues of poverty and equality are completely intertwined – generally and in respect of lifelong learning. Poverty is now largely defined in relative terms, by comparing the position of those at the bottom with the median income or some other comparator. It is not the absolute but the relative position of poor people which matters. Around 13 million people out of a UK population of 61 million are deemed to be living in relative poverty.

Poor people are very often poorly educated. Indeed, as Leisha Fullick observes in her IFLL Thematic Paper:

> *Education can reinforce inequalities. The explosion in training and education in recent times has itself contributed to the diminishing status of people who are poor, unskilled and unqualified. The explosion in learning as an aspect of consumption (for example, through health and fitness clubs and the new technologies) also has… become part of the complex patterns of inequality and exclusion, based not just on economic factors but on culture, behaviour and attitudes.*[19]

Amongst her main conclusions are that we need to:

- *strengthen the local infrastructure of lifelong learning* so that it can support better identification of the learning needs of disadvantaged adults;
- *achieve better integration with other aspects of anti-poverty strategy*, at both local and national level; and
- *develop more learning opportunities* to go with the grain of people's lives, needs and concerns, and which give them the capabilities they need to develop their own solutions to individual and local issues.

Technology

Technology is increasingly pervasive, across all areas of our life. It is no longer a question of IT skills as a necessary condition for holding a skilled job; being

---

[19] Fullick (2009).

Table 1: Household internet access and educational qualifications in the UK, adults under 70, 2008

Educational qualification	Internet access, 2008 (%)
Degree level or higher	93
Higher educational qualification	86
A-level	89
GCE / GCSE (A–C grade)	82
GCSE (D–G grade)	74
No formal qualification	56

Source: ONS (2008)

technologically literate is a prerequisite for taking part in society, as a citizen and consumer, as well as an economic contributor.[20] As Simon Mauger argues in his IFLL Thematic Paper,[21] the debate on the nature of digital divide is complex, but the figures on unequal access to information technologies are clear.

> *We are at a tipping point in relation to the online world. It is moving from conferring advantage on those who are in it to conferring active disadvantage on those who are without, whether in children's homework access to keep up with their peers, offer discounts, lower utility bills, access to information and access to public services. Despite this increasing disadvantage there are several obstacles facing those that are offline: availability, affordability, capability and relevance.[22]*

Digital literacy and capability has become so central a part of people's lives that we propose it as part of a citizens' curriculum, which should be universally available (see *Chapter 8* for more information). There will always be unequal access to technology, as richer people are more easily able to buy the technology or access to it. However, the technology is no longer a collection of add-ons; it is fundamental to social and economic participation. The point therefore is to ensure that no one is excluded from the technological access needed to participate. The guarantee should be of universal access to the technology and to the skills needed to make use of it.

---

[20] Department for Business, Innovation and Skills (BIS) and the Department for Culture, Media and Sport (DCMS) (2009); Morris (2009).
[21] Mauger (2009).
[22] BIS and DCMS (2009), p.11, paragraph 18.

Crime

Crime, like poverty, is closely correlated with low educational achievement. Half of all prisoners do not have the skills required by 96 per cent of jobs. Forty-three per cent have a reading level at or below that expected of an 11 year old; the figure for writing is 82 per cent. Only one in five can complete a job application form. Between 20–30 per cent of prisoners have learning disabilities or difficulties that interfere with their ability to cope within the criminal justice system.

Offenders also commonly have mental health and addiction problems, and come from unstable or chaotic backgrounds. This is not a plea for sympathy, simply the facts. As the IFLL Thematic Paper on Crime says:

> *The education system has not succeeded with the vast majority of offenders... It is not just the absolute low levels which matter. The disparities are significant in themselves. Area-based analysis of juvenile crime has revealed that growing educational inequality is associated with rises in convictions, and also with the numbers of racially motivated crimes (though not with property offences).*[23]

Large numbers of (mainly) young men disappear out of the public system into the penal one. With no qualifications, and often no other recorded achievements, they have no official identity other than a prison number. Compare this with the successful student passing through higher education. The gap which opens up in teenage years between offenders and those on a more normal path gapes very wide after only a few years. Although many offenders grow out of criminal activity around their mid-twenties, the chances of closing that gap are small.

Education cannot close that gap on its own, but effective learning opportunities, within prison and extending to cover the transition from prison, are an important route for reintegration.

Workplace inequality

In *Chapter 4* we show the inequalities which exist in access to training, which follow a largely predictable path – the more education someone has already had, the more likely they are to get further opportunities to boost their skills. This is not only a matter of access to organised training. The work environment of people with good qualifications is much more likely to be itself a rich one, where

---

[23] Schuller (2009).

people are regularly stimulated and learn as part of their work, compared with the 'restricted workplaces' where jobs are monotonous and suppress desire and opportunity to learn.

One of the most striking lines of argument to emerge from the UK Commission on Employment and Skills (UKCES) is the concern with inequality as a phenomenon which damages business.[24] This is not only because of the social costs it generates; excessive inequality is a drag on the collective work performance of most organisations. We refer later to the challenges this poses to the effective use of skills and potential.

Equality, social mobility, and recurrent meritocracy

Let us return to the three-step argument discussed earlier in this chapter and spell this out in a little more detail. Step one, the equalisation of chances for young people, is critical. Inequalities happen early, quickly and deeply. The speed with which very young children who test low on ability but come from well-off backgrounds overtake their contemporaries who test high but are from poor backgrounds indicates the scale of the challenge. This issue has been subject to very extensive debate. We stress only that if the whole system was generally seen to be one providing lifelong opportunities, there would be more scope for experimenting with different ways of achieving initial equality. This is because we could provide a more varied range of opportunities that could suit disadvantaged young people better than the current offer. But the important thing is that every effort continues to be made to close the gap.

However, problems occur if attention is focused exclusively on the elusive goal of equalising initial educational chances, or even achievement. It is entirely right to aim to open up the higher professions to young people from a wider range of social classes, to extend the opportunities for disadvantaged young people to enter higher education and so on.[25] But it is a fundamental error to construe the whole issue as if it is a question of getting everyone more or less to the same starting line for adult life – and then let the devil take the hindmost. The proper image is not one of a horse race, where the task is to ensure correct handicapping so that all have a fair chance of reaching the finishing post first. Life is more complicated than that, and the challenge is to provide recurrent opportunity – without the previous record determining the outcome beyond fairness or reason.

---

[24] UKCES (2009a), Chapter 1.3.
[25] Milburn (2009).

But now we have to push the argument further, and deal with the issues of social mobility and meritocracy. These two concepts throw up similar challenges. On both the right and left of the political spectrum social mobility is seen as a good thing – and political parties throw mud at each other for not doing enough to promote it. For the right, it's a sign that society can reward aspiration and achievement, from whatever level; for the left, it's a sign of greater equality. Everyone agrees that it is better for all members of one generation to have a similar chance of ending up in a higher social or occupational stratum, rather than this being determined by the position occupied by their parents. But here's the hard part: social mobility is perfectly compatible with high inequality. Even if we were to achieve a society of near-perfect social mobility, where there was no or very little correlation between a person's parental wealth or social position and where they end up in the social hierarchy, the equality issue could still be present. It's one thing – a good thing – for people to have equal chances to get to the top, but it's quite another to decide on whether the gaps between the top and the rest, or between the middle and the bottom, are fair. High social mobility (good) and high inequality (bad) can exist together, even if uneasily.[26]

An illustration comes from the current economic preoccupations with financier rewards. We might be pleased to note that access to elite positions in banks or hedge funds was fairly distributed, and not as reserved as it had been to the scions of the middle class; but this pleasure might be heavily overshadowed by our feelings about the huge disparity between the rewards they garnered pre-crash, and those of the rest of society.

The issue goes beyond rewards, though, to the machinery of selection and allocation of positions in society generally. Michael Young's *Rise of the Meritocracy* generated a term – meritocracy – which has entered common discourse. However, its meaning in today's parlance deviates significantly from the author's intentions. Young's book was a satire, and he pointed to the discomforts of a society where position was allocated on merit. These days 'meritocratic' is opposed as a positive alternative to patronage or other forms of unreasonable access to good positions. However, Young's imagination led him to pose the question of what a fully-fledged meritocratic system of allocation would do for our sense of social solidarity; those who fail initially may have failed more or less 'fairly', but the consequence is still

---

[26] There is a further issue. In so far as social mobility involves downward as well as upward mobility, it is predictable that those with the necessary means will invest still more in their children's education, to avoid them being part of the downwardly mobile. This could be a trigger for further polarisation.

that some people are consigned to a very dismal future. This subtle twist has been more or less submerged, but needs to be rediscovered. [27]

Taking meritocracy seriously in its original sense provides important support for the case for lifelong learning. The dangers which Young foresaw of a harshly meritocratic society would be alleviated if there was recurrent opportunity. If people are routinely able to access learning, they are not locked in a hopeless economic or social cell, and the key tossed away. The rewards which go to different strata may still be unfair, but they are not determined for life by an early allocation into higher or lower echelons. In other words, a *recurrent meritocracy* would have less of the dark side which Young suggested. It would reconcile the two senses of the term; more importantly, it would be an excellent organising principle, to which lifelong learning would have much to contribute.

There is one further step in this discussion of education and equality. The recent book by Richard Wilkinson and Kate Pickett, *The Spirit Level*, argues that many of our social problems derive from the mere fact of inequality. [28] Almost everyone loses from living in a very unequal society – even those at or near the top – since it produces higher levels of violence and crime, worse health, and lower trust and mutual confidence. The link between inequality and teenage pregnancy (see Figure 3) is particularly striking, in itself and because of what it signals for the probable educational futures of the mothers and of their children.

We shall return to this argument when we discuss expenditure, since it throws up major questions about how far high expenditure on its own achieves the intended goals. Here the lessons from their analysis are twofold. First, high levels of inequality affect educational performance; in other words, the significant causal direction is from inequality to educational performance, rather than the other way round. This is a sobering result for educationalists, since it casts doubt on how far education as a channel for social mobility can solve the problem of inequality. The second lesson, not drawn by the authors themselves, is that

---

[27] Young (1958). Reflecting sadly on the use and misuse of his book, Michael Young had this to say shortly before he died: 'If meritocrats believe, as more and more of them are encouraged to, that their advancement comes from their own merits, they can feel they deserve whatever they can get. The newcomers can actually believe they have morality on their side. So assured have the elite become that there is almost no block on the rewards they arrogate to themselves. … as the book also predicted, all manner of new ways for people to feather their own nests have been invented and exploited. Salaries and fees have shot up. Generous share option schemes have proliferated. Top bonuses and golden handshakes have multiplied. As a result, general inequality has been becoming more grievous with every year that passes, and without a bleat from the leaders of the party who once spoke up so trenchantly and characteristically for greater equality.' (*The Guardian*, 29 June 2001).

[28] Wilkinson and Pickett (2009).

Figure 3: Teenage birth rates and inequality

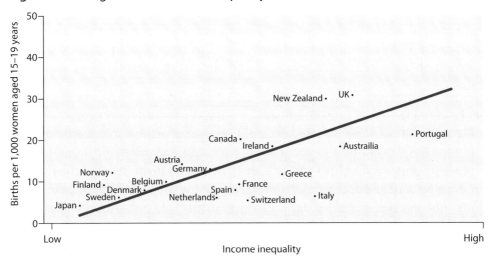

Source: The Equality Trust, taken from Wilkinson and Pickett (2009)

one of lifelong learning's important functions is to help people establish the kinds of solidarity – across classes, generations and other divides – which might enable a stronger move towards reducing basic inequalities. As the nineteenth century social commentator de Tocqueville observed about his native France, a great distance between top and bottom (aristocracy and peasantry in his case) reduces empathy, which he contrasted unfavourably with the relatively class-free interaction of Americans. Now the position of the countries has been largely reversed, at least in degree of inequality. Polly Toynbee and David Walker have shown how inaccurate the perceptions of rich people in the UK are in respect of what others earn.[29] The rich cannot conceive of people getting by on the incomes they do, so vastly overestimate the average wage. This level of insulation from reality does not make for good bonding. But the point here is that in most societies, learning to live together, in the Delors formulation, is a critical factor in at least enabling inequality to be reduced – and therefore in achieving the social outcomes which flow from greater equality.

To sum up this section, our goal has been to assert the importance of education to equality, and also to recognise its limitations as a solo instrument; to point out the need for action early in the life course, but also the inadequacy of seeing life as a race which just needs to get off to a fair start; and to show that even a highly social mobile and meritocratic society will still need learning opportunities if it is not to risk being an unfair one. This may be a surprising conclusion to some.

---

[29] Toynbee and Walker (2008).

In *Chapter 4*, which provides a stocktake on current expenditure and participation, we return to the question of equality and fairness across a number of dimensions. In *Chapter 5*, where we present a new model of the educational life course, we draw some conclusions on how these considerations should lead us to fresh thinking on the allocation of resources and opportunity across the extended life course.

My professional life has rested securely on the conviction that learning is a fundamental personal and social good. Educated and skilled individuals lead more prosperous and fulfilled lives. Much of history is the story of the rise of educated and skilled societies, often at the expense of those less accomplished. My time as chief inspector did nothing to dispel this certainty. It was spent largely in an attempt to raise the quality and status of learning at the margins, with new injections of commitment each time I saw some fresh example of inequity. In a third sector provider in Manchester it was impossible to ignore the fact that the young adult trainees were tiny, much like one imagines the doomed Pals' Battalions of the urban poor in the First World War to have been. 'Oh yes,' said the tutor, 'They sometimes grow six inches in two years when we given them decent food.'

For me, then, the collapse of adult learning numbers when state subsidies were reduced was a Damascene moment. Did it mean that adult community learning served the poorest and most vulnerable in our society? (The evidence suggested not.) Or did it mean, as the government seemed at first to believe, that adult learning was a branch of the entertainment industry; a discretionary acquisition, in competition with television, holidays, gym membership and a broadband subscription?

It is for an answer to that question that I have looked to this Inquiry. I wanted an answer that was rooted in the tough realities of adulthood and old age in Britain today, but that was less patronising than old models based on teaching 'them' a few of the things 'we' enjoy. I believe we have found it, in a structure of changing need and entitlement.

David Sherlock, Inquiry Commissioner and
former Chief Inspector of the Adult Learning Inspectorate

Costs and benefits

We return now to our discussion of the actual and potential benefits of lifelong learning. We have argued that it is often difficult to make what are regarded as rigorous assessments of the benefits. It is even more difficult to attach these to specific costs and thus make some estimate of the returns to investment in learning.

One strand of the Inquiry's work focused on the social productivity of learning, or the public value as it could also be termed. There are complex technical difficulties of making such estimates, including putting any kind of monetary figure on them. However, we have chosen three areas by way of illustration to illuminate potential benefits.

Dependency

Our first example draws on the demographic analysis provided for the Inquiry.[30] An ageing population means, almost inevitably, more people arriving at a point where for one reason or another they can no longer look after themselves. The average cost of providing residential care for older people is around £465 per week. What kind of assumption can we make about the potential impact of higher participation in lifelong learning? We have strong evidence from many individuals of how taking part in learning reinforced their independence and capacity to look after themselves.

Let's assume that the date of entry into residential care is postponed by just one month as a result of the person's participation in some form of learning. The net saving is not the full £2,015 – they still have expenses of living at home. Let's assume a range of saving between 15 and 30 per cent – quite modest. This frees up £302–£604 – in principle, it seems reasonable to say, a potential modest sum for investment in learning opportunities per person. With 60,168 adults aged 65 and over permanently admitted to registered care homes in 2007/08, this could release between £18.2 and £36.3 million per annum. In the same year, over 150,000 temporary admissions of older adults to registered care homes were also made, with the potential to further increase savings that could be made as a result of investing in learning.[31]

---

[30] McNair (2009a).
[31] The Health and Social Care Information Centre (2008).

This kind of calculation covers nowhere near the full picture. For example, the strain imposed on the family of a dependent member, the loss of income to a carer – these are costs which ideally should be factored in and could be given monetary value (note, though, that the carer might be more free to gain employment once the dependent person goes into care). Once again, such crude estimates are only the starting point for a wider debate on quality of life. [32]

Their crudeness is a reflection of the political reality. We are under no illusion that they will carry the day in the battle for scarce resources. The Treasury receives claims for 'preventative spending' (investments which should save money in the future) every year, which would probably absorb the entire budget for public spending. However, the calculations still need to be made and discussed.

Crime

It costs around £40,000 per year to keep someone in prison. Any overall estimate of the cost of crime should add in the costs to the victims and their families, the costs to the families of the offenders and the foregone output of the offender as a productive member of the labour force. (One hundred and fifty thousand children have parents in prison, and it is hard not to believe that this will affect these children's well-being, including their educational success.) One estimate puts the total cost at around £90,000, once these costs are added in. These are annual costs; you can multiply them to arrive at a much bigger figure for a lifetime offender.[33]

The Inquiry's Public Value strand of work included work which estimated the cost-effectiveness of training programmes for offenders, and showed large potential gains.[34] Our line of thinking here is broader and simpler. First imagine that a given investment in offender education reduces the recidivism rate by 2 per cent (low estimate) or 5 per cent (high estimate). This seems a plausible range – we claim no more than that. A rough average of estimates for the total cost of reoffending is around £13 billion. There are fixed costs; we cannot count in all the reduction as saving, so let's halve the effect of the estimated saving in each case; i.e. 1 per cent and 2.5 per cent. The results are £130 million and £325 million. The lower figure, as it happens, is very close to the total budget for offender learning.

---

[32] As the Treasury's so-called *Green Book* on evaluation and appraisal notes: 'Costs and benefits that have not been valued should also be appraised; they should not be ignored simply because they cannot easily be valued. All costs and benefits must therefore be clearly described in an appraisal, and should be quantified where this is possible and meaningful. Research may need to be undertaken to determine the best unit of measurement. Alternative non-monetary measures might be considered most appropriate.' (Paragraphs 5.76-77). HM Treasury (2003).
[33] Schuller (2009).
[34] Matrix Knowledge Group (2009a).

There are strong arguments against reasoning which translates everything into a common currency. Education and training are not the only paths to explore – expanded mental health and addiction services are arguably even more obvious as means of keeping people out of prison who should not be there. But as a way of broadening the debate on how to reverse the drift to hyper-incarceration, it's more than a start.

Mental health/depression

Like crime, mental ill-health has massive costs. Also like crime, the costs are borne by many people: by those who suffer ill-health; by their families; by their employers and colleagues at work; and by society as a whole. Estimates of the total vary enormously. A reasonably authoritative estimate comes from the Sainsbury Centre for Mental Health, who put the annual cost to employers at around £25 billion.[35]

There is already solid empirical evidence on the impact adult learning has on improving mental health, as John Field shows in his IFLL Thematic Paper on well-being.[36] Notably, using longitudinal data, Feinstein and Chevalier estimated that raising the educational level of women without qualifications could result in £230 million savings annually.[37] Again, this is subject to wide variation, depending on assumptions made, but it is not difficult to trace the pathways through which such gains could be made, for this group and for others. The effects endure to subsequent generations. At this stage, there is no need to make the case for a single approach to making the estimations. Sensitivity analysis introduces different assumptions to produce a range of possible results, and this is much needed to avoid the spurious precision.[38]

The recent Government Foresight exercise on mental capital pushed our thinking forward on this, in relation to ageing generally. It concluded:

> In a society where the mental capital of older people is seriously undervalued, it is unsurprising that there has been little investment to date in providing other than recreational cases for older students and very little research on its utility… Nevertheless, there are good grounds for supposing that such investments might be highly cost-effective.[39]

[35] Sainsbury Centre (2008).
[36] Field (2009).
[37] Chevalier and Feinstein (2006).
[38] HM Treasury (2003).
[39] Kirkwood et al (2009) p.61.

Once again, the goal is not to reduce everything to financial calculations. The suffering of depressed people and their families and friends cannot be captured in this way. But as a means of opening out our thinking, it is a legitimate exercise.

Conclusion

We make no attempt to disguise our faith in lifelong learning. In this field at least, faith is compatible with evidence, with logic and with common sense. We have mustered, in very compressed form, the evidence for the ways in which learning generates positive social outcomes. Evidence, we stress, comes in different shapes and sizes, and while we should always expect high standards of rigour, we can accept these different forms without assuming they will all conform to the same criteria. Even if we cannot always quantify the outcomes, the picture is overwhelmingly one of positive effects.

Having said that emphatically, we have also entered warnings against trying to claim too much for lifelong learning. We discussed the problematic issue of equality, and argued for a rethink of both social mobility and meritocracy; without structural changes in the pattern of inequality, these two seemingly positive social phenomena can have ambivalent effects.

Finally, we have tried to open up the debate on costs and benefits a little, without being able to spend much time on the technicalities. In conclusion, we need three things to give us a better grip:

- a broader set of criteria for judging the effectiveness of spending;
- a longer timeframe, which captures long-term effects; and
- a willingness to experiment with innovations, some of which will, inevitably, not have positive outcomes.

'We have an insufficient knowledge base to guide change towards a more effective and equitable system; and the different parts of the system do not talk to each other enough.'

3 What's wrong with the system?

This chapter identifies the key features which stand in the way of progress towards the kind of system we envisaged in the opening chapter.

One temptation is to produce a long list of woes, and deplore the fact that education and training do not do enough to solve them. We avoid this; our goal is to identify the strategic points. Because we concentrate on systemic weaknesses, the canvas is inevitably broad. We are more specific when we come to proposals for addressing these flaws in subsequent chapters. The point here is to focus attention on long-standing deficiencies, and whether we are actually heading in the right direction to correct them.

1. Initial education does not serve as a secure foundation for lifelong learning

Young people should leave school or college, at whatever age, with a desire to carry on learning, and the skills to do so. A joined up system of lifelong learning would have this as a goal for all parts of the initial education system. In a ruthlessly competitive global economy, young people need the skills to survive and flourish as soon as they leave. However, a system which achieves its immediate objectives of raising young people's qualifications, yet leaves them without an appetite to carry on learning, has failed.[1] Too much schooling is focused on heaving students over hurdles and into the next phase of education.

Too many leave school without basic skills or any qualifications, and therefore without the foundation for subsequent learning, as well as for adult life. The UK has made progress in recent years, but the picture is still deeply depressing. Having these fundamental competencies is arguably more important than achieving a minimum number of subject certificates.

Many of the fundamentals for learning are laid down early on. This is why a well-resourced foundation stage remains a priority. But it should not be at the expense of, or as an alternative to, investment in adult learning.[2] Both are essential for an

---

[1] Claxton and Lucas (2009).
[2] Alakeson (2005); De Coulon, Marcenaro-Gutierrez and Vignoles (2007).

efficient and equitable system. We need a distribution of resources which matches more closely the educational needs of the population as a whole, not a single segment.

There are three key challenges here:

- *families and parents* are the child's first educators, and are essential partners in laying the foundation, so we should sustain and strengthen the priority for early years;
- the right *incentives* should be in place, so that individuals and institutions in initial education are rewarded for success in instilling a desire to carry on learning. An obvious – but often ignored – corollary is that incentives which point the wrong way, and encourage practices that stunt this desire, should be removed; and
- how *staff* at all levels, from early childhood to higher education, are managed and trained should reflect this aspiration to instil a desire for learning. Most staff try their best to do this, but our sense is that their training and development does not help them to do it systematically. This is a key challenge to system and institutional leaders.

We address these challenges in *Chapters 8* and *9*.

2. The demographic challenge: the balance of opportunity and support for learning across the life course is wrong

Britain is an ageing society. Some parts of it, notably Scotland, are ageing faster than others. Most people already spend more than a third of their adult lives in retirement, and the number of people over 65 will accelerate rapidly in the next two decades.[3] Over the years, a series of initiatives on the implications of ageing (the Opportunity Age strategy, a Foresight exercise on ageing, and the Age Positive and Better Government for Older People initiatives) have paid little attention to learning, while educational responses have been slow to come from a system primarily focused on young people and on paid employment. The explicit recognition of this issue by the Government, in its *Learning Revolution* White Paper on informal adult learning[4] and its new Age strategy[5] are welcome, but modest in proportion to the scale of the challenge. The key flaws are as follows:

---

[3] McNair (2009a).
[4] Department for Innovation, Universities and Skills (DIUS) (2009a).
[5] HM Government (2009).

- diminishing rather than growing public opportunities for learning by older people;
- training at work diminishes very sharply for those over 55;
- the emphasis on economic purposes in our education and training system ignores the growing need for learning for life beyond work – now involving unprecedented periods of post-employment time;
- the positive value of intergenerational and family learning is insufficiently recognised; and
- failure to join up government initiatives like the various planned services to provide careers advice, and health checks.

Responses to demographic change can be scheduled over many years – but they do need to be set in train with a positive and visible impetus behind them. The classic instance is the reform of the pensions system, including the gradual raising of the pension age. Something similar is needed in education: a gradual but persistent adjustment of the system to reflect the changing demographic balance.

We address this in *Chapter 5* where we outline the need for a new model of the life course.

3. The system does not recognise the increasingly diverse transitions into and from employment

Both entry into and exit from the labour market are often protracted and meandering paths.[6] Many find their way along these paths with ease, or at least without too many problems. However, our system is still largely designed as if the transitions are quick and straight.

For young people, exploration of different pathways and identities is natural. Even so, they need some clearer signposts, and support in making the transition into adult working life. For those who are not on the established route of successful school and college, the map is confusing and discouraging. They easily get lost, and disappear.

For people at the other end who are contemplating finishing their working lives, the system does not offer an adequate range of opportunities to manage the transition effectively. For an increasing number, the Third Age is a time of fulfilment and exploration. However, as with young people, there is very unequal enjoyment of this privileged form of transition. Many face a transition from work with little

---

[6] Furlong (2008).

opportunity to learn how to make the most of the new phase – usually those for whom education has not worked so far.

We also address this in *Chapter 5*.

4. Educational inequalities accumulate over the life course

The current system has inadequate capacity to redress inequalities. Particular initiatives on this are there in plenty, but they are add-ons to a system which is structurally unequal. This is an immensely difficult task, as the efforts to change the social class profile of entrants into higher education demonstrate (targeting under-represented groups has been more effective in further education).

Financial assistance is often unclear and unfair. This applies in particular to student support, which in England discriminates heavily against those who do not fit the traditional full-time university mould. It applies also to tax relief for employers, whose effects are poorly understood. The system deters some, and provides others with regressive or poorly-targeted fiscal reward. However, the biggest failure is in the excessive concentration of resources on the initial stage of post-compulsory education, leading to a grossly unbalanced system.

Different aspects of inequality interact with each other. Gender and class interact, for example, in ways which see middle-class women at the top of the initial education pile and working-class males at the bottom – especially white working-class males. The gap is widening.

Lifelong learning cannot resolve these and other deep-seated structural inequalities on its own. It could indeed increase polarisation; the explosion of the private market in learning will necessarily favour those better off. However, addressing them systematically means providing recurrent opportunities designed to enable those who had not initially succeeded to have another chance. Our current system, if anything, does the reverse.

In addition to these all too familiar dimensions of inequality, there is a whole set of groups who are routinely excluded from opportunity – not deliberately but effectively. Equality concerns should extend to these more specific cases too. One test for the progress of any system should be: *How does it perform when seen from the perspective of a disabled adult, a cared-for child, or an ex-prisoner?* Some of our individual stories illustrate such issues.

We address these large issues in *Chapter 6*.

5. For all the rhetoric, a high-skilled economy is not what we have in prospect

The weaknesses of the British training system have been examined repeatedly. The particular merit of the most recent examination, the 2006 Leitch report on skills, was to insist on the fact that 70 per cent of the 2020 workforce are already in the labour market, and so to reinforce the need for a lifelong approach, but the response to this has been only partial. The key specific weaknesses commonly recognised are:

- simplistic notions of 'demand-led' training obscure the reality of workplace practices which do not encourage skill utilisation, and prioritise employer demand over learner or national demand;
- inadequate volume and poor distribution of training, but no consensus on where and how this should be most urgently improved;
- the pursuit of qualifications can overshadow the value of competence and the challenge of designing work environments which reinforce learning;
- inequality of access to training, but insufficient sense of how to develop a collective culture to address the problem;
- an imbalance between regulation and permissiveness, and between employer flexibility and the rights of employees as learners;
- particular difficulties with the level of training in small and medium-sized enterprises (SMEs) and for the self-employed; and
- insufficient awareness of the benefits of training among employers and employees alike, despite welcome initiatives such as the introduction of union learning representatives.

The emerging issues for the long term are as follows:

- the strategy for the future should concentrate on *aligning infrastructure, culture and incentives* to foster both demand and supply, through supportive regulatory frameworks and entitlements;
- *the quality of the working environment* demands far more attention than it has received: the effective use the environment makes of people's capacities, and the effect it has on mental health;
- *co-investment* will be crucial: employers, the State and individuals contributing money and time in different mixes; and
- in a turbulent economy, skills for *employability* need to be interpreted broadly. Informal and voluntary work should form part of this breadth, as sources of skill.

We address this in *Chapter 6*.

6. Finding a way through the system is complex, opaque and demotivating for many

Motivation to learn is crucial, for individuals and organisations. Individuals are frustrated if they cannot find a way to learning which interests them. Employers are frustrated if they cannot get the training that they feel they need.[7]

The phrase the 'qualifications jungle' is a cliché, but this does not rob it of its force. We have a mass of courses and qualifications whose status, meaning and validity are often obscure, even to those who have them.[8] Progression routes are too often hard to identify, if they exist at all. It is a tangle which needs massive simplification (a task which the UKCES is currently addressing as a priority).[9]

Information and guidance are important tools. Serious efforts to improve them are under way, with the adult advancement and careers service[10], and these are welcome. However, there are limits to the extent to which individual guidance can promote a culture of learning, and can reach out to excluded groups.

Informal learning has a big part to play in a culture of lifelong learning, recognised in the government paper, *The Learning Revolution*. There is excellent innovation here; for example, in museums and libraries, as well as local authorities' adult learning.[11] However, the balance between allowing informal learning scope to develop and linking it with formal modes is hard to strike, and we have not found it yet.

We address this in *Chapters 7* and *8*.

7. The governance of the system in England is over-centralised, insufficiently stable and does not trust its professionals enough

The relationship between central and local needs to give a stable framework for all to play their part. The pendulum has swung too far towards central control. This does not mean it should simply be tugged back to its previous position, or pushed even further towards localism. In England, it is currently difficult to identify where the driving force for local service coordination is located, although the same does

---

[7] See Simpson (2009). Our analysis of private training markets showed a yawning gap between private suppliers providing courses without qualifications, and public providers of training yoked to qualifications.

[8] Although it is worth noting that we have myriad degree courses without this causing problems of recognition.

[9] UKCES (2009a).

[10] In Scotland the equivalent is Careers in Scotland, an all-age service.

[11] See Innocent (2009); Brighouse (2009).

not apply throughout the UK. On this issue particularly, the situation in Scotland and Wales is radically different.

The centre itself has been remarkable for its instability.[12] Constant changes of departmental structure, and a whirligig of governmental ministers with varying shades of responsibility for lifelong learning, have created a climate of strategic uncertainty and high levels of policy mortality.

Accountability is, rightly, a major issue. However, if it takes the wrong form, accountability stifles innovation, destroys trust and increases costs. We need a better balance between accountability and earned autonomy. Professionals in all walks of lifelong learning need their trust in the system raised, along with the system's trust in them.

Our colleges have been subject to central direction, but this has too often been a series of disconnected rather than strategic changes. As the enrolment figures show,[13] they have been incentivised to move towards a focus on youth, and away from the lifelong comprehensive service which should be their true mission. The pressure has been for fiscal stability at the expense of innovation to meet local needs.

Our universities still have relatively high autonomy, and many of them use this creatively. But there is no willingness to use a common currency for credit in higher education, nor between further and higher education, making progression and mobility difficult. An increasing emphasis on research, coupled with fiscal disincentives which discriminate against part-time provision, has weakened universities' commitment to lifelong learning.

Clear guidance, incentives and frameworks are needed for all the partners to collaborate in delivering a full range of learning opportunities, with 'earned autonomy' as the touchstone.

We address this in *Chapter 9*.

8. Inadequate infrastructure: buildings, technologies and services are not well integrated

There has been substantial investment in education buildings in the past decade: in children's centres, in schools, and in further education and higher education (despite some major hiccups with college buildings in 2009). We have advances in access to technology, as with the People's Network in public libraries, and UK

---

[12] Tuckett (2008).
[13] See The Data Service (2009).

Online and its 500 learning centres. However, this does not mean we have an adequate infrastructure for lifelong learning. The challenge of the twenty-first century is to imagine and implement a suitable infrastructure which combines well-designed physical environments, the wider use of public spaces, accessible technological capacity and the people skills needed to integrate the two.

Good infrastructure design needs different sectors to come together. These must include the people who deliver learning through it, and a strong learner voice. People are often the forgotten factor in infrastructure design. There are two essential aspects here: effective co-production, with those who use the service being involved in design and development; and giving enough training to those who are to make the infrastructure hum.

Infrastructure also includes links with other services. Even at local level, these are often lacking. Co-location of learning with other services – notably health – is something which will demand increasing attention and imagination. The benefit system can be a major block to lifelong learning, providing disincentives.[14]

We address this in *Chapter 9*.

9. The 'system' is not sufficiently intelligent

We have an insufficient knowledge base to guide change towards a more effective and equitable system; and the different parts of the system do not talk to each other enough.

This report gives an overall picture of the resources which go into the system from various sources. The picture is still very sketchy. Some of the sums bandied about in the public debate, notably the suggested £38 billion of employer expenditure in England, are calculated from a fragile basis.

Our knowledge of participation patterns is more secure. We have information that is consistent over time, but it is still quite superficial, notably in relation to the duration of learning. The inequalities are clearly apparent, and yet it is not easy to bring them all into line with each other.

We are still far away from a consistent way of assessing the results or outcomes of all the effort put into learning. Qualifications are an imperfect measure of human capital, and more direct measures of competence at work would be

---

[14] The reference to health prompts a possible parallel: we may need a 'national learning service' to make the effective connections between the different parts of the system.

a great advance.[15] Wider social outcomes are not adequately integrated into overall evaluations. Lifelong learning has multiple objectives – better economic performance, stronger social cohesion and greater social mobility, to name but three – yet we have no agreed means of assessing overall progress in any detail.

To be intelligent, a system needs good information. We need more systematic information on participation, expenditure and outcomes. In particular, we need stronger and more varied ways of estimating the benefits and costs of learning, including, but going well beyond, the economic aspects, and longer-term research to strengthen the knowledge base. We also need more room for creative experimentation, to help build our understanding of what works.

We address this in *Annexe A*.

Conclusion

Concentrating on flaws in the system, this chapter has inevitably struck a negative note. The purpose has been to open the way for the analyses and proposals we have in subsequent chapters. We need to stress that the Commissioners' discussions, and the bulk of the consultation meetings which have been held, had a thoroughly optimistic and positive tone. This reflects the abundance of good practice, and the potential which everyone sees for the future, in spite of current difficulties.

---

[15] OECD is now trying to add this to its array of influential comparative analyses, through the PIAAC programme.

'We have, for the first time, aggregated up all different forms of expenditure: direct expenditure on teaching and course provision, student support costs, and the costs of organising and managing the education and training.'

'We do believe that there should be a better balance in the distribution of resources, and that additional money is needed for some areas, in some cases urgently so. However, pumping up expenditure is not the solution to every problem.'

4 Where are we now?

Summary

This chapter presents a stocktake of the current position on lifelong learning in the UK. It is organised primarily around two main axes: participation and expenditure. On participation, we begin with some comparative figures, to gain an idea of how the UK compares with other countries. We show how participation rates have changed over the last decade, to get an idea of the trends involved, and the direction of travel. We also show how participation rates vary in a number of dimensions, including sex, social class and geography, in and out of the workplace. This is a crucial basis for understanding where we need to move in order to meet the challenge of greater fairness in our system.[1]

On expenditure, we bring together a very wide range of figures in order to get a sense of what is spent on all the different forms of post-compulsory education and training. This has a number of different components:

a) expenditure by *public authorities* of all kinds. As well as programmes for the public, a major component is spending by public authorities on their own employees' training. We break this down by broad categories, according to purpose;

b) expenditure by *employers*, public and private. This means primarily vocational training.

c) expenditure by the *third (voluntary) sector*. As with public authorities, this covers both programmes for the public or particular groups of the public, and training for third sector employees; and

d) expenditure by individuals and households.[2]

---

[1] The participation analysis was carried out by Fiona Aldridge of the IFLL Secretariat and NIACE.
[2] Analyses of a, b and d were commissioned from Nigel Brown Associates: Nigel Brown, Mick Fletcher and Mark Corney. Analysis of c was commissioned from MakesFive (Solihin Garrard). We are grateful to the authors for their work. Responsibility for the use made of it here is ours.

Bringing together all these forms of spending is not something that has been done before, to the best of our knowledge. The sums involved look very large, but our aim is not to impress with their scale, nor is it to bemoan their miserliness. The overview is far from perfect, but it does provide a basis on which to build a better knowledge base for future decisions on lifelong learning. We discuss below what the sums actually mean.

Key results from this include the following:

- total expenditure on adult learning amounts to approximately £55 billion or 3.9 per cent of Gross Domestic Product (GDP);
- roughly £26 billion of the total is spent from the public purse; £20 billion on training by private and non-profit organisations; £9 billion by individuals, including the self-employed;
- the scale of public subsidy on vocational training is large; our estimate is that the various forms of tax relief amount to £3.7 billion; and
- of the total spent on teaching provision for colleges and universities, the split is roughly 1/3:2/3; for student support the split is 10:90. The weighting is heavily in favour of young, full-time students.

We also present some small but original analysis of time use data. This gives us some understanding of how much time people spend on learning of different kinds. The most detailed information on this is dated '2000', but it serves to give us a handle on this important dimension.[3] In particular, it opens the way for our calculations in *Chapter 5* of how learning expenditure is distributed across the life course.

Participation in lifelong learning: trends and distribution

The good news is that millions of people across the UK take part in learning of one form or another. For the most part they gain from it, at work and/or in personal terms, and they enjoy it. There is a huge range of providers, including voluntary sector programmes, which reach out to those for whom participation in education is particularly difficult. Innovative schemes are there in plenty. The less good news is that the overall numbers have been sliding; certain parts of the system are in a significantly unhealthy state. Meanwhile, some groups participate much less than others, accentuating initial inequalities in educational achievement.

Before we move to the figures, we need to say something more about the values which lie behind our interpretation. Our assumption is that high levels of learning

---

[3] The time use analysis was carried out by Muriel Egerton. We are grateful to her; use of the results is our responsibility.

are not just a personal good, but a sign of a healthy and a civilised society. In *Chapter 2* we have given some of the reasons for this: learning is linked to all kinds of desirable outcomes, both individual and collective. Learning makes people healthier, happier, more active citizens and so on, even if there is no easy direct read-off between increasing educational achievement and these outcomes. But the effects also spill over into wider society. For the most part, and in very general terms, we all benefit from each others' learning as well as our own.

There are two important caveats to this. The first is that formal education is not the only, and not necessarily the best, way of achieving these desirable outcomes. It is not obvious that someone will benefit more from signing up for a class than, for example, participating as secretary for a local hobby club. Of course, they may do both, but there are always choices to be made about how to spend time. Raising levels of formal participation is less of an obvious plus if it comes at the expense of a decrease in other less formal types of activity that may produce similar levels of well-being, for the individual and society. The class bias that we can see so clearly in the participation figures to some extent reflects cultural preferences, and we should not ignore this.

The second point has a very different significance. Put brutally, the advantages which some people gain from raising their levels of educational achievement benefit them *at the expense of others*. In some respects, education is a positional good.[4] For example, if you get a better job by gaining a qualification, someone else does not get that job who otherwise would have, because you have leapfrogged them in the queue (which may be done entirely on merit). Or your education gives you the confidence to use a public service legitimately to your own advantage, for instance in asserting your right to a hospital appointment, but in a world of finite numbers of doctors, giving you that appointment means that someone else doesn't get it. This is known, a little unfairly, as the 'sharp middle-class elbow'. In other words, the person who receives education achieves an advantage (perfectly legitimately) over others, so the net benefit may be zero, or even negative.

This is one more reason why the question of fairness and equity is so important. When we argue that more should be done to equalise participation rates, this is not just out of a conviction that many people are missing out on a valuable experience with tangible benefits. It is also because the greater the inequalities that exist in participation, the greater the disadvantage which results *from education itself*. This is an uncomfortable conclusion, but one that demands attention. It is a matter of social justice, not paternalism.

---

[4] Hirsch (1976).

The participation trends

International comparisons

First, we can put the UK position in some kind of international context. The European Union (EU) gathers information on participation in adult education and training. The survey covers both formal and non-formal learning. Figure 4 gives some of the results. How well does the UK do in relation to other comparable countries?

The broad picture from the EU's Adult Education Survey (the Survey covers 17 EU countries plus Norway) is that on the simple measures of participation the UK does relatively well. On these measures we are an associate member of the Scandinavian club – not a full member, but quite close to it. This means that we have quite high gross participation rates, nearing 50 per cent. Of the countries listed, only Norway, Finland and Sweden do better than this. The UK is high on both formal and non-formal learning.

Moreover, on at least some measures of equal access, we also do well. The gap between highly qualified and unqualified people's participation rates is smaller for the UK than anywhere else other than Sweden. The same is true in respect of age, where we appear to have a relatively small gap between the participation rates of older and younger people, compared to our European neighbours.

Figure 4: Participation in formal or non-formal education and training, age 25–64, 2007

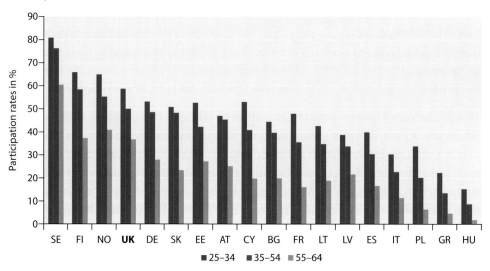

Source: Eurostat Adult Education Survey, taken from Eurostat (2008)

All this looks encouraging. However, there are some major qualifications to this apparently rosy picture. First, we should note that the data is good but limited. If we dig below the gross participation rates and look at duration – how long people spend in their period of adult education, rather than simply whether or not they took part – a different picture emerges. Here, the UK is out on its own (see Figure 5). For non-formal learning, there is not much variation between countries as far as duration is concerned; those who take part do so for quite similar lengths of time. But when it comes to formal education, the picture is dramatically different: for whatever reason, UK learners take part for much shorter periods than their European counterparts, averaging not much over 100 hours, compared to more than twice that amount for most countries. This is a striking difference indeed.

Such a difference needs closer analysis, which is not easily available. It would be possible to give the figures a reasonably positive spin: they show that the UK enables a lot of people to take part, in short chunks. Isn't this exactly what the doctrine of flexible provision proposes, and a preferable pattern to one of fewer people doing long courses? Maybe. But it is more likely that both the high rates and the short duration derive from the same source: that the UK figures include quite a high percentage of episodes such as induction training, which can be very brief indeed – a matter of a few hours (remember that the figures are averages, which cover up the range of distribution around them). Figures from the Learning and Skills Council (shown in Figure 6) show that for about a quarter of employers,

Figure 5: Mean instruction hours spent by participants in education and training, age 25–64, 2007

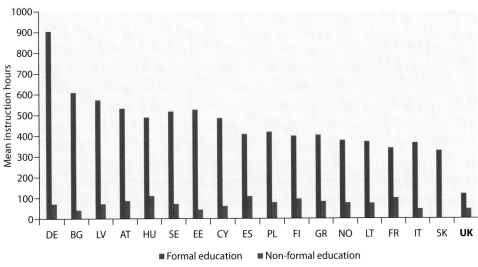

Source: Eurostat Adult Education Survey, taken from Eurostat (2008)

Figure 6: Proportion of training accounted for by health and safety or induction training

Source: LSC (2007)

at least half of the recorded training is on induction and statutory items such as health and safety. These are important, certainly; but they are hardly an adequate index of a learning culture as most of us would understand it, so high participation rates disguise what is often superficial engagement in learning.

As this suggests, figures on their own can tell us only a limited amount, which is why league tables are often so misleading. We need to locate them in some kind of context, however cursorily. This means looking not only at the education and training statistics, but at the way lifelong learning as a system forms part of a wider economic and cultural profile: the values which a society upholds, for example in levels of equality and social cohesion; the climate of industrial relations, notably the extent of collaboration between the social partners; and the expected role of government in social and economic affairs. We cannot go into this in any detail, but one increasingly accepted categorisation is threefold: the Anglo-Saxon neo-liberal; the Continental European social market; and the Nordic welfare regimes.[5] The last are often idealised, perhaps exaggeratedly so, but nevertheless succeed in combining overall high levels of participation with quite equal distribution across the population, and with strong state support for a variety of provision. The Anglo-Saxon model has its strengths, allowing diversity and flexibility, but it has nowhere near the same coverage as the Nordic model. Many more people fall through the gaps, accentuating inequalities. This is particularly evident in the sphere of workplace training, where the UK has a 'long tail', with many of its population lacking basic skills and having no or few qualifications.

---

[5] Esping-Andersen (1999); Green *et al* (2008).

Participation at work

According to the UKCES,[6] in international rankings we are now seventeenth on 'low' level skills, eighteenth on 'intermediate' level skills and twelfth on 'high' level skills. While the overall UK skills profile is improving over time, too many people are still in danger of being left behind: one in eight adults of working age still have no qualifications; more than a quarter are not qualified to Level 2; and just under half are not qualified to above Level 2. Moreover, as other countries are improving their skills profile too, our relative position has changed little. Indeed, many countries are improving faster than we are.

Understandably perhaps, employers tend to give training to their most educated staff. Those who perform routine tasks – cleaners, factory workers and kitchen hands, for example – tend to be neglected by their employers' training plans. According to the City and Guilds Centre for Skills Development,[7] professional and associate professional staff – the more highly paid – receive the most training; unskilled and low-paid employees receive the least.

These cultural considerations are crucial for any view of the future of lifelong learning. They spread into the nature of workplaces – whether they are 'expansive' or 'restrictive' in the encouragement they give to learning at work[8] – and more broadly into the role society sees for learning. We will return to these questions later. What we have done here is sketch an outline of the UK's place in relation to other countries. It is certainly not at the bottom of the league, and has many features to celebrate, but it also has major flaws.

Class and inequality

A single snapshot would not tell us much, so let's look at the overall trends over the last ten or more years. The results come from a variety of sources, but mainly from the annual series of surveys carried out by NIACE. The essential points are:

- the single most salient feature of all the participation data over time is that participation is very closely related to social class. A series of indicators all point constantly and unambiguously in the same direction: it is not only the direct measure of socio-economic group, but all those related factors such as highest level of qualification, income and occupational status. The higher up you are, the more likely you are to take part in learning. However you define it, social class fundamentally shapes the participation profile;

---

[6] UKCES (2009a).
[7] Gosling (2009).
[8] Unwin, Felstead and Fuller (2008).

- attachment to work also appears continually as a powerful factor. Most obviously, people in paid employment participate more, but even being registered unemployed is more likely to mean participation than having no connection at all to the labour market. Even being in a low-ranking job gives you a better chance of learning than being out of the labour market altogether;
- the younger you are, the more likely you are to participate. The age pattern is one of direct decline. This is far greater than could be explained by any age-related decline in individual capacity; and
- having a disability discourages participation. Some of the reasons for this are self-evident: lack of mobility, difficulty of access to buildings or the non-availability of appropriately designed learning materials. Others may be to do with personal factors such as confidence.[9]

Table 2: Current or recent participation in learning by socio-economic class – 1996–2009 compared (%)

Social grade	1996 %	1999 %	2002 %	2005 %	2008 %	2009 %
Total sample	40	40	42	42	38	39
AB	53	58	60	56	51	53
C1	52	51	54	51	46	48
C2	33	36	37	40	33	33
DE	26	24	25	26	26	24
Weighted base	4,755	5,205	5,885	5,053	4,932	4,917

Social Grade A includes the upper and upper-middle classes, and is generally grouped with Grade B, the middle classes. Grade C1 includes the lower-middle class, often called white-collar workers. Grade C2 mainly consists of skilled manual workers. Grade D comprises the semi-skilled and unskilled working class, and is usually linked with Grade E, those on the lowest levels of subsistence such as old age pensioners and those dependent upon welfare benefits.
Base: all respondents

Source: NIACE Adult Participation in Learning Survey, taken from Aldridge and Tuckett (2009)

---

[9] Forthcoming analysis from the National Equality Panel shows that the relative position of disabled people with poor qualifications has worsened over the last 30 years – see http://www.equalities.gov.uk/

Figure 7: Current or recent participation in learning by age, 2009

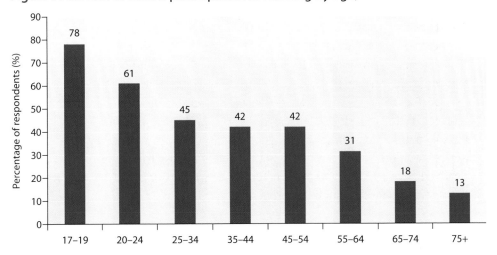

Base: all respondents

Source: NIACE Adult Participation in Learning Survey, taken from Aldridge and Tuckett (2009)

These headline conclusions should be enough to show that adult learning holds up a mirror to society's inequalities. There is hardly a single factor where participation patterns run counter to the wider patterns of disadvantage. It is the classic Matthew effect: to him that hath shall be given.[10]

Again, let's see how this plays out in the workplace – the office, the production line or the virtual workplace. We have noted above that being in employment is better than being out of work as far as general access to learning is concerned, but we need to look further into the distribution of opportunities across different kinds of work. What do different occupations and different jobs mean for access to learning? The picture is predictable; the gaps are wide. There is no total correspondence between where you are in the hierarchy of jobs and your chances of getting access to learning, but the fit is pretty good. Professionals – generally, the 'knowledge workers' – have good access, the intermediary levels do quite well, and then there is a very steep drop-off (see Figure 8). There are one or two exceptions to the pattern – energy workers, for example, seem to do better than one might expect from their position in the occupational hierarchy (see Figure 9) – but overall it is clear and consistent with the picture already sketched.

---

[10] 'For to all those who have, more will be given, and they will have an abundance; but from those who have nothing, even what they have will be taken away.' From the Bible, the Gospel According to St Matthew, 25:29.

Figure 8: Participation in job-related education and training in the 13 weeks prior to interview, by socio-economic classification, Q1 2008

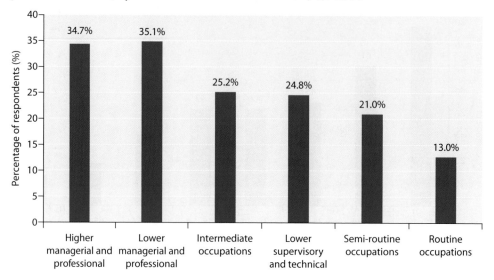

Source: ONS Labour Force Survey, Q1 2008, taken from ONS (2008b)

Figure 9: Access to training at work in last 13 weeks by sector

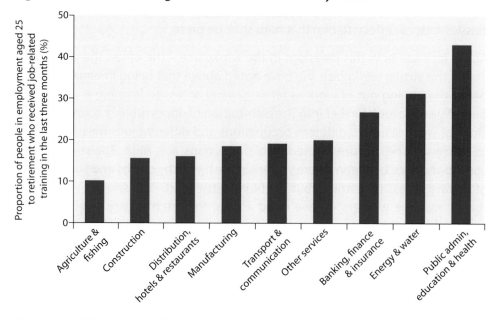

Note: the data is for the average for 2006 to 2007, UK, updated March 2008

Source: ONS Labour Force Survey, taken from ONS (2008b)

Table 3: Job-related training by highest level of qualification in the UK

Qualification	1998 %	2003 %	2008 %
Degree or equivalent	39.9	42.4	37.2
Higher education	38.7	40.9	35.4
GCE A-level or equivalent	24.3	27.3	25.6
GCSE grade A–C or equivalent	25.6	27.9	24.4
Other qualifications	17.1	21.9	18.7
No qualification	7.9	10.2	8.4
All levels of qualification	25.0	29.0	26.6

Note: data is 12 months ending March, not seasonally adjusted.

Source: ONS Labour Force Survey, taken from Clancy (2009)

One other dimension of the distribution of learning at work needs to be stressed. Working in the public sector raises your chances of accessing learning very considerably. Over 40 per cent of public sector workers participate compared with 21.8 per cent of those in the private sector. Naturally, there are two ways of looking at this: as a dubious privilege, or as an example of good practice which should set the standard for organisations elsewhere. We prefer the latter.[11]

Gender: a more ambiguous picture

The Matthew effect, however, takes us on to gender: the Marthas along with the Matthews. Here the picture is less clear-cut, and the variations across age groups produce some intriguing patterns (see Table 4).

For this table we have used the age groups which form the basis of the four-stage model we describe in the next chapter. Men participate more in the first stage, but this switches in the second stage, with women clearly doing better in the second stage. Above 50, the rates are more or less equal for both sexes.

Arguably the single most striking trend in education in the last 10–15 years has been the way women have overtaken men in educational achievement,

---

[11] This is not to say that all public sector training is good value; for instance, some of it is arguably more to do with risk avoidance than with learning.

Table 4: Current or recent participation in learning across the four life stages, by gender, 2009

	18–24 %	25–49 %	50–74 %	75+ %
Total sample	64	44	30	13
Men	66	41	29	12
Women	62	46	30	13
Weighted base	533	2,146	1,686	464

Base: all respondents

Source: NIACE Adult Participation in Learning Survey, 2009

at every level, in almost every subject and in almost every OECD country. This is a huge shift in the educational picture, which has attracted remarkably little analysis, both as a sociological phenomenon and as a trend with major policy implications. Its implications for lifelong learning are many, but here we point to only one. The general pattern of participation, as we have seen, is that those who succeed initially go on to enjoy better access to learning opportunities later on. As women now outstrip men in initial educational achievement, what will that do to subsequent patterns of participation? Will the gap between female and male participation widen at all stages in the life course?

Participation is not only a function of previous education. Motivation and barriers are the major factors which shape participation, but the gender difference is so significant because of its cultural lessons and implications. These are to do with the attitudes of peer groups to learning and its advantages. Men are more likely to learn at work or independently, and women are more likely to learn at publicly funded institutions or community facilities. Research evidence on why this should be so is scarce, but very strong anecdotal evidence suggests that women encourage each other more to learn, and support each other in their learning, at all ages. Peer group effects – their social capital – are very strong. The question is, what lessons does this have if we are interested in creating a general culture of learning?

Ethnicity

Data on ethnicity shows that black and minority ethnic adults and the larger white population participate overall in broadly similar proportions. A more detailed analysis of particular groups, however, reveals markedly different levels of participation among adults from different communities, with fewer than one

Table 5: Participation in learning by gender and ethnicity, 2006

	All %	Men %	Women %
All respondents	62	65	59
All respondents from minority ethnic groups	61	63	58
White	62	65	59
Black African	73	75	71
Black Caribbean	61	60	62
Chinese	66	66	67
Indian	61	65	56
Pakistani	47	52	42
Bangladeshi	38	42	34

Base: all adults

Source: ONS Labour Force Survey 2006, taken from Aldridge, Lamb and Tuckett (2008)

half of Bangladeshi and Pakistani adults participating in learning. For women within these communities, the rate is lower still – 34 per cent from Bangladeshi and 42 per cent from Pakistani communities (see Table 5).

The challenges of offering educational pathways for Bangladeshi and Pakistani adults, and women in particular, are compounded by the pattern of participation by age – with learners with a Bangladeshi background over 35 years of age participating at less than half the national rate.

Geography: differences between and within nations

We noted already that this report covers all four nations of the UK, although it cannot cover all the differences between them. One particularly salient difference is in participation levels. Scotland appears to be worse hit by the overall decline in participation than the other nations, whereas Wales and Northern Ireland show up well (see Table 6). However, it is true that people from different countries can respond differently to questions about whether or not they participate, and some of the Scottish response may be because they set the threshold slightly higher – that is, they discount very short episodes.[12]

---

[12] Schuller and Field (2000).

Table 6: Current or recent participation in learning, by UK nation, 2002–2009 compared (%)

	2002	2005	2008	2009
Total sample (UK)	42	42	38	39
England	42	42	39	39
Wales	39	42	38	41
Scotland	44	36	31	33
Northern Ireland	40	37	40	42
Weighted base	5,885	5,053	4,932	4,917

Base: all respondents

Source: NIACE Adult Participation in Learning Survey, taken from Aldridge and Tuckett (2009)

The other key geographical variation is in the relationship between demand and supply with regard to skills and qualifications. This applies to regions as well as nations. The generalisation of a shift in employment patterns towards high-skilled work therefore applies only in some parts of the UK. Outside London and the south-east, it is a gross over-simplification. There are often more qualified people than there are jobs to match their skills. Without going into the complex issue of 'over-qualification' and 'mismatch' it is clear that we should be looking as much at how skills are used as at how to raise qualification levels.[13]

Expenditure on lifelong learning

We spend a lot on lifelong learning. People usually find money interesting, but there are limits on how far the details of these calculations will hold the average attention, so we have consigned these details to the IFLL website and provide here only the broad outlines. Our estimate of the total varies according to the method of calculation chosen, but the lowest estimate for the global amount, combining public, private and individual expenditure is about £55 billion. A figure such as this is slightly less dazzling than it once would have been, overshadowed by crunch-inducing bank losses and recession-busting government expenditure, but it is still very large. This is in part because we have covered all forms of lifelong learning, and we have, for the first time, aggregated up all different forms of expenditure: direct expenditure on teaching and course provision, student support costs, and the costs of organising and managing the education and training.

---

[13] UKCES (2009a); Felstead (2009).

Costs of provision

Tax payers, employers and individuals all contribute to this big overall pot. One reason why it is important to bring it all together is that overall investment depends on the sense that everyone is contributing, and contributing on a reasonably fair basis. We argue later on that 'co-financing' – the sharing of costs by two or more of the stakeholders – is a key to levering in resources for learning. Leaving everything to the Government (the tax payer) has to some the attraction of appearing 'free', but it will not maximise investment or help create a culture of commitment to learning, nor will expecting employers, or individuals, to shoulder all the burden. Things work best – most support is given financially, but also in terms of genuine commitment – where all parties are substantively involved in supporting learning. Of course, there will be debate and disagreement on who should pay how much for any given provision. For example, should employers pay for basic skills, since in principle people should not leave the school system without such skills? Should individuals pay for their own higher education, since graduates generally earn more because of their publicly funded degrees? What proportion of the costs of so-called 'leisure courses' should be paid by the individuals consuming them (especially now that we have evidence of how these courses improve older people's health and well-being)? All these are genuine questions, which are currently up for debate. People naturally seek to reduce their financial obligations where they think others will step in. However, a society where everyone recognises that they have a stake in learning, and where there are collective as well as individual returns, will produce higher rates of investment in it.

Before we discuss the results, a few more words on terminology. We talk mainly about 'spending' and 'costs', but also about 'investment'. Some would argue that money spent on education, from whatever source, should be treated as an investment. In an organisational balance sheet, it should go on the asset side not the expenditure side. We naturally have a lot of sympathy with this position, since it turns learning from a cost into an asset that accumulates, which should in turn make those holding the purse strings (public or private) more sympathetic. In most cases, learning is indeed an investment which produces returns (not necessarily economic returns). However, the money comes from somewhere and represents a cost to someone, so in general we choose here to talk of expenditure – and then later on to spend time examining the benefits which flow from that expenditure.

What is the spending for? Everyone has their own view on what learning is or should be for. Even very instrumental learning – dentistry, for example, or plumbing – can count as a contribution to the country's cultural development, as dentists and plumbers acquire all kinds of other learning along with their technical skills. Almost any subject can be learnt for personal gain as well as occupational relevance, and vice versa.

The 1997 Dearing Report defined the aim of higher education as being to sustain a learning society, and its four main purposes as follows:

- 'to inspire and enable individuals to develop their capabilities to the highest potential levels throughout life, so that they grow intellectually, are well equipped for work, can contribute effectively to society and achieve personal fulfilment;
- to increase knowledge and understanding for their own sake and to foster their application to the benefit of the economy and society;
- to serve the needs of an adaptable, sustainable, knowledge-based economy at local, regional and national levels;
- to play a major role in shaping a democratic, civilised, inclusive society.'[14]

These were for higher education, but almost all forms of learning could be fitted somewhere under these labels, suitably adapted. However, there is no such common set for classifying expenditure. Table 7 and Figure 10 use three general headings: 'national performance', 'public programmes' and 'employee development'. These are very broad labels, but they give us a reasonable way of clustering all the different types.

- *'National performance'* covers all the most obvious forms of post-compulsory education which takes place in colleges and universities. It deals with the costs of teaching and student support, including what is needed to build and run the institutions within which learning takes place. We label this 'national performance' to indicate that our position as a nation depends on it, but as the Dearing goals indicate, performance is not solely related to economic goals. Diplomas, undergraduate and graduate degrees all fall within this category, whatever the subject.
- *'Public programmes'* refers to provision which supports other public goods. They have no close link to employability, but cover broader citizenship and other public value programmes. They may be part of the formal education system, but figure strongly in the voluntary and informal sector.
- *'Employee development'* refers to the training of staff for organisational ends. This covers the public, private and third sectors; that is, not-for-profit as well as profit-making organisations. There are particular difficulties of classification here. Many forms of training are relatively informal: they are intentional; i.e. they do not happen by accident, but they occur as part of everyday life in the

---

[14] NCIHE (1997).

organisation. For example, mentoring is a form of employee development which is growing in scale and which many consider to be particularly effective, but it is usually not so structured that it can be recorded and costed. The distinction between formal and informal learning is a very important one – for one thing, people who have not been successful in their initial education often prefer more informal modes, as they are the least likely to remind them of their early failures, so supporting informal learning has a strong equity component. However, it is not one which makes the life of data-gatherers easy.

Who spends what on lifelong learning?

There are two overall totals of expenditure on adult learning. Both are likely to be underestimates. The two figures are:

- £55 billion: this excludes all the estimated cost of time spent on learning,
- £93 billion: this includes expenditure on provision and the cost of time spent on learning.

Table 7: UK expenditure on adult learning provision by investor and learning purpose, 2007–08

	National performance	Public programmes	Employee development
Public sector	£12.9 billion	£1.2 billion	£7.7 billion £3.7 billion tax relief[a]
Private sector[b]			£16.2 billion[c]
Voluntary and community sector	£0.13 billion	£0.5 billion	£3.15 billion[d]
Individuals	£4.68 billion	£0.82 billion	£3.9 billion[e]
Total	£17.71 billion	£2.52 billion	£34.65 billion
Grand total: £54.88 billion			

[a]*Includes Corporation Tax Relief and PAYE Tax Relief (for self-employed businesses).*
[b]*The private sector supports some adult learning for the general public, through union learning centres opened to families and local communities, and Corporate Social Responsibility initiatives to name but two.*
[c]*Includes expenditure on employee development for businesses operated by self-employed people.*
[d]*This includes a calculation of the cost of volunteer training.*
[e]*Expenditure by self-employed people on their own business-related training.*

Source: IFLL

Figure 10: Distribution of expenditure on the costs of learning provision (£ billion) by category of investor, 2007–08

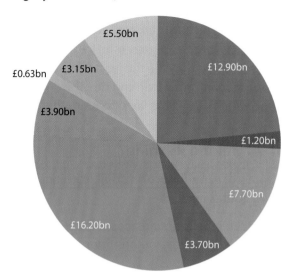

■ Public expenditure on national performance

■ Public expenditure on public programmes

■ Public expenditure on public sector employee development

■ Tax relief

■ Expenditure on employee development by private for-profit organisations

■ Expenditure by self-employed people on their own business-related development

■ VCS expenditure on national performance and public programmes

■ Expenditure on employee development by VCS organisations

■ Individual expenditure on learning

Note: VCS = voluntary and community sector

Source: IFLL

Table 7 shows how the £55 billion total is broken down and Figure 10 shows the distribution of expenditure on the costs of learning provision.

The cost of time

The figure could be far bigger. Economists would, reasonably enough, include the costs of learners' time, on the basis that while they are learning they are not producing. This is the approach adopted by the National Employer Skills Survey (NESS), which reported that in 2007 employers in England[15] spent £38.6 billion on training, including the wage costs of those undertaking training, both on and off the job. To extend the NESS approach to all learners would add in many billions to the total. One set of our calculations includes that, and this would boost the global

---

[15] Our figures are for the UK.

Figure 11: Breakdown of expenditure on cost of provision and cost of time by category of investor

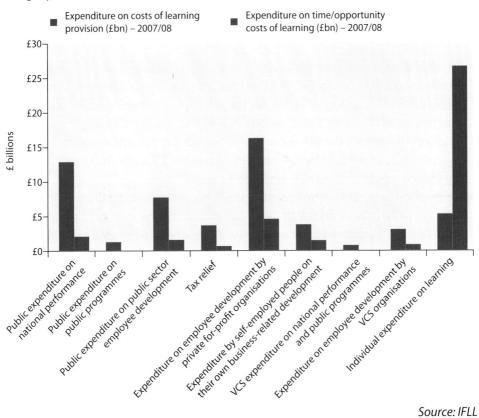

■ Expenditure on costs of learning provision (£bn) – 2007/08

■ Expenditure on time/opportunity costs of learning (£bn) – 2007/08

Source: IFLL

total to £93 billion. On this basis, the cost of time accounts for £38 billion, 40 per cent of overall expenditure. Individuals overwhelmingly commit the most – nearly 70 per cent of the total cost of time is met by them, and 19 per cent by employers supporting off-the-job training. Figure 11 shows this but we have excluded these calculations from our overall baseline calculation, because it would unreasonably skew the whole picture. We do not think that an hour's training for a top banker or footballer earning a £1 million salary should be counted as the same investment as, say, five weeks of full-time training for a low-wage employee, even if that were a realistic prospect.

Our estimates of the cost of time spent learning have raised some key issues. There is no agreed methodology for calculating the opportunity cost of individuals' time invested in learning. We have adapted the approach used in the National Employer

Skills Survey,[16] but believe this issue would merit further study, as part of further work we recommend on valuing co-contributions to learning (see *Chapter 6* for more information).

The key messages from our analysis are as follows:[17]

- Expenditure on *all post-compulsory and adult learning provision in 2007–08 amounts to 3.9 per cent of GDP.* Of this total, £25.5 billion (47 per cent) was public expenditure (including for public sector employees and tax relief for companies on the cost of training). £19.3 billion (35 per cent) was for training of employees and volunteers by private for-profit and not-for-profit organisations, including by companies operated by self-employed people. £9.4 billion (17 per cent) was by individuals, including self-employed people.
- Of the total expenditure on learning provision, just over £20 billion (37 per cent) was on provision in principle available to all citizens (National Performance and Public Programmes). The remaining expenditure of around £35 billion (63 per cent) was only available to employees of the investing organisations.
- Tax relief, including on corporation tax and PAYE, is a major component. It amounts to £3.7 billion annually, or several times the current Train to Gain budget.
- Sixty-five per cent of total public expenditure[18] on post-compulsory education (£9.75 billion) was spent on HE, three-quarters of which we estimate went to learners under 25.[19]
- Of the £11.8 billion expenditure on provision of mainstream post-compulsory education,[20] £7.9 billion (67 per cent) went to higher education (HE), £3.9 billion (33 per cent) to further education (FE).
- Approximately 90 per cent (£1.9 billion) of the £2.1 billion maintenance loans and grants/learner support expenditure goes on HE maintenance loans and grants, and just 10 per cent on FE student support.
- Of the £1.2 billion public expenditure on public programmes, £0.3 billion expenditure from the Department for Business, Innovation and Skills (BIS) supports the Adult Safeguarded Learning budget, the LSC Offender Learning

---

[16] We have used the £12.26/hour wage figure from NESS for economically active people. For others we have used the National Minimum Wage 2007 figure of £5.52/hour.

[17] A more detailed summary of the findings of the Inquiry's expenditure research will be on the Inquiry's website: www.lifelonglearninginquiry.org.uk

[18] Including maintenance loans and grants.

[19] Corney, Fletcher and Brown (2008) suggest 70 per cent of HE expenditure (approximately £6.8 billion) goes on 17–20-year-old full-time undergraduates.

[20] Excluding maintenance loans and grants.

Budget and the Science in Society Programme. The balance is principally investment in public services such as libraries and community development.[21]

This analysis raises key questions about the balance between expenditure on different types of provision, on different groups, and by different parties. These questions are considered more fully in *Chapter 5* where we propose a new model for the educational life course.

Our estimates of tax relief on employee training suggest this is a significant public contribution to private employer training expenditure. We argue in *Chapter 10* for tighter conditions and greater transparency in accounting for tax relief in company accounts. Equally, our work on tax relief has highlighted the absence of general tax relief for individuals investing in their own learning. This appears inequitable to us. We favour a review of tax relief arrangements for individuals investing in learning as part of a new framework of incentives and entitlements.

This is the first time that we have been able to see an overall picture of expenditure on adult learning. The data on which the research has been based is imperfect and partial, often not designed for the purpose. However, we are confident that they represent reasonable 'orders of magnitude' estimates of the pattern of expenditure and the relationships between major parts. As a 'first analysis' it highlights areas for further work. In *Chapter 10* we call for a joint initiative to improve the way expenditure on adult learning is recorded as a basis for encouraging a more strategic approach to future investment decisions.

The point of this analysis of overall expenditure is not to argue for additional money as such. We do believe that there should be a better balance in the distribution of resources, and that additional money is needed for some areas, in some cases urgently so. However, pumping up expenditure is not the solution to every problem. We have only to look at the US, which tops the world league in its spending on health without achieving even a respectable position in international league tables on health performance. (Arguably, indeed, health in the US is negatively affected by the stresses caused by the expense of their system.) We need stronger measures, of both fairness and effectiveness, in order to judge how well the resources devoted to lifelong learning in all its forms are used, and how well they are distributed. We outline these in *Chapter 5*.

---

[21] This is likely to be an under-estimate and this area would merit further study in light of the commitment to opening up public spaces and supporting community learning champions in *The Learning Revolution* White Paper (DIUS, 2009a).

Time on learning: age ratios

Time and money go together, so to get a more detailed idea of how much time people spend on learning we commissioned an analysis of available data, drawn from detailed diaries. The diaries were kept by around 17,000 people as part of a UK Time Use Survey carried out by the ONS in 2000–2001.[22] This is a large sample, but because the diaries only covered a single weekday and a weekend day, the actual number of people who recorded themselves as studying on the day in question was much smaller, at around 770. However, the big advantage of this dataset is that it goes into great detail: respondents completed the diaries by recording the way they used their time in ten-minute slots, with careful distinctions being made between primary and secondary activities. Therefore, although the information is now quite dated, this is a valuable complement to the broader-brush surveys referred to earlier.

The results confirmed many of the patterns listed above, in the class patterns of overall participation. For our purposes the key novel information is in the distribution by age group of time spent on formal and on informal learning. The results are shown in Table 8.

Table 8: Average hours of formal and informal study, by age group

	All (hours)	18–24 (hours)	25–49 (hours)	50+ (hours)
Formal study	50	303	32	6
Informal study	13	35	14	7
Base	16,967	1,798	7,904	7,265

Source: UK Time Use Survey, 2000; calculations by Muriel Egerton, Oxford University

This produces some surprisingly rounded ratios in the relative amounts of time spent by the three age groups. (We return to the age grouping in *Chapter 5*.) For formal learning, the ratios are almost exactly 50:5:1 – in other words, the youngest age group spent about ten times as much time in study as the middle age group, and fifty times as much as the oldest. For informal learning, they are exactly 5:2:1. The roundedness of the ratios is surprising, but comes directly from the data. The explanation for the scale of the age differences in time spent in formal learning is very obvious, namely that a high proportion of the under-25s are in

---

[22] ONS (2000).

full-time education. However, the fact that it is obvious does not take away from its significance, and we use these ratios to make some significant calculations on the balance of the system overall in the next chapter.

'We can, with only a small leap of the imagination, do far better than we currently do in reducing the arbitrariness of age, and the distorting impact this has on our lives. In the context of lifelong learning, there are major reasons for moving to a different model.'

5 Meeting the challenge of change
A new model for the educational life course

Summary

In this chapter we set out proposals to alter the way we think about the distribution of learning over the life course. This means escaping from the habits and mindsets which currently dominate our thinking – and our education and training practice. Our basic proposal is a very simple one: to think of the life course in terms of four main stages, broadly up to 25, 25–50, 50–75 and 75+.

There are three powerful motors which provide the rationale for this realignment: demographic, economic and social. An ageing society and extended transitions into and out of employment combine to require a new approach, jettisoning more arbitrary dividing lines such as 60/65.

The essential counterpart to this four-stage model is that there should be a new contract between the generations. The 'contract' – a matter of social attitude rather than law – is based on the mutual advantages which flow if all generations have access to learning.

The four-stage approach opens up prospects for a better balance in the distribution of resources and opportunities. It applies to learning in, at and for work, as well as for personal and community development. It means innovation to meet the needs of the Third and Fourth Ages, and recognising the way learning in one generation generates value for all. At the same time, there should be a strong emphasis on mixed-age, family and intergenerational learning. The four-stage structure in no way suggests that education and training should be age-segregated.

The new model also opens up the way for a better balance in the triangle we put forward in *Chapter 1* of human, social and identity capitals. A new intergenerational contract means more opportunities for people to contribute economically; to stay connected; and to achieve meaning in their extended lives.

Why a new model?

We need a structure that better reflects demographic, labour market, social and cultural realities. These have changed dramatically over past decades, but our conceptual and administrative categories have remained remarkably static. As a result, our current policy set is inconsistent, unfair and inefficient in its response to the changes.

Almost all age-based divisions are to some extent arbitrary. The age at which you are regarded as an adult, or start school, or qualify for free or reduced travel: these all have some approximate justification, but could be very different. In Scandinavia, for example, primary school starts at seven. This is only two years difference from most of the UK – but two out of seven is significant. An equivalent divergence might be for one country to have a retirement age of 60, and another of 80. A moment's reflection shows us just how arbitrary these divisions often are in the light of the changes we have pointed to.

Some would argue that we should ignore chronological age entirely. However, this is just not realistic. We need ways of grouping people: for policy purposes and for our own social practice. It would be hard to imagine quite how we could do without ages altogether. Yet we can, with only a small leap of the imagination, do far better than we currently do in reducing the arbitrariness of age, and the distorting impact this has on our lives. In the context of lifelong learning, there are major reasons for moving to a different model.

Our model is a simple one, of four quarters or stages: under 25, 25–50, 50–75, and 75 and over. Of course, there will be sub-divisions within these stages. Most obviously, the first stage will be sub-divided many times, as babies become children, young people and adults. However, these stages provide a basic framework, founded on critical demographic, social and economic lines. We have already defined the Inquiry as primarily, though not exclusively, concerned with post-compulsory education and training, and with adult learning. For us, therefore, the first stage refers primarily to 18–25.

In one sense, the precise chronological ages we have chosen as dividing points do not much matter. However, 25, 50 and 75 all have a genuine significance beyond their mathematical symmetry. However approximate, they are points where for large proportions of the population, physical, social and labour market factors come together in a different mix. Of course, they are not single 'big bang' moments; the numerical ages are just indicators. But whatever figures are chosen for the transitions, the essential point is to achieve a proper recognition, in policy and in social attitudes, of these three issues:

- most young people do not emerge as independent adults until later than they used to, in terms of identity, earning and residence;
- people will want to, and need to, go on working longer, but they will move to doing this on a different basis from their earlier employment; and

- increasing numbers of people will live very long lives, and seek meaning for the final stage of these lives.

In the course of the Inquiry's consultations we heard repeatedly of the need for a new 'language' or 'discourse', which would get people thinking differently about what we mean by lifelong learning. We cannot invent a new vocabulary as such, but a new model of this kind offers the jolt that is needed to conventional thinking.

Simple as it may seem, significant practical implications flow from the four-stage model. It forces us to abolish or downgrade some of the more irrational age-based barriers which currently block people's personal or professional development. Linked to our proposals on learning entitlements it provides a structure for developing greater choice across the life course, in and out of the workplace. Linked to our proposals on a citizens' curriculum, it provides a broad, fresh framework for developing educational content. Finally, it challenges knowledge-gatherers – statisticians and researchers – to present us with a different image of ourselves in a complex, unstable and ageing society.

A further overarching rationale is equity. This has both a vertical (across age groups) and a horizontal (within age groups) dimension. However successful a society is in providing good and fair schools for all, initial education can never ensure that lifetime chances are enjoyed by all on an equitable basis. Proposals to widen participation in higher education or recruitment to the professions are good, but they focus primarily on giving all a fair start. A four-stage framework provides a broader basis for ensuring the *recurrent* provision of opportunity, to those who have missed out or fallen behind for whatever reason, as well as those who are well established in their learning careers. It counters the cumulative effect of inequality (the Matthew effect) in a way that no front-loaded system can.

In short, this new approach to defining the life course would:

- enable society to treat each age group more coherently and more equitably, strongly promoting policy coordination – for example, by reviewing the learning needs of young offenders and young full-time HE undergraduates in the same frame;
- remove definitively some fundamental barriers, notably 60/65, as the line which defines 'dependency', allowing due recognition of the diversity of exit paths from the labour market;
- respond also to the diversity of extended entries into adult life;
- enable coherent debate on the balance of resource allocation over the life course, notably in recognising the implications of demographic change; and
- encourage the development of appropriate learning materials, recognising the way learning needs change with age, but without corralling people into age groups.

Thinking in terms of the four stages gives a framework, not a straitjacket. It does have a normative side, in that it suggests that there are points in the life course at which people may wish to think particularly about how they will spend the next stage of their lives. However, it is geared to expanding not restricting individual choice. Of course, the population cannot be divided into homogeneous groups according to these ages. Any dividing line is arbitrary. People will move from one stage to another at different chronological ages, influenced by gender, culture and class; and the transitions between stages are usually an extended process, not a single passage. None of these are adequate reasons for sticking with a set of divisions that are outmoded and which block our thinking on how learning contributes to a better life.

We fully recognise the so-called 'de-standardisation' of the life course, meaning that people do not make transitions at the same time, or even in the same sequence, to the extent that they used to. For example, leaving school, getting a job, getting married, then having a baby can happen in exactly the reverse order, or indeed in any order. But the fact that these patterns are now more varied calls for a new way of structuring the life course, not the total dissolution of any structure.

Demographic change interacts with labour market and social trends

In his IFLL Thematic Paper on *Demography and Lifelong Learning*, Stephen McNair identifies the following key changes in the shape of the British population:[1]

- the population is growing but ageing: as a result of rising life expectancy, improvements in health, and through immigration;
- life patterns are becoming more complex, and less predictable: with more job changes for many, more geographical mobility, more frequent relationship break-ups, second and lone parent families, and more multi-generation families;
- there are fewer young adults: the number of young people entering the labour market is shrinking, and they are taking longer to establish themselves in long-term careers and adult identities;
- there are far more people in the Third Age: with most people spending a much larger share of their lives in potentially healthy and active retirement, which lasts for much longer; and
- there are more people in the fourth stage, with more people (mainly in the final years of their lives) dependent on others for some aspects of daily life.

---

[1] McNair (2009a).

The last of these in particular reminds us that there are major gender variations, as more women live well into the fourth stage. These intersect with other social factors such as ethnicity. We deal with some of the specific implications of these variations as they occur.

McNair concludes (p. 7):

> 'For lifelong learning policy, the two most important issues are that:
>
> - *most people are experiencing more frequent, and less predictable, life transitions.* Transitions are more frequent, including entering and leaving the labour market, migration (into, out of and within the UK), childbearing and family formation, divorce, second families, caring for others, and bereavement; and
>
> - *most people are spending more of their lives outside the labour market* than their parents did: in 'retirement' of some kind, and carrying out unpaid caring roles (for children and older dependants).'

Demography therefore is the main driver, but the change in the age structure interacts with changes in the labour market, and with social trends. More women at work; more young people staying on longer at home and in education, and making extended transitions into established careers; changing family structures; the growing numbers of people with long-term health problems: these all combine to make a fresh approach necessary. As the demographer Sarah Harper observes: 'policy on education has been developed in the context of a traditional pyramidal population structure and linear life courses.'[2] This does not match current reality.

One direct implication is for information and research. We should begin now what will certainly be a long and tortuous process of changing the categories for gathering statistics, notably on the labour market. The primary recommendation here is to move towards a different end age for employment statistics, later than the current 60/65, and with a common date for men and women. We would prefer a move directly to 75, as the four-stage model suggests. If this is too big a leap, an alternative would be a staged move, to 70 and then to 75 two decades later. Changing statistical bases is a major operation. Either case will require international collaboration, and therefore take time; we need to start the ball rolling now. This is more than simply a major technical adjustment; it has all kinds of powerful symbolic meanings and practical implications.

---

[2] Harper (2009).

Figure 12: UK population, 2002, 2050

a) 2002

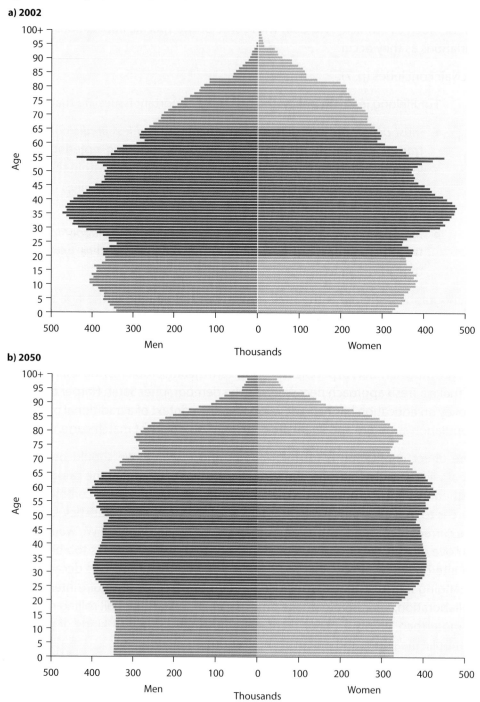

b) 2050

Source: GAD 2002-based principal population projection, UK Pensions Commission analysis

The four stages

We turn now to the rationales for the specific stages.

The first stage (up to 25): recognising prolongation

For young people and those who cater for them, the transition to adulthood is marked by multiple arbitrary and often conflicting dividing lines. Instead of helping young people to move consciously into adulthood, the current system is a confusing tangle. In many respects, it serves only to prolong dependency and child status, whilst apparently allowing adulthood. Educationally, it is also deeply unfair. It gives some groups far more access, not just to more education on some meritocratic basis, but to more opportunities to develop and grow. These should be equally available to all and not only to the more successful. The contrast between young offenders and full-time students is glaring; even though the former have more money spent on them, the benefits are far fewer – to them and to everyone else.

This first stage has more, and clearer, sub-divisions than the others. At the very start, developmental paths can be tracked in terms of weeks or months. Then there are divisions at ages four or five and at 11 for most. There has to be a distinction between 'children' and 'youth', probably at around 14. However, there is no justification for drawing deep lines (which endure in their effect) at 16, 18, 19 and 21 as is currently the practice.

There is mounting evidence that young people continue to mature for longer than was originally thought, physiologically and otherwise. This shows itself in many different ways. Neuroscience does not reveal a magical age at which the brain becomes adult, but some brain areas continue to develop for much longer than was thought – well beyond adolescence and into the twenties.[3] Exploration of professional and personal identities does not stop at 25, but most people have achieved some definition of themselves by then – even those whose pathways have been disrupted or unsettled. Young people now regularly stay at home longer – especially young men – but leave at around the age of 25.[4] Most offenders have stopped offending by their mid-twenties, and need a clear transition to socially integrated adulthood.

---

[3] Blakemore and Frith (2005). We return to the continuing plasticity of the brain in the context of ageing.

[4] In 2006, 58 per cent of 20–24-year-old men and 39 per cent of women were living with their parents; for 25–29-year-olds, the figures drop to 22 per cent and 11 per cent. (Social Trends 27, 2007, Table 2:8, quoted in Moynagh and Worsley, 2009).

The age of 25 as a dividing line already has considerable *de facto* support. It exists, for example, in the distinction between youth and adult apprenticeships in England, and in the EU's definition of a young person for travel concessions and 'young citizenship'. 'Young adults' are increasingly defined as those aged 18–25, for example, in relation to qualifications and social mobility.[5] However, these unsystematic references have insufficient leverage to resolve the divisive muddle. We want to demolish the walls which rise, quickly and often irrevocably, between different groups of young people, especially now that the initial period of education has become such an extended one for about half of them. Getting a common understanding of youth as extending to 25 would, paradoxically, help us treat this very heterogeneous group more coherently and fairly.

Young people's entry into adult working life is complex, variegated and full of uncertainties. Andy Furlong and colleagues have shown this in great detail with their picture on non-linear transitions, as shown in Figure 13.

Some young people have effectively dropped out of education well before the official school-leaving age. Others leave as soon as they can; the UK has one of the poorest records on early school leaving within the EU. There is a 'royal' road of progression from successful school to full-time higher education and then into employment. The road is both longer and broader than it used to be: many more people enter higher education, and increasing numbers stay on to do postgraduate work. (The proportions doing this are roughly equivalent to those doing first degrees in the 1970s.) Even this royal road is rockier than it used to be, and quite a few drop out from it. Student debt was relatively rare in the UK until recently; its level has risen remorselessly. This is not necessarily wrong, but it means that the relatively comfortable position of university students until the 1990s has now changed dramatically. It is still extremely advantageous to go to university and get a degree, but graduate employment is now more precarious, and the graduate premium is set to decline for many graduates.

Away from the 'royal' road is a myriad of other paths. Some of them are quite well signposted – via apprenticeships or other forms of vocational training, and into stable parts of the labour market. However, for many, the path is very uncertain. The position of those who do not go to university has been made worse by expansion, which has drawn in many more of their peers into higher education. Financial support for them is much less generous than for full-time university students, however much the latter groan under their student debt. Many young people disappear from sight, being neither in education nor in employment. Alarmingly large numbers go to prison, where they disappear physically from public sight,

---

[5] Uberoi *et al* (2009).

Figure 13: Youth transitions: non-linear

Schools　　Youth training scheme　　Part-time work　　Unemployment

Higher education　　Full-time work　　Further education　　Housewife

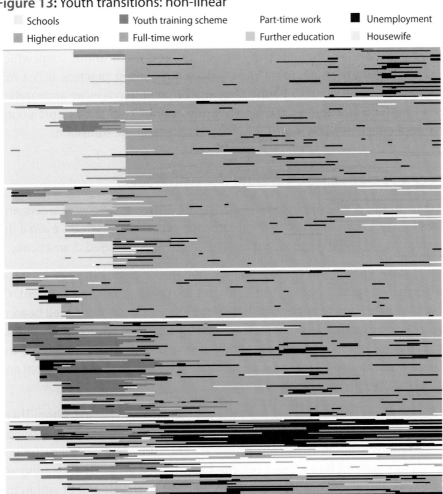

Each horizontal line plots the trajectory of an individual in and out of different statuses between the ages of 16 and 23

Source: Furlong et al (2003)[6]

or become homeless. Teenage pregnancies are extraordinarily high by European standards. If there are 'republican' roads to set against the royal one, they are far less well constructed and maintained.

The net result is that a young person's passage into adult life is more likely than before to be prolonged and unpredictable, even for those at the lucky end. For some, there is no visible transition, and they drift into long-term unemployment

---

[6] Furlong, A., Cartmel, F., Biggart, A., Sweeting, H. and West, P. (2003) *Youth transitions: Patterns of vulnerability and processes of social inclusion*, Scottish Executive, Edinburgh.

or a repetition of dead-end jobs. For others, the process is a more positive one of exploration of personal and professional identity. The point of drawing a line at age 25, rather than at 18, 19, or 21 is this: to recognise the prolonged nature of the transition, and to offer a socially recognised end point to this stage which fits the overall pattern much more closely than our current practice. It is a mix of recognising what is actually happening, and of providing a more appropriate focus for the transition process. This, we argue, would help us support young people more effectively and more fairly in accomplishing the transition.

The second stage (25–50): ending the rush hour

The second stage is when the great majority of people make their careers and raise families. This has a very dated ring to it; however, it remains true – even if the notion of a 'career', and the forms that families take, have changed dramatically.

Gender is obviously a particularly salient difference here, though there is convergence between the sexes in the rate of participation in employment. Of course, careers and family responsibilities start before 25 and extend well beyond 50 – we insist on exactly that point for the next stage too. But we are talking about the broad patterns which shape people's learning priorities. For this stage, the priorities for learning will tend to be concentrated around their occupational and family needs, albeit in very different mixes.

There are far fewer crude dividing lines than is the case for the first stage. There are not the same administrative or legal distinctions as for younger people. Giving quasi-psychological labels to discrete decades – the 'turbulent thirties' or 'furious forties' – is fun, but not much use. Even the biological limits of child-bearing are eroding, so that family demands are even more diverse. Development within the stage is not smoothly continuous. People change jobs, locations and partners. All these transitions generate learning needs.

This stage, 25–50, is the one where most people feel an acute time squeeze. The European Foundation on Living and Working Conditions has labelled the whole stage 'the rush hour'.[7] This is especially true in the UK, with its long hours culture; it is not surprising that the EU data on barriers to learning shows UK respondents citing 'work' more often than most. Forty-four per cent of UK respondents said training conflicted with the work schedule, and 42 per cent said they did not have enough time because of family responsibilities. In families where both parents are working, this can mean constant pressures on reconciling careers with time spent with children and partners. Single parents are also torn between work and child-

---

[7] IFLWC (2006).

Figure 14: Pattern of happiness

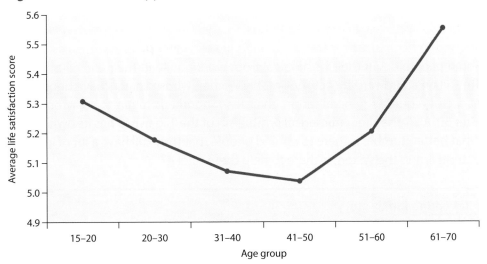

*Source: Oswald, A. and Powdthavee, N.
(authors' calculations using the British Household Panel Study)*

rearing. Adding learning time to these other commitments can seem impossible. The consequences for mental well-being – and for productivity – are clear from the evidence (see Figure 14). The challenge is to look for new mixes of work, study and family time.

There are also consequences for the next generation. As the Government Equalities Office observes:

> *Around three-quarters (74 per cent) of working parents said they would take their children on more days out if they had more time. Half (51 per cent) of parents of 11–16 year olds reported they would like to 'help with homework' if they had more time. Around one in two (56 per cent) parents of children under the age of six said they would 'read to them' if they had more time.[8]*

The aim must be to spread things out more evenly over the extended life. Moving to a conception of working life as generally running from 25 to 75 (though not meaning full-time work – and not quite immediately!) would not only put us in a better position to meet the pensions challenge, it would also enable a smoother distribution of working time – and allow more time for learning.

---

[8] Government Equalities Office (2009) p. 4.

Drawing the end line for the second stage at 50, which may seem surprisingly early, has a strong rationale. It encourages both individuals and social institutions to do two apparently conflicting things: to encourage the extension of working life, and to begin the preparation for later life earlier than is often the case today. Some people begin their withdrawal from working life in their early 50s. Others are still on an upward trajectory, notably women whose careers have begun late. As a crude but fair generalisation, their learning needs begin to splay out more after 50. Also, the sheer numerical symbolism of the 'big five-o' has its own power. What better number is there to remind people that they still have a lot of learning potential, and the system is there to help them fulfil it?

Tai-chun's family story[9]

Tai-chun knew it was going to be a difficult day. Her new job with the genetic engineering business was putting a lot of pressure on her. Managing the virtual meetings with the companies in China made her homesick. But that's why they had hired her – Cantonese was her first language and her English was pitch perfect. It was useful to have the ThroughLanguage suite standing by, but she didn't really need it. This had been the first job she'd applied for where they actually seemed to appreciate her skills instead of interrogating her about her qualifications and their equivalence to EUQual.

As she got Hao settled to have his breakfast, she screen-allocated the patch of wall in front of him so he could watch his Dad's latest message. In came the media link to her phone every evening, updating her on his job hunt and with a cheerful message and sometimes a story for Hao. How come he was this clever and he couldn't find a job?

Hao had finished his breakfast. Rushing now she almost forgot to pack Hao's own PA. The nursery had made such a fuss about their quality systems and how she could monitor where and how he was any time day or night. Tai-chun didn't like leaving Hao overnight at the nursery, but her alternate shifts started at 7.00pm and she really had no option – but sometimes she wondered whether he would think his Mum and Dad appeared more on screens than in the flesh.

---

[9] This story and the next one in this chapter (Jane's) are fictional ones set in the future, drawn from the Inquiry's work on scenarios for learning infrastructures. They explore possible future links between technology, architecture and people. We use them here to illustrate potential changes in life course patterns.

Having left Hao at the nursery Tai-chun hurried to the Civic Centre. She loved the library, or rather the museum part of it where all the books were kept. She could have got her PA to download some of the texts she wanted to look at, but she needed to talk to a real expert to save herself the time of going through so much potentially useless information. And she couldn't afford the new Web 4.0 applications that everyone seemed to be talking about. Just in time for her appointment, she waved her PA at the sensor and settled down into the chair, waiting for the screen to light up so she'd be through to the librarian.

Later, as she thought about her session at the library, Tai-chun realised how lonely she felt. Here she was, making the decision on cell augmentation for her mother back in Guangzhou, to make it possible for her to fly out to the UK, so the family could be all together – and yet her husband and child weren't with her for most of the time. She had to snap out of it. She had a job after all – that was the main thing for the present. Sitting in the learning area of the tram, she plugged in her PA. She just had time to do the next module of her induction programme.

The third stage (50–75): valuing a new mix

At some point after 50, most of us make the transition, suddenly or gradually, from paid employment to 'retirement'. For many, moving into one's 50s may not involve much change. For others, it can be the start of alternative careers, new interests, a new mix of paid and unpaid work, or new family patterns. For an unlucky few, it heralds the onset of long-term illness and disability which will drive them out of work and into isolation and poverty.

The key reason for defining this quarter century is to banish the artificial and outdated barriers of 60 and 65, which are such blocks to creative thought and action on good practice at this stage. These dividing lines should be fading away anyway with changes in pension ages, improving health and other trends; but anyone who thinks that this is happening smoothly should look at how labour market and other statistics help define what is 'normal', and reflect on the way that published 'support ratios' define a group of largely healthy, active, and potentially contributing members of society as 'dependants'. Furthermore, the separation of male and female ages (65 and 60 respectively) has long been perverse, and the Government's decision to abolish it is best seen as 'better late than never'. These dividers need a very firm shove to remove them from our collective mindset, from the statistical frames we use and from the influence they have on our social practices.

Furthermore, the very notion of 'retirement' as a brief respite between work and death is quite obsolete when most people will live for at least 20 years after leaving paid work, and many for 30 or 40. We agree with the Cabinet Office report which suggested that: 'It would be useful in the short term to blur, and in the long term to abolish, the concept of retirement.'[10]

However, moving in this direction will increase people's sense of risk and uncertainty, as well as opening up new horizons. Managing this shift requires new skills. Learning, and social engagement with others through learning, can play an important part in helping people manage the reshaping of lifestyle, social networks and activity.

There is now a very broad consensus on the need to enable people to carry on working longer. This is both for reasons of public finance – the pensions burden would be unsustainable if this did not happen – and personal well-being. Most older people want to carry on working if the right work is there, in the right form; however, many have to work, whether they like it or not. The Third Age[11] is the age of disparity as well as opportunity, with huge variance in wealth and health. All this means much better training opportunities are needed, across the board, to enable older people to stay in the labour market. However, currently, training at work drops off dramatically for older people, leaving them far less supported than they should be to sustain their employment, or to make the transition into a new phase. There is no alignment between training and employment policy.

Nearly 50 per cent of men aged 60–64 are economically active (in full or part-time employment or self-employment) and 61 per cent of women aged 55–59. However, if we go beyond the 'normal' retirement ages we find that about 16.5 per cent of men aged 65–69, and 30 per cent of women aged 60–64 (13 per cent of women aged 65–69) are still economically active. The proportion of women and men that will be economically active beyond 60 and 65 are very likely to grow – and will certainly do so if given the right circumstances. It is increasingly absurd to write them off as awkward statistical additions.

Speaking at the Inquiry's Demography Seminar, Chris Humphries, Chief Executive of the UK Skills and Employment Commission, drew attention to the growing trend for 'deferred adulthood' – the pattern for young people to defer entry to 'serious career-minded jobs' until their mid-to-late 20s (confirming by this our specification of the first stage as running to around 25): 'Combined with a 10 per cent drop in the youth cohort between 2010 and 2020, this will present

---

[10] Cabinet Office (2000).
[11] In general, we use 'stage' to denote the four quarters, but the Third Age is already an established term – cf. Third Age Universities as a recognised and widespread initiative (www.u3a.org.uk).

challenges for organisations… Employer practices do not, on the whole, reflect what employers say about their support for older workers; their willingness to support flexible working for older workers is not proportionate to demand.' Humphries called for a campaign to help 'sell the benefits of older workers'.[12]

Those in the Third Age make a massive unpaid contribution to society. They volunteer in greater numbers than other age groups; they care for each other and for those older and younger than themselves (see Figure 15). Arguably, they are the major source of social capital today.

Theirs is a diverse set of experiences, combining widely varying levels of paid employment; diverse processes of exiting from employment, often into other forms of work; and changing demands of family life, notably in respect of caring responsibilities. Again, these experiences are not unique to this stage, but the Third Age has some broad characteristics which have their own implications for learning. It is the group whose numbers are growing by more than any other. Arguably, it is the life stage where most change in self-perception and social position has occurred over recent decades, and where the largest source of

Figure 15: Participation in voluntary and community activities, by age, 2003

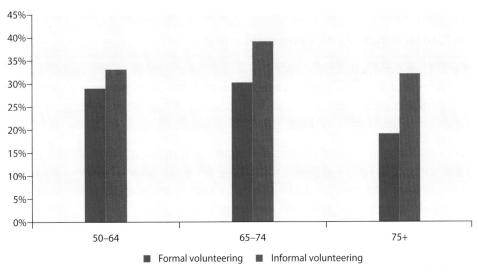

Source: ONS (2005)

---

[12] The Government recently announced a review of the industrial opportunities in an ageing society. This will include 'a review of opportunities that are being created – both in manufacturing and services – and the likely future skills needs and technological opportunities; for example in relation to leisure needs and care, as well as the drug treatments for those affected by illness related to age.' Department for Business, Enterprise and Regulatory Reform (BERR) (2009).

Figure 16: Involvement in unpaid care by people aged 50 and over, by sex, 2001

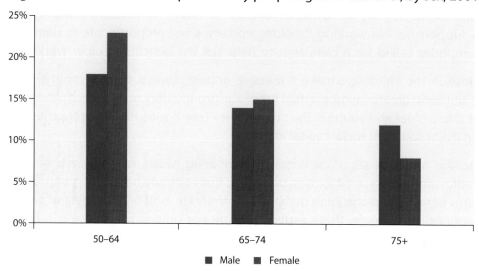

Source: ONS (2005)

potential skills and capabilities resides. To let these skills and capabilities develop and flourish, we need a fresh approach.

The fourth stage (75+): growing fastest

However we qualify it, identifying 75+ as a separate stage is perhaps the most controversial of the four. The argument against is that it stigmatises people who do not wish to be thought of as 'very old', or any of the more derogatory terms that are sometime applied. The argument is powerful but not decisive.

There are now many more people in this age group. Many – not all, but a high proportion – have issues of health and dependency, including chronic illness; it is around this time that the probability of 'accelerated decline' increases in respect of some of these chronic illnesses (see Figure 17).[13]

There is also the inescapable fact that they are in the final stage of their lives, and may wish to come to terms with this. That process may or may not be tranquil. It raises questions about meaning and purpose. We need to allow for 'disengagement' – the tendency of some older people to withdraw from some conventional day-to-day activity. But this does not at all suggest that older people necessarily confine themselves to more restricted circles.

---

[13] Kuh and Ben-Shlomo (2004).

Figure 17: Older people reporting a limiting long-term illness, by age and sex, 2001

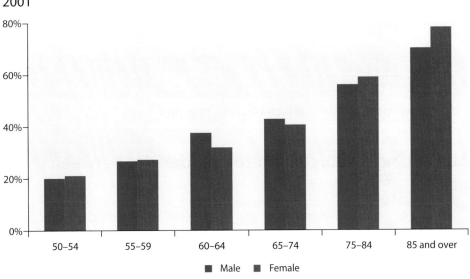

Source: ONS (2005)

The fourth stage implies the likelihood of some degree of dependency, but this does not mean that there is a simple dividing line. The fact is that life expectancy is now lengthened to a historically unprecedented extent, generating new learning needs. The increasing size of this age group poses specific challenges to the goals and meaning of lifelong learning policy and practice. On balance, we argue that identifying 75+ as a stage in the broad sense we have adopted opens up positive opportunities for innovation, and meaningful learning.

Once again, there is a strong gender dimension here. Women make up a far higher proportion of this age group than any other. The invisibility of old age is a major form of gender discrimination. This is especially the case now, since the current generation of old women has benefited least from education. Therefore, taking seriously the learning needs of the fourth stage has a real equity pay-off, and will be of major benefit to health and social care budgets if it delays morbidity.

To sum up: all divisions based on chronological age look arbitrary from some angles. However, the way the major divisions are made influences our outlooks in significant ways, so we should not ignore them. The sociologist Zygmunt Bauman writes eloquently about the flux we live in – he calls it a 'liquid world'.[14] If he is correct, the 'liquidity' includes age-markers, and we have the capacity to change them. This matters because:

---

[14] Bauman (2006).

- it influences our self-perceptions: what we are capable of, and what we need to realise those capabilities;
- it influences our perceptions of others, what they are capable of and what they need;
- it influences how resources are allocated: which groups get access to what, and why; and
- it should, if we get the way we handle the markers right, strengthen the intergenerational contract which binds us together.

Rebalancing resources: interdependencies between the ages

> There is, perhaps, no branch of our educational system which should attract within its particular sphere the aid and encouragement of the State than adult education. How many must there be in Britain […] who thirst in later life to learn about the humanities, the history of their country, the philosophies of the human race… [This] demands the highest measures which our hard-pressed finances can sustain.
>
> Winston Churchill, letter to TUC, 1953.

In *Payback,* her reflections on debt, Margaret Atwood tells the story of the Canadian writer Ernest Thompson Seton, whose father presented him with an odd bill on his twenty-first birthday. It was a record kept of all the expenses connected with young Ernest's childhood and youth (NB, to 21 only...), including the fee charged by the doctor for delivering him. Ernest is said to have paid the bill. 'I used to think that Mr Seton Senior was a jerk,' says Atwood, 'but now I'm wondering.'[15] Our debts and responsibilities to past and future generations are a fertile source of philosophical debate as well as psychological turmoil.

The current distribution of resources for learning is heavily weighted towards initial education. It is inevitable that the system should be 'front-loaded'; i.e. that it will concentrate primarily on equipping young people with the values, competences and attitudes needed to give them the best foundation for life. However, the weighting is too strong. We show this by drawing on our analyses of expenditure and participation.

First, though, we need to emphasise two points. The analysis below covers expenditure on learning after school age, which we now take to be 18. We have not tackled the whole question of how school resources might be brought into

---

[15] Atwood (2008).

the debate – though other Inquiry outputs address the implications for different sectors.[16] We need to reiterate the point that a schooling system that enables all young people to achieve to their potential, and to retain a love of learning, is an essential part of a lifelong learning system.

Secondly, we reject entirely the opposition that has sometimes been made between investing in early years (0–5) and investing in adult learning. On the contrary, we entirely endorse the need for sustained commitment to, and investment in, early years learning; and there is a strong symbiosis between successful early years learning and adult learning, as our frequent references to family learning make clear.

In short, the rebalancing we propose relates only to the very broad post-compulsory sector of education, training and learning.

We have calculated the current allocation of resources across the life course in the following way. We have used the participation figures to derive an estimate of the numbers within each of the four age groups that currently participate in learning. The overall proportions participating are shown in Table 9.

We then draw on the analysis of time use to estimate what this means in terms of the *average duration of participation*. It's obvious that young people not only participate more, but their participation on average also lasts a lot longer (mainly because many more of them are in full-time higher education). Our calculations need to reflect this. We have differentiated between formal and informal learning, since the ratios are significantly different.

The respective ratios are:

- for formal learning: 50: 5: 1: 0.5 (estimate only for fourth stage). In other words, the average participant in the first stage spends ten times as many hours learning as one in the second stage, and fifty times as many as one in the Third Age. As we noted in the previous chapter, these ratios look suspiciously round; but they are in fact derived directly from the empirical data; and
- for informal learning: 5: 2: 1: 0.5. Exactly the same comments apply as above.

Table 9: Current or recent participation in learning across the four life stages, 2008

Age	18–24	25–49	50–74	75+
Percentage participation	65%	45%	27%	11%

Source: NIACE Adult Participation in Learning Survey, 2008.

---

[16] See *Annexe C* for the full list of Inquiry Sector Papers.

We then simply multiply these two figures (i.e. the participation rates and the duration ratios) to give a calculation of the gross amounts of time spent by each age on learning. We call these the *weighted participation ratios*, as shown in Table 10.

Finally, we apply these to the sums which we have calculated are spent on provision, by government, employers, voluntary organisations and individuals.[17] This gives us an indication of the overall distribution of learning resources across the age groups, shown in Table 11 and Figure 19. Of course, this is a very crude index, but we doubt if it is misleading in its overall picture.

Table 10: Weighted participation ratios across the four life stages, 2008

	18–24	25–49	50–74	75+
Formal learning	3,250	225	27	5.5
Informal learning	325	90	27	5.5

Source: IFLL

Table 11: Expenditure on formal and informal learning across the four life stages, 2008

	18–24	25–49	50–74	75+
Total expenditure (£ millions)	£47,141	£6,057	£1,397	£285
Percentage of total expenditure	86%	11%	2.5%	0.5%
Expenditure per head of population	£8,045	£283	£86	£60
Expenditure per learner	£12,395	£633	£319	£542[a]

[a]This figure looks artificially high for two reasons: (1) The time use weighting for the 75+ group is an estimate; (2) relatively small numbers of 75+ are currently participating in learning.

Source: IFLL

---

[17] £54.88 billion. See *Chapter 4*.

Intergenerational support

The imbalance in the aggregate and the per capita figures is dramatic. How do we decide if this is a) fair, and b) effective as a way of collectively allocating our spending on learning? These two questions require very different kinds of answers, but they are interconnected. The first crucial point to be made is that the discussion on this should be seen as part of a new intergenerational contract, and not as a zero-sum game in which each generation battles against the rest for a larger share. Investment in the first stage is necessary for everyone's future well-being. The younger generation will be providing, over time, the economic performance needed to maintain the prosperity in which all will share. They will produce the innovations for future progress, and will finance the welfare services needed. They are already paying for this themselves to some extent, via student loans, but obviously they cannot shoulder this all themselves. The second and third stages are the ones already producing the investment needed, for themselves and for the first and fourth stages. They shoulder most of the tax burden – directly as tax payers and indirectly as employees. Investment in the fourth stage not only provides them with the benefits of learning in their old age. It also demonstrates to younger generations that they too will accede to these benefits in the future. It should also reduce the costs of dependency, as older people maintain independence longer and learn to manage their own health and their use of health services. Sectional interests – each group arguing its own case – should not dominate the debate.

Figure 18 shows schematically how these flows work. Overall, *public* money goes 'upwards' towards the fourth stage in the shape of pensions and healthcare, and 'downwards' to the first stage for initial education. However, *private* money flows downwards from those in the Fourth Age also, to assist younger people. Bear in mind that this picture shifts over time, as each generation ages; because we cannot know what exactly the position will be when we reach the next stage, the notion of an intergenerational contract is crucial for binding the arrangements together.

The interdependencies should be clear, even from this very summary account. It is difficult to overstate their importance at a time when we are likely to see increasing stresses and strains in the way public and private resources are distributed. Already we hear of the 'locust generation' – the post-war boomers who as a cohort benefited most from public expenditure, and some of whom

Figure 18: Investing in learning: intergenerational links

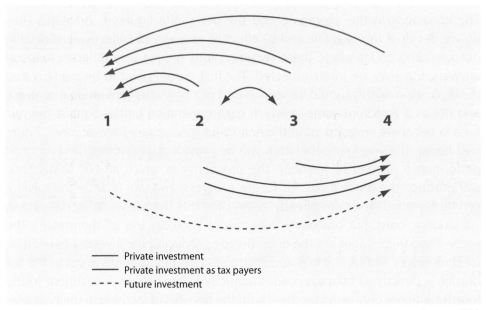

1   2   3   4

——— Private investment
——— Private investment as tax payers
- - - - Future investment

Source: IFLL

are enjoying pensions whose payment depends on future generations. Conflict between generations will not help us along, so we need to articulate and defend these interdependencies.

But however powerfully we make the case for interdependence, this will not provide an automatic formula for dividing up available resources. In thinking about how we should sensibly and equitably allocate resources, we cannot simply use the numbers provided above. Per capita equivalence across all stages is not a sensible proposition. As we acknowledge, front-loading is inevitable, but the ratios we have revealed must prompt reflection on whether we have the right balance, and if we do not, what kinds of change we might envisage.

We have no magical formula for this. Our main task here has been to lay out the situation in a way that has not been done before, to give a framework for future debate. However, the case for lifelong learning is strong enough that we have no hesitation in concluding that the current balance is wrong. In order to give a lead on this, we suggest the following as a basis for rebalancing over time. We should move from the current estimated distribution ratio of 86: 11: 2.5: 0.5 to a ratio of 80: 15: 4: 1 by 2020.

A rebalancing of this kind reflects the demographic changes we discussed earlier. The 18–24 population is set to decline by 9 per cent by 2020, while the third stage and fourth stage populations are set to rise by 18 per cent and 28 per cent respectively. The additional £3.2 billion for stages two to four which results from this demography-related adjustment would go a very long way towards rebalancing the system, and would underpin our proposals for extending entitlements beyond age 25 in *Chapter 6*. The pie charts in Figure 19 show how the change in ratios would alter overall expenditure in each of the four stages, and how this compares with the projected population changes for each age group to 2020.

We have to reiterate that this is not a recommendation directed at shifting the balance of public expenditure alone. We make the argument elsewhere that co-investment is the name of the future game – bringing in resources from all the

Figure 19: a) Current population and b) 2020 population projections (millions); c) current total expenditure on provision and d) proposed rebalancing (£ millions)

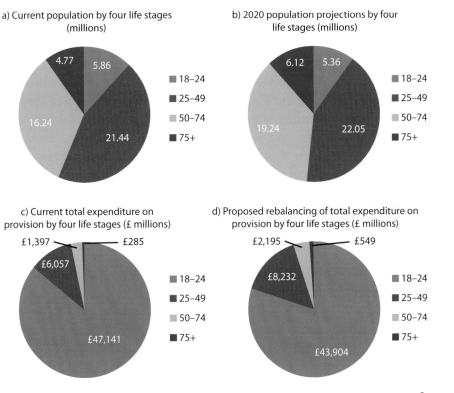

a) Current population by four life stages (millions)

b) 2020 population projections by four life stages (millions)

c) Current total expenditure on provision by four life stages (£ millions)

d) Proposed rebalancing of total expenditure on provision by four life stages (£ millions)

Source: IFLL

different stakeholders (for once the term is truly apt – all have a stake in the project). It may be that we should ask individuals to save more for their learning throughout life – with suitable tax incentives from the State, and with encouragement from employers in the form of time off for learning. (As Martin, one of the learners we spoke to during the Inquiry said, 'We need to drum home to people that a ten-week course, although more expensive than it was, still costs less than a ticket to watch the football.') We discuss this in the next chapter on entitlements. The point here is simply to provide some overall guidance on the strategic evolution of intergenerational finance for learning.

Finally, we need to repeat that we accept the very powerful evidence for the impact of good investments in early education. In particular, the evidence from the EPPE work is all the more convincing because of the way it combines different types of research method to produce a complete picture of the effects of good quality early years provision.[18] Our two points on this are:

- these arguments should make us look carefully at how our efforts are best deployed across the life course – extending downwards as well as upwards, and not assuming that the expansion of formal schooling is the answer. This is exactly in line with our own overall case for putting more into adult learning; and
- the case for efficient investment – i.e. what pays off most – changes as our focus moves across the life course. There is a strong premium on investment in initial education, because there is a longer payback time (as Margaret Atwood could, we are sure, beautifully describe). The payback period for adults is shorter, and for older adults may be quite short indeed. However, the 'intensity' of the payback can be high, if older people are able to maintain their health and independence, and lead fulfilling lives,[19] and the moral case for investing in learning at every age remains constant.

Implications for educational content

Briefly, the new life course model and the intergenerational contract open up the following as areas for significant new development.

---

[18] Sylva *et al* (2007).

[19] On average, around half of the total spent on an individual's health is spent in the last year of their life. This will always be high, but greater independence and better self-care capabilities could surely reduce it considerably.

Third Age capabilities

The Third Age is the time when more people will be doing more things differently than at any time previously in history. They will combine traditional employment roles with new careers, whether full time or part time. They will continue to do unpaid work as volunteers in a whole range of capacities. They will combine traditional family roles with new responsibilities as grandparents, step-grandparents and carers. They will also be conscious of the next stage. Not all of them, of course, will be doing all of these; this is the generalised picture of the age group as a whole.

They will be the prime beneficiaries of the citizens' curriculum we outline in *Chapter 8*. 'Third Agers' undertake a range of civic activities – voting (which they do disproportionately), participation in voluntary work, and so on. They are likely to be conscious of their financial position and its future consequences to an above-average degree. They are also likely to be conscious of health issues, and the need to manage their own health. Their digital capability will vary greatly; this will be a significant factor if they wish to stay connected with family, friends and the world outside. This leads directly to the enhanced role of technology in learning for all ages, but certainly including older learners. We illustrate this with a story from the Inquiry work on scenarios.

Jane's story[20]

Jane stared at the 3D image in front of her in utter incomprehension, thinking of the injustice of it all. How could she be expected to keep up with the younger generation? Of course, there had been plenty of predictions about the changing age demographic, but when it came to it no-one had been really prepared for the consequences. The GenUp Learning programme that Jane was on was supposed to prepare her for a new role in society, whatever that meant. Not that she had much option of course, unless she wanted to lose her meagre State Pension. In fact, GenUp was making Jane feel even more isolated from the new world of jobs and technology. The Well-being Council might go on about the 'connected society', but their sheltered housing was void of the ultra-sophisticated systems that those in employment had in their own homes.

---

[20] See footnote 9.

Jane recalled how there had been a European Federation-wide Initiative to get people over 50 back to work. Now that was all but abandoned, and the latest political spin was all about the 'social capital' possessed by the 'veteran generations' and how that must be deployed for social good. At first she had been enthusiastic about the Initiative. But nobody in the guidance teams she encountered, virtually or otherwise, seemed really knowledgeable or even interested in how someone over 29 could ever gain re-employment. There seemed to be those whose working lives, or perhaps personal lives, had given them much more experience of the sort of communications technology life seemed to require nowadays. It was these people who now seemed much more comfortable with the interactions the Initiative required, while Jane still set great store by the idea of physically visiting the establishments and people in question. But once away from work, Jane realised how the non-work-allocated public transport systems had declined and anything else was hugely expensive.

There were what they still called Community Centres, but those that were not linked with the commercial training companies just hadn't got the funds to maintain staff or equipment. And Jane simply hadn't realised the extent to which the public libraries had declined. The only one near to Jane resembled the dark ages of the early Internet and could hardly be used with the advanced AI systems supported by the global 'educationaries'.

Fourth stage capabilities

We need to repeat: identifying the fourth stage as a discrete category does not mean segregation. It means choice and tailoring. In many respects, the needs of older people overlap with those of preceding ages, although their vocational learning needs will largely disappear. However, there are at least two distinct sets of learning challenges which are inherently more specific to fourth stagers than others. Both are integrally linked to the notion of individual empowerment and choice.

The first set again derives from our outline for a citizens' curriculum. The focus here is likely to be on health. Old people should be able to continue to learn how to manage their own physical and mental health as far as possible. This includes managing their relations with the providers of health and other services (for instance, as holders of personal budgets, and therefore as quasi-employers). However, financial capability is also likely to figure. 'Financial elder-abuse' is not a pretty term, nor is the phenomenon it points to: the vulnerability of old people to exploitation by others. This ranges from outright theft to more delicate issues to do with sharing or ceding control over their own finances to children or other family members. Helping people understand their financial position is fundamental to trust and security.

The second set is existential. Ever since the *Monty Python* film, it has been almost impossible to talk about 'the meaning of life' without quotation or exclamation marks.[21] However, there can be few more important learning tasks than learning to make sense of the life you have lived. We have drawn inspiration from the Children's Society report, *A Good Childhood,* for its model of evidence-based and value-informed analysis and prescription.[22] We lack *A Good Death* as an equivalent, but learning to die well is unarguably a fundamental right.

During the Inquiry, scientists reported that the number of people with dementia was expected to reach 1 million in the next few years. Speaking at the Inquiry's Well-being and Happiness seminar, Suzanne Sorenson from the Alzheimer's Association explained that educational achievement can be a factor in slowing the development of dementia, but it is very difficult to separate education from other lifestyle factors. However, she went on, 'there is evidence of the effect of "cognitive reserve" – an apparent resilience to cognitive damage – masking symptoms of dementia. Lower-educated people with clinical symptoms start to show a slow decline earlier, whereas those with "higher cognitive reserve" and good social skills can mask their symptoms. Once their symptoms are revealed, however, those with higher levels of education tend to decline faster.'

Dementia and lifelong learning

Public sector broadcasting is designed to ensure there are programmes to 'educate, entertain and inform', but there is much more that could be done to reach those with dementia. Many programmes are too fast and busy to be followed, yet broadcasting in all its platforms could be used to encourage lifelong learning among those with dementia by assisting them to retain their memories. Drawing on archive material and using evidence about the condition of Alzheimers and other forms of dementia, programmes could be designed that connect with people and provide customised lifelong learning for people with memory loss. BBC Wales is exploring this as a possibility.

Professor Teresa Rees, Inquiry Commissioner
and Pro-Vice-Chancellor, Cardiff University

---

[21] But see Eagleton (2008).
[22] Layard and Dunn (2009).

Intergenerational and family learning

Finally, to reiterate the message that our four-stage model does not imply stronger age segregation, we give a particular mention to learning which explicitly seeks to span generations. An ageing society does not only mean that there are more older people. It also means changes in the shape of families: longer (more generations) and thinner (fewer children per adult), with more dissolved relationships and reconstituted families. This makes for a complex structure.

On top of these demographic trends are social ones which put further stress on families. Soaring rates of imprisonment mean that 150,000 children have a parent in prison. Greater mobility means physical distance between generations. Technology can do something to counter this – another reason why digital capabilities are so important – but learning together is a crucial form of intergenerational solidarity.

A recent NIACE report for DIUS provides evidence on how family and intergenerational learning contributes to all four essential categories of Public Service Agreement:

- sustaining growth and prosperity;
- fairness and opportunity for all;
- stronger communities and better quality of life; and
- a more secure, fair and environmentally sustainable world.[23]

This wide relevance does not, however, guarantee that this kind of learning receives its due attention. If we use only individual measures – qualifications, achievement, and so on – we will not get a true picture of the learning system. We need also to use families as our units – not necessarily conventional families, but in whatever shape they come.

Having a positive impact on children's lives from behind bars

Storybook Dad started as a prison tutor's small idea in HMP Dartmoor. In just three years it had become a registered charity, spread across 40 prisons with 17,000 imprisoned parents participating. The project caters for prisoners of all ages (including young offenders) and women prisoners. Forty-three per cent of prisoners have had a family member convicted of a criminal offence. Storybook Dads aims to try and break this familial cycle of re-offending.

---

[23] Lamb *et al* (2009).

Prisoners are recorded telling a story to their children, using a microphone and a mini-disk recorder: the stories are downloaded and edited on computer; music and sound effects are added; the final story is put onto CD and then sent to their children. Poor readers and non-readers alike can participate. Some prisoners write their own story and make a book using computer graphics, which greatly enhances their IT skills. Others gain valuable skills in digital editing and can work towards an OCN qualification in Sound and Audio Production.

Recommendations

A new model

a) A four-stage model should be used as the basis for a *coherent systemic approach to lifelong learning*. All those with a stake in any form of education and training (policy-makers, social partners, practitioners) should directly address the implications of extended lives, and of extended entry into and exit from employment. More generally, *official information-gathering* should use the four-stage model as a framework, as appropriate.

b) The first age (up to 25, but starting at 18 for our practical purposes as people move into the post-compulsory phase) should be looked at as a whole – a very diverse group, but a group nevertheless, with all of its members having claims to *learning and development as young people*. This is a fundamental change of perspective from the current approach, which constantly divides and re-divides young people.

c) Learning in the second stage (25–50) should be seen not only as a key measure for sustaining productivity, prosperity and strong family lives, but as part of a *new mosaic of time*, exhibiting different mixes of paid and unpaid work and learning time. Ironically, the unemployment crisis opens up scope for the UK to move away from the second stage time squeeze, where career and family responsibilities result in huge pressures which reduce well-being.

d) The Third Age[24] is central (50–75): more people need and want to work longer, and consequently to carry on learning at work. *Training and education opportunities* should be greatly enhanced for those over 50. Policy, including learning policy, should treat 75 as the normal upper age limit for economic activity, replacing the outmoded 60/65. This will unblock a better general

---

[24] We use the title Third Age as this is already common currency for this stage. The same does not apply to the other stages.

distribution of working time across the life course. This is not a call for everyone to work to 75, but a recognition that 'retirement' will increasingly become a gradual process lasting several years.

e) The implications of demographic trends for the *content of lifelong learning* should be explored systematically and creatively (these two not being in opposition). In particular, the emergence of the Fourth Age means that we urgently need to develop an authentic *curriculum offer in later life*.

f) *25, 50 and 75* should be identified and used as *key transition points*. Of course, people do not make the transition at the same age or in the same way, but focusing on these points gives a useful structure, for personal development and for policy. Special information and guidance arrangements should be in place for those making the transition to enable them – if they so wish – to review what part learning might play in their lives.

Rebalancing resources

a) Public agreement is needed on the *criteria for fair and effective allocation of resources for learning across the life course*. The debate should include both efficiency and equity: what do we need to do to make sure that resources have maximum impact, and how are they used to include all segments of society. The current discourse is still rooted in investment in education as an initial phase. It should be framed around the interdependence of generations, so that investment in learning for all ages benefits all other ages.

b) As a starting point, we propose the very broad goal of shifting from the current *86: 11: 2.5: 0.5* allocation across the four quarters, to approximately *80: 15: 4: 1* by 2020. This combines all public and private spending. This should be seen not so much as a specific target, but rather as a guideline to be used in monitoring the system, as we suggest should be done through a triennial *State of Learning* report to ensure that genuine progress is being made (see *Annexe A*).

c) Within each age group, including the first stage, specific attention should be given to the fair and equitable distribution of resources. Which groups benefit most, especially but not only from public investment; which are excluded; and is this a pattern we are comfortable with? This is an essential mechanism for a continuing commitment to equalising opportunity. It covers equity both between sectors (HE, FE, community, etc) and within them.

d) We outline the dimensions of an *intergenerational contract*, as a way of conceiving how all generations benefit from investment in each others' learning, now and in the future.

e) Finally, to counter any sense that we favour age segregation, we recommend redoubling efforts in support of *family and intergenerational learning*. Investing in families, broadly understood, is an absolute win-win strategy, and the outstanding way of breaking the cycle of disadvantage.

'Guaranteeing some level of entitlement is potentially a hugely important mechanism for removing barriers and increasing choice. It offers great flexibility and can be tailored to fit many different circumstances.'

'Conventional patterns of working time are very much up in the air, with unemployment, short-term working and greater flexibility all growing. There is opportunity in this crisis to generate innovations in time which will pay off in the future.'

6 Enabling demand for learning
An entitlements framework

Summary

In this chapter we examine a crucial mechanism for expanding lifelong learning, and for rebalancing the system: the establishment of a range of different entitlements to learning. The goal is to provide an overall framework within which entitlements can be developed, devised and tailored to suit the particular context.

First, we discuss what entitlements are, and what they might be. Actual and potential entitlements take many different forms. They may be universal or targeted. They may be underwritten by the State or employers or other organisations. Importantly, entitlements may attach to individuals, or be developed as collective benefits, for groups of people. We argue that entitlements should be seen as a way of maximising the commitment of everyone involved.

Our framework comprises:

- three *general entitlements*: to basic skills (literacy and numeracy); to a qualification which can function as the foundation for future competencies; and to 'learning leave' as part of employment. The first builds on existing policy, but extends it in various ways. The second is to a qualification giving the competences required to function in tomorrow's global society. Currently, this is usually seen as Level 2, but this is already regarded by some as inadequate; they argue for Level 3 as the minimum. However, not just the level but the content of the minimum will need to be regularly updated in the light of economic and other changes. We therefore favour the uplift towards Level 3, but this must be broadly interpreted. Thirdly, we propose a general move towards learning leave, as an entitlement in a looser sense which good employers will progressively build into employment contracts, as part of a new mosaic of working time patterns; and
- a set of *'transitional' entitlements* targeted to emphasise the particular importance of key transition points in people's lives, professional or personal.

The framework is underpinned by a universal infrastructure of access to digital technology, and of advice and guidance.

We envisage a system of *Learning Accounts* as the main vehicle for building and using entitlements, allowing contributions from different stakeholders over time. These should be set up from the age of 25, marking the transition into the second stage, but linked to earlier forms of support. We suggest ways in which such Learning Accounts could be taken forward, drawing on current savings and fiscal measures. In particular, we suggest they should be kick-started by diverting into them at least part of the current Child Trust Funds.

What is an entitlement?

Probably the single biggest measure supporting adults returning to learn was the US GI Bill, which enabled millions of American servicemen and women to go back to college after the Second World War. Item 1 of the Bill which President Roosevelt signed into effect on 22 June 1944 read:

> It gives servicemen and women the opportunity of resuming their education or technical training after discharge, or of taking a refresher or re-trainer course, not only without tuition charge up to $500 per school year, but with the right to receive a monthly living allowance while pursuing their studies.

The Bill did more than offer generous financial support to the veterans to help them reintegrate; it encouraged them to aim higher, to raise their educational sights. In the peak year of 1947, veterans accounted for an amazing 49 per cent of college admissions. By the time the original GI Bill ended on 25 July 1956, 7.8 million of 16 million Second World War veterans had participated in an education or training programme.[1] This was a learning entitlement on a major scale. It helped to propel the US into pole position in the post-war expansion of post-secondary education – a position which President Obama now intends them to regain.

In 2008, the GI BIll was updated once again. The new law gives veterans enhanced educational benefits that cover more educational expenses, provide a living allowance, money for books and the ability to transfer unused educational benefits to spouses or children. This last feature is particularly interesting as an example of collective entitlement.

There are dozens of other entitlement initiatives around, though not on this scale. In the UK at present, government-sponsored individual entitlements include the following:

---

[1] OECD (1975).

- student maintenance, for full-time HE students. This is on a means-tested basis. Students in England and Wales get up to £2,906. Financially, this is by far the biggest form of entitlement, amounting to approximately £1.9 billion annually;
- Education Maintenance Allowances, providing £30 per week for young people aged 16–18 from poor households;
- all employed apprentices must receive a wage of no less than £95 per week (increased in August 2009 from £80 per week);
- an entitlement for those without Level 2 to free training to gain that qualification, provided the employer participates in Train to Gain; and
- free tuition for those under 25 who wish to obtain a full Level 3 qualification.

Services' Learning Credit schemes

The Ministry of Defence's Standard Learning Credit (SLC) scheme provides annual financial support for small-scale learning activities. The Enhanced Learning Credit (ELC) scheme provides larger-scale support in the form of single, annual payments (to a maximum of three years) to help pay towards the cost of higher-level learning. All personnel are eligible to claim SLC support to cover 80 per cent of fees (to a maximum of £175 per annum) paid to civilian bodies for certain personal development learning programmes, examinations and support. The ELC scheme provides up-front funding, available at two tiers: up to £1,000 per annum for those with four or more years' eligible service, and up to £2,000 per annum for those with eight or more years' eligible service. Personnel may make ELC claims in up to three separate financial years, either while in service or for up to ten years after leaving. In 2008–9, over 13,000 Army personnel took advantage of the schemes (2,913 on ELCs and 10,510 on SLCs).

Individual Learning Accounts in Scotland

ILAs support low-income learners aged 16 and over; i.e. people whose individual income is £22,000 or less, or those on benefits.

The new ILA500 support for advanced-level study part-time students was introduced for autumn enrolment in 2008. This can benefit up to 20,000 part-time students. This offer provides £500 per year to support part-time learners studying for HNC/HND awards, undergraduate degrees, Professional Development Awards and Continuous Professional Development courses.

The ILA200 offer provides up to £200 per year for learners to fund a wide range of shorter courses (below 40 credit points). Many courses focus on vocational learning, but it also supports those learners furthest away from learning to do shorter 'bites' of learning to encourage a more lifelong learning approach for all.

Examples of courses which may be vocational or lifelong learning are: Cookery; Financial Capability; Photography; English for Speakers of Other Languages (ESOL). Over 130,000 people have opened an ILA and over 70,000 learners have attended over 105,000 courses. Currently, there are over 330 registered ILA Scotland learning providers offering almost 20,000 courses. This includes universities, colleges, private training providers and local and community-based learning providers.

France's 'congé individuel formation' and 'droit individuel à la formation'

France has introduced rights for individuals to learning leave. The 'congé individuel formation' (CIF – individual training leave) is financed through a 0.2 per cent payroll tax on companies with 20+ employees, paid to a mutual organisation (Opacim/Fongecif). It allows an employee who has completed at least two years' service (six months in the case of a fixed-term employee) to apply for leave for up to one year full time, or 1,200 hours part time, with their salary and contractual rights maintained. The purpose of the leave is to change occupation, or achieve a higher level, and is linked to a qualification. If Fongecif approves, the employer can defer but not refuse the leave. In 2007, over 40,000 people exercised this right (nearly 80,000 applied), with an annual length of 754 hours.

More recently (2004), the 'droit individuel à la formation' (DIF – individual right to training) was introduced. The right here is to a shorter leave – up to 20 hours a year, cumulable for six years – and it is managed through joint agreements by industrial sector. The employer can refuse the time off if they judge it inappropriate. The DIF is geared primarily towards reducing inequalities. Approximately 500,000 employees took advantage of the DIF in 2007.

Entitlements vary considerably in scale and ambition, but also on a number of other dimensions, and these are worth spelling out before we outline our framework. We define the principal goals of entitlements as some or all of the following:

- to make a public statement that society, or an organisation, values learning and wishes to support it;
- to tap actual and latent demand for learning, generally or by a particular group;
- to increase choice, generally or within some constraints;
- to cater to needs genuinely throughout the life course, including at key points of transition;
- to promote equity between groups and over time; and
- to leverage contributions from different sources.

Most entitlements will aim for most of these. A national set of entitlements (as distinct from any single entitlement) should aim to cover all of them, and do so without incurring excessive administrative or transaction costs.

Population: who's it for?

The entire population has a right to education, formally recognised, but this only goes as far as the end of compulsory schooling – indeed, it is, as it were, an enforced right. Beyond that there are various entitlements, nationally established, for groups such as those lacking in basic skills, and others which apply to specific organisations, not across the country.

Qualifying criteria: who gets it?

Where the entitlement is not universal, the distribution can be determined by a number of factors; for example, *need*, as with English language; *age*; or *length of service*.

Entitlement to what?

The entitlement may not be to anything more than a *decision process*. This is the case with the proposed 'right to request time for training'; no one was forbidden to make such a request previously, but the proposed right would place an obligation on the employer to think about and respond formally to it. Alternatively, it may be to *information and guidance* – from a one-hour session to more generally available advice and support.

However, the key factors are money and time. *Financially*, the entitlement may be to waiving or discounting of direct costs such as tuition fees; to travel expenses; to educational materials (books etc); or to maintenance costs. The assistance may be in terms of grant or loan. Some of these exist already, notably in relation to higher education. They have hugely varying financial implications, as our discussion of 'rebalancing' has already highlighted. *Time* is money, up to a point, but it is also a separate form of entitlement. There have been many examples of paid educational leave (PEL), where time off from work is granted, full time or part time, with maintenance of pay. The maintenance can be of basic salary or full salary. The time involved may be capped at different levels, from a few hours to a year, or even more. University sabbaticals are a prime example.

A major distinction is between entitlements which are tied to a specific *type of learning* – most obviously, in the case of employment-based entitlements, whether or not the learning is job-related.

Finally, the entitlement may of course be to a combination of all or some of the above.

Where does it apply?

The entitlement may be a matter of *national policy*, or of *local/regional* policy, through discretionary action; for example, by a local authority. It might cover a *sector,* or be devised for a particular *organisation*, as with the Services scheme.

Individual/collective

An entitlement may be an entirely *personal* one. This is usually the case, as the name 'Individual Learning Accounts' suggests; but it can be designed to cater for a *group* as a whole, as with the Collective Learning Funds currently being piloted.

Single-source or joint funding

The resources supporting the entitlement may come from a single source (individual, employer, state) or from a combination of two or more of these. In some cases, there can be a contribution from one which triggers contributions from others, as with ILAs.

The strength of the entitlement

The strength of the entitlement ranges from a legally enforceable right, through formal or informal agreements where there are some constraining conditions on how or when anyone can claim the entitlement, to a publicly declared aspiration, such that the entitlement gives only a general indication of an intention to promote learning opportunities.

Finally, an entitlement is not something which only results from additional funding for a particular initiative. It should be part of the system for supporting learning on a sustained basis, not a temporary measure (though of course it would be reasonable to pilot specific entitlements to see how they worked, before implementing them fully). This distinguishes (though not always very clearly) entitlements from the incentives offered by government or employers for particular learning goals.

We use 'entitlement' in ways which spread across most of the senses just discussed. This variety may lead to some loss of clarity. However, it compensates by the flexibility it gives for developing arrangements tailored to particular circumstances. This is essential if it is genuinely to promote choice.

We have some reservations over the use of the word 'entitlement'. In some usages it carries a 'something for nothing' flavour: but there is a very close link between learning and intrinsic motivation: people learn best when they want to learn, rather than because an entitlement exists, and entitlement can suggest that personal commitment is not needed.[2] However, guaranteeing some level of entitlement is potentially a hugely important mechanism for removing barriers and increasing choice. It had a central place in the Scottish Parliament's 2002 Inquiry into Lifelong Learning. It offers great flexibility and can be tailored to fit many different circumstances. After all, entitlement sits snugly with the overall perspective we gave in *Chapter 1*, springing from the notion of education as a human right. Our point here is that entitlements bring with them some sense of reciprocity, an implicit contract between learners and the organisation or community which supports them.

Learning leave: a story still to tell?

In the 1970s there was a fair head of steam behind the notion of paid educational leave. Optimists saw this as a logical further step from paid holidays, which had only become a matter of general practice some 40 years earlier, notably with legislation from the French administration of 1936. They hoped that it would soon become as normal a part of working conditions as paid holidays already were – indeed, that it would seem as unacceptable for employment contracts not to have PEL as a standard feature as it would be if you were told a job had no holiday entitlement. The arguments were similar: PEL is needed,

---

[2] William Beveridge once said: 'benefit in return for contributions, rather than free allowances from the State, is what the people of Britain desire. (Cited in *Options for New Britain*, Uberoi *et al*, 2009 p.63). This is too sweeping. Entitlements need not be contribution-based, but we see them as part of an implicit contract: learning benefits both learners and the rest of society.

as holidays are, to refresh the workforce, to the benefit of their productivity as well as their well-being.

The International Labour Organisation (ILO) approved its Convention 140 on Paid Educational Leave in 1974, drawing explicitly on Article 26 of the UN Declaration of Human Rights. The intergovernmental thinktank, the Organisation for Economic Cooperation and Development (OECD), commissioned analysis of legislative and negotiated agreements on educational leave, which fed into their policy recommendations on lifelong learning.[3] However, it didn't take off as a universal right – either at the level of legislation or through collective bargaining – though in some countries and some sectors there remains strong traces of it.[4] In the neo-liberal climate of the 1980s and 1990s, governments were reluctant to give legislative support to an occupational benefit of this kind. It seemed counter-cultural even to suggest it, though it was arguably of benefit to all parties and, in the ILO format, highly flexible. If legislation was not a promising route, neither was collective bargaining. The dominant economic focus of the last two decades, and an ever-increasing pace at work, left little space for temporal innovation. People were too busy working, and organisations too fixated on ever-increasing growth rates to incur the cost of giving time off. As the Swedish sociologist Steffan Linder observed, the richer you are, the more your time costs.[5]

However, the idea of PEL – meaning the integration into employment conditions of time off for learning – is not dead. In fact, it occurs routinely, although usually not as an entitlement but as part of a decent job. Professionals often have it built in (for example, Scottish teachers are entitled to 35 hours CPD per year, and FE teachers in England are entitled to 30 hours, including a pro-rata entitlement for part-timers). Trade unions have embraced learning and skills, which now figure increasingly as part of the collective bargaining agenda. Good employers routinely offer access to training with time off and some financial support, for fees or examination expenses. However, only some fall into this category, and often the leave is offered only to those already highly educated and skilled.

Ironically, the current recession may have opened up new space for real innovation in this area. The prospect of large-scale unemployment is forcing us to rethink old assumptions about work and income, and how these are distributed.

---

[3] OECD (1975).

[4] France is the most commonly cited example with its legislation on congé formation, introduced in 1971. This has been regularly updated, most recently in 2003 (see box on p. 118). The rationale in the law for the right to educational leave is impeccable and the form remains quite inspirational; but the bureaucratic structure which controls it has become divorced from the reality of the workplace, so the effects are limited.

[5] Hence his book's title 'The Harried Leisure Class'. (Linder, 1971).

Organisations are experimenting with new ways of distributing working time, in order to preserve jobs during a downturn, to maintain loyalty and conserve expertise. In some cases workers have chosen, where consulted, to maintain jobs for all, even if this means accepting reduced working time and/or pay levels. The opening is there for different mixes of work and other time, including both learning and leisure, spread over different periods.[6]

Often, parallels can be helpful in expanding our horizons. We have already noted paid holidays as the obvious one. An interesting trend here is for holidays to become dispersed more over the calendar year, not all taken in chunks during one or two summer months. It would clearly be absurd to think of educational leave as coming in tidy two- or three-week packages of learning in the same mould as regular holidays. Today, it is even more the case that learning will take place in variable chunks – not all bite-sized, or even bite-shaped, but variable and interspersed with other activities. (See *Chapter 7* on new qualification frameworks.) Dispersed and variable patterns of holidays fit well with this greater variety in the rhythms of learning.

Occupational pensions are another parallel. They are not universal in the same way as paid holidays are, but have a much more variable incidence across different sectors and levels. The interesting parallel is that they often embody a combination of employer and employee contributions, with the State helping further via tax relief. This tripartite model of co-investment is something which has powerful relevance for learning. Of course, state pensions also come as a universal benefit (if still gender-discriminatory); this would be analogous to a universal floor entitlement to learning, on which the co-investment model builds.[7]

---

[6] European Foundation for the Improvement of Living and Working Conditions (2006). Recent examples include *kurzarbeit* arrangements in Germany, or the nine-day fortnight under debate in New Zealand; and the Spanish bank BVBA offering up to five years leave break, including support for training.

[7] A further parallel occurs here, with personal budgets in care services. Personal budgets mean that funding is transferred to the individual, so they can make their own choice of service, with advice. Instead of receiving a service which is free but over which they have no control, they are entitled within limits to define what kind of service they want and to commission it. So an elderly person might want someone to read to them, and choose this over what the local council will previously have defined as best for them. See www.communitycare.co.uk for more information. Here, there is a potential overlap with educational entitlements: access to learning could be built into this personal budget, either as an earmarked component or part of a recommended list of options.

A framework: infrastructural guarantees, general entitlements and transition entitlements

We move on now to lay out an overall framework within which different kinds of entitlement can be located. This is in tune with our strategic approach: not to prescribe in detail, but to set the terms on which progressive developments can be debated and taken forward. Table 12 is a guide. We divide it into three parts:

- infrastructural guarantees, which commit public authorities to ensure a certain level of service;
- general entitlements, which focus mainly on the population as a whole; and
- specific transition entitlements, which address key points when learning is particularly likely to make a big and lasting difference.

Table 12: An entitlements framework

General entitlements	Specific transition entitlements

• A *legal* entitlement of free access for all who need it to learning to acquire basic skills, i.e. literacy and numeracy, up to Level 1.
• A *financial* entitlement to a minimum level of qualification needed to be able to play a full contributing part in society; this is currently Level 2, but will rise and change over time.
• Both these entitlements should extend to all, regardless of age.
• A *'good practice'* entitlement to learning leave as an occupational benefit to be developed flexibly and over time as part of mainstream employment conditions.
	• To help people use learning to make potentially difficult transitions; for example:
	  – guaranteeing access to learning for those leaving prison or institutional care;
	  – moving between areas or countries; or
	  – on their 50th birthday
	• These to be developed flexibly over time.

Underpinned by infrastructural guarantees	
• Universal access to advice and guidance. • Universal access to a minimum level of digital technology (currently broadband at 2Mbps, but this will rise and change).	

Infrastructural guarantees

There are two fundamental services which need to be in place for people to be able to take advantage of their entitlements, at every stage. Both deal in information, in complementary ways: the first with personal advice and guidance, the second with access to the digital world.

Access to advice and guidance

The new adult advancement and careers service should mean that everyone will have access to good advice and information. This must be available to the population as a whole. It should be holistic, covering a wide range of advice, centred around individuals' needs and not separating these into unrealistic compartments; so it should address, not only people's professional learning but also their other concerns. It is an integral part of our citizens' curriculum (see *Chapter 8*). For people to acquire the various capabilities which comprise this, they need to have well-founded and impartial guidance. There is no need to specify more at this general level; we have more to say on some specific points at which access should be particularly supported (see below on staging posts).

Access to the digital world

Digital inclusion is the contemporary equivalent of universal access to the postal service, for so long taken for granted. Universal access to broadband is already established as the goal for 2012 (see the *Digital Britain* report).[8] This is essential for there to be full democratic participation, and to counter the divisions which occur in digital access. The guarantee will need to be updated as technology progresses and broadband at 2Mbps is surpassed as a tool; we therefore phrase it in terms of a minimum level of digital inclusion. We urge that libraries should be supported to play a full part in this, as places of universal access serving the community.

These two services underpin the system. They should be completely universal, so that access is genuinely available to all. They should not be subject to the vagaries or the special interests of commercial competition.

General entitlements

We propose three general entitlements: a *legal* entitlement to literacy and numeracy as basic skills; a *financial* entitlement to a qualification giving the competences required to function in tomorrow's global society; and a *'good practice'* entitlement to learning leave. These general entitlements pick up directly

---

[8] BIS and DCMS (2009).

on the values and issues identified in earlier chapters. The basic skills entitlement addresses above all the issue of *equality*: it is geared to helping those who have not yet reached the level of education which is the minimum for effective participation in economic and social life. However, we reiterate here that there is a business as well as a social justice case for greater equality, as the UKCES has made clear. It covers people in all four stages of the life course. The more diffuse entitlement to learning leave addresses the issue of *aspiration and culture*; it is designed to encourage employers and employees to think of learning as a natural part of a longer and more varied working life.

We remarked at the start that the idea of entitlements is not a strange one. It exists already in forms which are quite familiar to many people, such as student grants. We need to consolidate both the idea and the reality, extending it to a wider range of people and circumstances. In particular, the system should allocate the entitlements as far as possible to those who need them most and who can make best use of them.

In fact, good progress has already been made in recent years in several respects, and especially in respect of our first general entitlement, to a basic level of achievement. Our proposals build on the current position in three major respects:

- we make a clearer differentiation between entitlements in stage one (up to 25) and those in subsequent stages;
- we extend entitlements which relate to 'working life' to cover the full age range of 25–75; and we argue that there should be an equivalent for those beyond working age; and
- we suggest a shift in the overall balance of support for entitlements, with a stronger employer contribution in stages two and three, more state support in stages three and four (but not from the education budget alone), and encouragement for more individual contributions across the life course.[9]

General entitlement 1 – basic skills: literacy, numeracy and language

The fundamental and strong right to education which we mentioned at the very start of this report has to include the right of any adult to all the support needed to achieve the basic skills of literacy and numeracy.

The scandal of so many people lacking basic skills was half hidden until the Moser report on adult literacy exposed the 'national disgrace of over 6 million adults with functional illiteracy and many more with numeracy skills below the levels

---

[9] We discuss levers for securing higher levels of employer engagement in learning more generally in *Chapter 10*.

achieved by most 11 year olds' (see IFLL Commissioner Nick Stuart's comments on Basic Skills later on in this chapter).[10] Definitions of literacy and estimates of the exact numbers are controversial. However, the numbers are not only very large, but inexcusably so for an advanced society with at least 11 years of schooling.

Great strides have been made in recent years. In 2006–7, 215,000 people achieved a first Level 1 or above literacy qualification (or the equivalent in ESOL), and 84,000 achieved their first Entry Level 3 or above numeracy qualifications. This is evidence of great headway made to solve the problem, but the task remains great.

Our first general entitlement is a *legal* one, for free access to provision for all to achieve these basic skills of literacy and numeracy. This is similar to what is currently offered in England, with free tuition for all those who have not attained at least functional levels of literacy at Level 1 and numeracy at Entry Level 3.[11] It is excellent that the Government has extended the entitlement to include all progression towards these levels, though what 'progression' means still needs to be carefully thought through. Recent evidence shows clearly how literacy and numeracy provide the essential foundation for acquiring employability skills.[12]

Making this entitlement a reality must be an absolute priority. It means mobilising support, notably through intermediaries such as union learning representatives and through family learning initiatives. It means designing assessment appropriate to learners' quite varied motivations, and embedding basic skills in a way that relates realistically to what they need to learn and do.

A closely related area is that of English for Speakers of Other Languages (ESOL). Learning English is essential for proper integration into our society (and indeed is increasingly recognised across the world as an essential condition for anyone to participate in the global economy). It is a means of making diversity a true social asset. There is currently an entitlement to provision with some state support, though there is an expectation of a contribution from the individual and/or employer if they can afford to pay. We agree with this, but there are groups to whom we would wish to extend the entitlement: to asylum seekers, immediately

---

[10] Moser (1999).

[11] The PSA target for 2008–11 aims for 597,000 people of working age to achieve a first Level 1 or above literacy qualification; and 390,000 to achieve a first Entry Level 3 or above numeracy qualification.

[12] Reder and Bynner (2009).

rather than making them wait six months; and to newly arrived spouses who lack access to social networks.[13]

Basic skills

The Learning Age[14] contained an insignificant sentence – so insignificant that some in Whitehall wanted to drop the idea altogether – announcing the establishment of Claus Moser's inquiry into adult literacy.[15] His report exposed the national disgrace of over 6 million adults with functional illiteracy and many more with numeracy skills below the levels achieved by most 11 year olds. At last the penny dropped.

Since 2001, the Government has invested £5 billion in the *Skills for Life* programme: 5.7 million adults have taken up over 12 million learning opportunities and over 2.8 million adults have gained a first qualification. This is a remarkable success story. But the task is unfinished. To reach the target of 95 per cent of adults achieving functional literacy and numeracy skills by 2020 set by UKCES's World Class Skills report[16] will require a further kickstart to the strategy. In particular we need:

- a new focus on priority groups and those working at Entry Level who have barely been touched in the past decade and are likely to be further ignored on present plans;
- a less narrow definition of employability; to concentrate too narrowly on this aspect fails to recognise the social dislocation and alienation experienced by those whom current programmes bypass;
- a new and more compelling strategy to tackle numeracy, which remains largely untackled but is still a startling national weakness; and
- greater attention paid to adults with learning disabilities and difficulties; they are virtually left out of account. That neglect must end.

Nick Stuart, IFLL Commissioner and Chair, NIACE Company Board

---

[13] The argument for expansive ESOL provision is fundamentally one of social justice and integration. There is also a solid economic argument. Many of those who cannot speak English have good educational levels and skills (see Convention of Scottish Local Authorities, 2005; Welsh Refugee Council, 2007). Lack of the English language means these skills risk being wasted. Human capital can disappear quickly, as people become discouraged from seeking work appropriate to their level. NIACE has put it well: 'Language is a lifeline and language is affordable'.

[14] DfEE (1998).

[15] Moser (1999).

[16] UKCES (2009a).

General entitlement 2 – future competencies: a platform

We know that the skills of literacy and numeracy are necessary but not sufficient for effective participation in economic and social life in the future. The difficulty is in specifying a given level of competence which might be regarded as a sufficient minimum. The goalposts move, but not in any simple direction. The level of competence regarded as adequate for one generation may not suffice for the next; and the range of competences changes, notably as a result of technological developments. Can we say what will be needed by 2020? Any attempt to set a threshold or floor level of qualification will always be to some extent arbitrary and ill-fitting.

Level 2 is the most widely accepted minimum standard. On this, the UKCES *Ambition 2020* report makes the point:

> *Our current position has not changed much from that reported in the Leitch Review in 2006: we are now ranked 17th on low-level skills… While the overall UK skills profile is improving over time, too many people are in danger of being left behind: one in eight adults of working age have no qualifications; more than a quarter are not qualified to Level 2; and just shy of half are not qualified above Level 2.*[17]

Its sobering projection is that seventeenth place will turn into twenty-third by 2020.

What is to be done? The current arrangements offer free tuition to all those 'of working age' studying to achieve a Level 2 qualification. We broadly endorse this for pragmatic reasons, because it gives direct purchase on the current system, but with amendments put forward below.

The target of raising the proportion of UK adults qualified to at least Level 2 is already daunting. However, we know that in some sectors Level 2 is already regarded as inadequate, and there is therefore a move to adopt Level 3 as the threshold. Our approach to how this entitlement should evolve is rather different. We do not think it wise to think in terms only of these different hierarchical levels as defining a minimum. It should be open to a broad interpretation, to allow for the range of skills and competencies which will be needed as a foundation, without tying these into a rigid straitjacket of defined levels. For the future, Level 3 should be accepted as the target; but the scope of the entitlement should be routinely reviewed – not just to upgrade it in terms of level, but to redefine it as appropriate to future changes: economic, technological and social. This is why we describe it as a platform for

---

[17] UKCES (2009a) p. 53.

future competencies.[18] It is a *financial* rather than a legal entitlement. It will need to change over time. What is needed is sufficient support to allow people access.

We have three further amendments to the current position:

- following the logic of our four-stage model outlined in the previous chapter, the definition of 'working age' should be extended to age 75;
- the current entitlement to achieve a full Level 2 qualification should be achieved universally via a unitised credit route, so that access is on a much more flexible basis than it has been in the past (see *Chapter 7*); and
- an equivalent offer should be made to those aged 75+, many of whom did not benefit from current or earlier drives to raise basic levels. This offer should be regarded as part of the 'rebalancing' which we suggest for the system overall, and will need to be publicly funded.

General entitlement 3 – 'learning leave' in a new mosaic of time

PEL, or its twenty-first century equivalent – 'learning leave' – is something which deserves serious consideration, both as a universal entitlement and as one which can be taken up by individual organisations or sectors who want to demonstrate their commitment to learning. We relate learning leave particularly to the second and third stages of the life course. In *Chapter 5* we identified the time squeeze as a major feature of the second stage. The UK has a distinctively long hours culture, closely allied to low pay. Its government has also been uniquely resistant to the European Working Time directive – often wrongly identified with setting limits on weekly working hours, whereas it has a far more flexible application to annual working hours. Both time and money are precious to many caught in this squeeze, which is exactly why its grip is so painful. It squeezes hardest on women with children, whose time burden is heaviest.[19] A system of time entitlements for learning which meshed easily with work and family commitments would be a major step forwards for those in the second stage, and for gender equality.

Is this facing backwards, trying to rekindle an ambition which belongs to the past? We do not think so. Rather, we are promoting greater flexibility across the life course. Remember that an essential part of the rationale for dividing the second and third stages in the way we suggest is that employment would last longer, but on a more evenly distributed basis. This would generate a profusion of patterns of full- and part-time work with a similar profusion of non-work activities (in fact, the

---

[18] For an interesting and much broader attempt to define such 'future competencies', see the report of that name from Nordic Network for Adult Learning (2007):
http://www.nordvux.net/download/2624/ntt_rapport_sum_en.pdf
[19] Women and Work Commission (2006).

distinction between full time and part time should soon evaporate for work, as we recommend it should for studying). It opens up the way for learning to be more fully integrated with work and holidays in a new mosaic of time.

We propose the development of 'learning leave' – a somewhat broader concept than PEL – as a *good practice* entitlement which should be an increasingly accepted part of employment conditions. This is best developed incrementally, tailored to the context of the sector or organisation. We would expect to see this featuring as a sign of good practice, in such models as the Investors in People template. Public employers should lead the way, but this is an issue on which procurement policy could be used to push things along; in other words, progressive employers, public or private, could use the leverage of their contracts with others to promote this as a matter of good practice.

Learning leave is part of employment conditions, and its basis should be paid for by employers. However, as with some other occupational benefits, there can be variants of this which draw in other contributions. State support might come from reviewing and redeploying the £3.7 billion corporation tax relief currently granted for training. Employees might contribute with their personal time. In line with the Inquiry's general approach, we do not favour compulsion, but prefer to work with the grain of good practice, encouraging good employers (and their associations) to match the best. For small and medium-sized enterprises (SMEs), where there may be particular problems in granting time off, the arrangements may need to differ. The exact design of the learning leave is best left to negotiation between the interested parties, as appropriate to organisation, region or sector.

However, it is only realistic to anticipate that good practice will not spread of its own accord. 'Short-termism' and 'free-riding' mean that it will be necessary for the Government to retain the option of introducing further measures, including legislation, where employees are not being given reasonable and fair opportunities.[20] Some employers currently choose not to invest in training, and not show any interest in learning leave schemes. In its annual report on skills, the UKCES could be asked to identify sectors where such particular action is needed, or may be if there is not rapid improvement.

Learning leave can also be designed to match the stage in the life course. So for those in the Third Age, learning leave arrangements may be geared wholly to their paid work, if they are still in regular employment, but the focus of the leave may well be on changes in their pattern of work: a shift to part-time work, which is more likely to occur in this stage, to a different type of career, or to a mix of paid

---

[20] This is analogous to the new minimum entitlement to an employer pension where the employer would otherwise provide none.

and unpaid work. The leave would therefore be used to enable people to make the transition to a new employment status, whatever that may be.

Relatedly, the balance of support might shift across the life course; for instance, with employers contributing more strongly in stage 2 and the State contributing in stage 3 (including through tax relief to individuals). However, this is a matter of degree, of mixing the different components in different proportions, and not of switching wholesale from one support source to another.

Variation and experimentation, suited to local circumstances are therefore important. However, a universal feature should be an obligation on all employers, public and private, to publish certain minimal details of their investment in training, and this should include where they have introduced learning leave as an entitlement. This would give shareholders and potential investors a clear indication of their commitment as employers to human capital growth.

> People often ask me what unions have got to do with learning. Most people think unions are just about going on strike to get more pay. Actually, unions are rooted in learning. 'Educate, Agitate, Organise' was the slogan on the earliest union banners. From the early Guilds to today's unions, members' education was and is central. Why? Because members want a better life for themselves and their families. That does not just mean more pay; it also means personal development and gaining skills to get on at work. That is why unions and the TUC are passionately committed to providing learning to union members and representatives. Union learning includes bargaining skills, employment law, health and safety or equal opportunity laws; but it also covers languages, computer skills, literacy and personal development. Union members want bread and roses.
>
> Most employers work well with unions on learning. Unionised companies have both higher levels of investment in training and higher returns to that investment, in the form of qualifications gained, completion and progression rates. But there are still far too many UK employers who spend little or nothing on training; who operate within a narrow, controlling, short-term mindset which will simply not survive in tomorrow's knowledge economy. We cannot continue to allow the employers who train to be undercut by those that don't. Like other countries, the UK needs to find ways of ensuring that all employers pull their weight. We have to encourage a more generous attitude to training which does not begrudge and question the value of qualification, but looks positively at how work can be made more interesting and more valuable – so as to make best use of the higher skills and expectations which employees are increasingly bringing to their work.
>
> *Tom Wilson, IFLL Commissioner and Head of Organisation and Services, TUC*

Specific transition entitlements

Life is full of transitions, large and small. In some philosophies, it is nothing but transitions – or is even only one rather ephemeral transition. Philosophising apart, learning is often most effective when it comes just as people are moving from one situation to another, whether of their own choice or not. These are often crucial moments, when the opportunity to learn can have a decisive influence on the track followed. We focus later on four specific transition points, with different clientele, where a real emphasis on learning can make a lasting impact. But first we deal with chronological transitions, familiar to us all, though affecting us as individuals in very different ways.

Big birthday bonus

Entering a new decade has a particular status. It sometimes affects people particularly strongly. This is of course an effect of pure mathematical roundness; there is no intrinsically greater change in the passage of a single day which takes you from 39 to 40, 49 to 50 and so on from the day before or after. However, it often has a psychological effect – positive, negative or mixed. We propose to take advantage of this to remind people of their continuing potential for learning. Learning Accounts could be topped up every decade with a further entitlement. However, a stronger entitlement – perhaps a double top-up – at 50 would signal the continuing potential for learning of those moving into the third stage. This could be universal or means-tested, for example, according to whether people had already benefited from publicly supported higher education. Whether generous or minimal, it would have powerful symbolic meaning.

The other transitions are by way of example. There could be many others. We select these to give an idea of the range.

Release from prison

Offender education is improving, but there is still work to be done in enabling ex-offenders to get themselves on a positive track, as opposed to relapsing into previous habits and company ('dependency paths' is an apt term here). A guarantee of a place on a course in a local college would give offenders a goal, an identity and a social context where they stand a far better chance of establishing a new life. The course could be vocational or for personal skills and development. The way to this should be paved beforehand, as part of pre-release preparation. A model for this already exists in the resettlement provision made for those leaving the armed services.

E-learning entitlement for parents of young children

This recommendation comes from a proposal made by the National Skills Forum in *Closing the Gender Skills Gap*[21]. The transition is both into being a parent and, sometimes, into leaving work, even if only temporarily. The former at least should be a delight; but it may mean some loss of adult identity. Parents of young children will often find it difficult to leave home. An e-learning entitlement would give them access to learning from home. They might wish to explore new areas; or it could give them the opportunity to maintain their existing skills, so that re-entry into work is easier. It is a creative extension to parental leave provision.[22]

Leaving care and other institutions

Children in care get one of the worst deals in society, on almost every count. Certainly, the education system fails them badly. The transition from a care institution can be traumatic, even if the quality of the care may not have been high. This applies to institutional forms of care generally. The proposal in the 2009 review of *Skills for Life* is very promising:

> *'The National Care Advisory Service (NCAS) is working with local authorities to develop and test models to support care leavers into employment. As part of this work we will ensure that, from September 2009, all suitably qualified care leavers will be offered an Apprenticeship place. We intend to make this a legal entitlement from 2013.'*[23]

A strongly supported entitlement to participation in learning would indeed give an invaluable lifeline to many.

Children from care

Looked-after children are statistically more likely to go to prison than into higher education. This is particularly the case if they have had an unstable upbringing as opposed to going to boarding school or having stable, long-term foster carers. Affordability is a real blight on ambition without financial support after leaving care. This neglected group needs far more attention in fostering motivation and raising aspiration, as well as financial surety during studying. Universities are not designed for young people without homes to go to in vacations, and the financial packages that are available can be highly

---

[21] National Skills Forum (2009).
[22] We recognise that parents of young babies may be very keen to get out of the home occasionally, into the adult company which classes provide (see Brassett-Grundy, 2004). This entitlement should not be an alternative.
[23] DIUS (2009b).

bewildering and invite considerable risk-taking. The Frank Buttle Trust has drawn attention to the challenges and risks attached to looked-after children seeking a university education. All higher educational institutions should review their policies to ensure that transition is made as smooth as possible, through, for example, year-round accommodation, a single point of contact for financial advice and appropriate support packages for those without families behind them.

Professor Teresa Rees, IFLL Commissioner and Pro-Vice Chancellor,
Cardiff University

Moving places: a welcome entitlement

The IFLL Thematic Paper, *Migration, Communities and Lifelong Learning*, makes the proposal that any incomer to a local authority should be entitled to a free course, on a subject of their choice.[24] This would apply both to internal migrants (i.e. those moving districts within the UK), and to those migrating here from a different country. The entitlement would encourage the incomer to find out more about the new locality – if only where the college or other provider is – and give them a chance to make social contact with the host community. It is a creative contribution to social capital.

In each case the entitlement will obviously be limited, not open-ended, though it may be more generous in some cases than others, in the length of course or level of financial assistance offered. We would, for example, expect the care-leaver entitlement to be greater than the welcome entitlement.

Here we can add an element of reciprocity to the idea of entitlement, by encouraging participants to contribute their skills and experience, as well as learning themselves. We can do this via our notion of a Local Learning Exchange (LLE – see *Chapter 9*). The LLE would be the natural place for those in any of the above categories to go for guidance on what their learning opportunities are. If the entitlement was not sufficient for the chosen course (since they will be limited), the LLE could advise on possible sources of support. However, the LLE could also log the potential of the person to contribute their knowledge and skills, as teacher as well as learner. They could if they wished offer to tutor, or to play some other role in helping others learn – hence the reciprocity.

---

[24] McNair (2009b).

Staging Posts and MyFutures Folders

We have already given support to the current proposals for a strengthened and universally available adult advancement and careers service, emphasising that this should be available to all throughout their adult lives. However, it would be particularly helpful if at the beginning of each life stage there were a distinctive opportunity for people to take stock of where they are, where they want to go and what they might need in order to do that. These 'staging-post' reviews would enable people to think about what they need to know in their several roles as citizen, worker, family member and individual. They would find out about local and web-based opportunities for further learning. They would be connected to relevant networks, and they would know about what entitlements they have, to financial and other support.

The service should be an independent one, free of commercial interest. Trusted intermediaries could play a part in encouraging people to take full advantage of it (see *Chapter 8*).

The reviews could be organised around something called a MyFutures Folder: a web-based tool, through which people could gather information and ideas on all the topics listed below. These would be, as it were, different files within the folder. They could update these files themselves on a regular basis. The main areas are likely to be:

- learning for work, so people can plan new careers;
- learning for financial capability, so they can get a better idea of what they need to earn and save;
- learning for health – looking after yourself, and making best use of services to improve your well-being;
- learning for volunteering and other civic roles; and
- learning for personal interest and hobbies.[25]

These broad headings are relevant to people at any stage in their lives, except that people in the fourth stage would be far less likely to retain an interest in learning for paid work. The balance of interest, though, would naturally change as people moved through the stages. For those entering the third stage, it should include updated pre-retirement education. The 'big birthday bonus' would give particular encouragement to learning at this stage. The issues surrounding health and finance are likely to be different at this point, as circumstances change. Similarly, for those entering the fourth stage, the priorities would be likely to change again.

---

[25] This is similar to the proposal for 'life profiles' made by Moynagh and Worsley (2009, p.220). They also suggest that the balance of content would change at different stages, and point out how the profile could be used, at the individual's discretion, for social or professional networking.

At this stage, people might be particularly interested in personal reflection, and in maintaining links with younger generations. However, the essence of the opportunity to take stock remains the same across all stages, and there is no suggestion that the issues should be age-specific in any deterministic way.

Funding the entitlements

This set of potential entitlements may seem like a grossly optimistic shopping list. It is not. We have already emphasised its pragmatic nature and its flexibility. It builds on existing practice, and focuses on key points where impact should be greatest. Progress can be made as and when it is judged right. This judgement will be made in different ways in different organisations and households up and down the country. Any underpinning legislation will need to be carefully developed to maintain this flexibility.

There will be two balances to be struck: in the volume of resources committed; and in who contributes. The Chartered Institute for Personnel Development (CIPD)'s suggested approach is:

- where training is very relevant to the job, the employer should pay the full cost;
- where it is quite relevant, the costs should be shared; and
- where learning is not related to the job, good practice encourages employers to make a small contribution.

This is a reasonable formula. We can elaborate slightly, as follows:

- the infrastructure is the responsibility of the State;
- for the first of our general entitlements (basic skills), it should be the State that pays;
- for the second, (future competencies) it should be primarily the State, with the employer contributing as appropriate; [26] and
- for the third (learning leave), it should be primarily the employer, along with the State and perhaps the individual, and with the proportions shifting as appropriate.

For the transition entitlements, there will be much variation, but similar reasoning should apply. We believe that this is a framework which will allow good practice to develop, to mutual benefit.

---

[26] We discuss ways to secure greater levels of employer investment in learning more generally in *Chapter 10*.

Learning Accounts: a common vehicle for entitlements

Individual Learning Accounts (ILAs) were launched as an imaginative and bold venture in 1999, but in England the initiative was closed in 2001. It was very successful in attracting learners, including from groups which did not traditionally participate, but it had proved vulnerable to fraudulent activity, as unscrupulous people claiming to be learning providers exploited a weakness in the system. This is a weakness which can be quite easily remedied, and the principle of ILAs remains sound. Indeed, Wales has maintained them and Scotland has relaunched them, to good effect (see box on p. 117).

There is no reason why we should not learn from the initial problems and from subsequent experience, and design a better and more comprehensive scheme. The lessons are there to be learnt, and the technology for running the scheme more easily available. The Skills Accounts currently being piloted in England are a step forward, but too tentative and narrow in their approach. Learning Accounts would allow contributions to be made by the State, employers, and individuals and their families. These could be very diverse and flexible. They could build up over time. They would benefit from tax relief for individual and corporate contributions. They could be spent only on learning from approved providers (but this does not mean public sector providers alone). This reduces the range of providers, but is a necessary safeguard against fraud.

The level of contributions would depend on a variety of factors, notably the financial positions of the State (public finances), the organisation, the community or the individual and their family. All of these will decide, in their own ways, how much they can afford at any given time. The Learning Accounts can be a channel for public policy, in the sense that government could decide to target support to certain groups through Learning Accounts, as the Scottish ones are currently geared to low-income households. This would be a key tool for ensuring more equality over the life course. However, they would also be a natural mechanism for organisations and communities to use for stimulating demand and increasing choice. Parents and grandparents or other family members could contribute (and, of course, children and grandchildren might reciprocate), making it a collective investment.

All of these inputs would vary, in the light of other claims on public, organisational and household finances. There should be some level of stability, especially on the part of government funding, so that people can plan their learning futures, but the scheme can and should be highly flexible and responsive to changing circumstances.

Collective Learning Accounts

One design feature to be strongly supported is that Learning Accounts should be pooled as well as banked. That is to say, people should be able, not only to store up their entitlement until it is a good moment to use it, and until it reaches an adequate amount for the learning in prospect, but also, as far as possible, to contribute their entitlements into a pot, for family, community or other collective use. A group of employees could pool their Learning Accounts into a 'collective learning account', perhaps tailored to suit the needs of their sector of work and with union learning representatives as advisers. This would help employees to learn together, and employers to train a group, both of which are often more effective ways of going about learning – and which might therefore attract additional government or employer support.

Alternatively, a community might decide to pool their entitlements, and use them to promote particular learning opportunities for particular groups. For example, a village may want to strengthen its twinning arrangements with a village in another country, and people would therefore make part of their entitlements available for the learning of the relevant culture or language, even if they as individuals did not participate. Their turn might come the following year. These are the kinds of local arrangements that a Local Learning Exchange might take forward (see *Chapter 9*).

Launching Learning Accounts

An initial platform could be provided by adding into the public finance available part of the current fiscal contribution made to training through tax relief. We estimate this to be £3.7 billion. If even 5 per cent of this was earmarked for Learning Accounts, it would mean over £185 million available annually.

However, a more radical suggestion, originating from the City & Guilds, is that Child Trust Funds could more usefully be devoted to enhancing Learning Accounts rather than being a simple financial asset to be inherited at 18. We agree with this, but would extend it. Instead of the total accumulated being released at age 18 as a cash asset, to be spent without constraint, at least a proportion of the Child Trust Fund should remain untouched until the age of 25, and be paid into the individual's Learning Account. Children are now allocated £250 at birth, and £250 at age seven (an additional £250 at each stage for poorer people), with added contributions possible from parents or other sources. Assigning the second £250 to a Learning Account would be likely to be a far better investment than releasing it all immediately as cash; and releasing it at 25 would be more likely to produce effective returns, and would be a suitable way of marking the transition into the second stage. If half of the public contribution to Child Trust Funds was converted to Learning Accounts as we propose, that would help to encourage private contributions to these also. Family members and others might feel that anything they put in would be of more lasting benefit than a cash gift at 18.

We suggest that Learning Accounts are launched at age 25, as people move from the first to the second stage. Financial arrangements for supporting students in the first stage are already in place (and see our proposal on Dearing grants in *Chapter 7*). For those who don't use these in the first stage, there should be opportunity for them to secure broadly comparable state funding in stages two to four. Other forms of support, such as Career Development Loans, would need to be integrated in these arrangements.

Learning Futurescard

We suggested above that a system of entitlements should make intelligent use of technology. The mechanism for carrying the Learning Accounts would be an electronic card – a Learning Futurescard, modelled on the electronic travel cards which now operate widely. This could be stocked up in a number of ways, for use in a variety of contexts. It would allow transactions to be recorded, in easily accessible form. It could carry finance for fee payments, for example, usable with accredited providers. More expansively, it could also be used to log achievements, including formal qualifications within the credit system that we discuss in the following chapter. This is the direction taken by e-portfolios.

The Learning Futurescard could be linked to some of the emerging developments in personal budgeting. For example, if learning becomes part of social care – and we have outlined the case for learning as a powerful means of postponing dependency and improving the quality of life for those in need of social care – this would then form part of the personal care budget. We would not want to exaggerate how far technology can of itself link up different services, but it can certainly play a part.

Conclusion

We have provided a framework for a system of entitlements, and filled in that framework with a set of proposals for a range of different entitlements. Some of these describe or build on entitlements that already exist, or ideas already in play; others are relatively new. The key point is to provide a structure which will enable further development, so that the State, employers, communities and households can develop their own initiatives and solutions. There is a huge amount to be gained from experimentation within a coherent overall framework – this is part of the 'intelligent' system which we are aiming at. We have suggested that the notion of 'paid educational leave' (or PEL), prominent in the 1970s, be reshaped for modern times as 'learning leave'. This is particularly worth doing at a point when conventional patterns of working time are very much up in the air, with unemployment, short-term working and greater flexibility all growing. There is opportunity in this crisis to generate innovations in time which will pay off in the future.

We do not expect immediate, universal implementation. We are all too aware of the cost pressures in a changing global economy. It is worth stressing, however, that in the likely circumstance of relatively high conventional unemployment for some years to come, the time costs will go down in the classical counter-cyclical calculus. This is why we stress the broader picture of change in the way people spend, and value, their time.

Some of the proposals are for government to consider; we would expect the governments of the four nations to differ in the way they take the entitlement agenda forward, as we already see in Scotland and Wales on ILAs. Some are for employers, perhaps coming together in sectors, or through strong local employer networks. Some – and we hope this is a route which will particularly flourish – will be the product of partnerships between different stakeholders. A model for this is the collective agreement between employers and unions, with learning representatives in active support; and with public support through tax relief, and through incentives to public and voluntary sector providers such as the Workers' Educational Association (WEA) to meet the emerging demand for learning. Promoting such arrangements could be a responsibility of the local authority in its strategic role, fostered by the Local Learning Exchanges that we suggest in *Chapter 9*.

The scope and diversity of entitlements are already broad, and could be even more so. Here we identify three key axes for their development.

- Entitlements should be designed to raise *joint commitment to learning*. They should be more than a taken-for-granted subsidy from the State, or a concession wrung from employers. The most effective entitlement will be one where all the players in the game are keen to make it work, whatever they expect to get out of it. However, joint commitment does not mean that each player contributes in the same currency. A very likely combination is for an employer to put in money, for example, the cost of a course, and the employee to put in at least some of their own time.
- Increasingly, entitlements to learning should form *part of a wider range of entitlements* or benefits. We have just referred to the growth of personal

budgets in social care;[27] integrating a learning component into personal budgets would be a natural prompt to people to participate.

- Technology should be used to make the system work *flexibly and across different areas*. The growth of loyalty and other cards should make the operation of entitlements easier and cheaper – even allowing for the impressive capacity of IT systems to achieve the opposite. It would link to the introduction of individual learner numbers, and to e-portfolios, to make it easier for people to keep a record of their learning. Hence our proposals for a Learning Futurescard, and for MyFuture Folders, sketched out above.

We recognise that there will be tight limits on both public and private resources, even when we move out of the current recession. However, we stress that these entitlements are investments which bring economic as well as social and personal benefits to individuals, but also to the wider society. Even quite small investments in learning can make differences which will continue to pay off over a long period. Enabling a young person with a difficult early career to make a positive transition to adulthood has long-term consequences. At the other end, postponing dependency makes economic as well as social sense, notably in respect of health budgets which will be a primary focus of public expenditure in the future. Our framework of entitlements provides opportunities for all to gain to mutual advantage. That is why we cast it as part of a new social contract.

Recommendations on entitlements

1. The development of a *national system of Learning Accounts*. These should draw on the current experience of Skills Accounts and the Scottish and Welsh Individual Learning Accounts (ILAs), and the past experience of ILAs in England. The goal should be to have a comprehensive, flexible system which will enable and encourage all stakeholders to increase their investment in learning; and which will stimulate and support individual choice and participation. Learning Accounts should be set up when the individual reaches the age of 25, at the transition into the second life stage. They should receive an initial input: we propose that the current Child Trust Fund scheme should be revised so that 50 per cent of the public funds allocated should be placed in a Learning Account – a far better asset for the individual, a better investment for all, and one that is more likely to draw in further contributions.

2. A *clear overall framework* is needed within which a set of learning entitlements can be developed. We propose two key categories for this framework:

---

[27] Leadbeater, Bartlett and Gallagher (2008).

a) *General entitlements:*
- A *legal* entitlement to *basic skills*, covering literacy, numeracy and language;
- A *financial* entitlement to a qualification judged to be the *appropriate minimum platform* for the competencies needed in the future; the standard for this is currently Level 2, but should be pushed upwards and outwards; and
- a broader, '*good practice*' entitlement to *learning leave,* an occupational benefit to be developed flexibly and over time as part of mainstream employment conditions.

b) *Specific 'transition' entitlements,* designed to help people learn their way through difficult or challenging points in their lives, such as leaving prison or care. One specific example is for *big birthday bonus entitlements*, contributing to Learning Accounts at the turn of each individual's decades, with a double bonus at 50 to signal arrival into the Third Age.

3. There should be *universally guaranteed access* to:
- adult advice services, tailored to appropriate stages and circumstances;
- the digital world: broadband, and then to the next generation of technological infrastructure.

4. The advice service should give particular emphasis to 'staging-post' reviews, at or around the ages of 25 and 50. These would offer comprehensive and impartial advice across a range of areas, enabling individuals to explore what their learning needs might be, and what support would be available to them for this, for instance in their Learning Accounts.

MyFutures Folders would be set up, on a voluntary basis, enabling the individual to hold information which will help them make social or professional plans, and to carry a record of their learning and other achievements.

'The effects of a shift to mode-free funding will be significant... The timescale for implementing this should therefore be quite long. However, the political need is for a commitment to do this to be made, so that the planning can begin. It is not good enough, as we have heard, for policy-makers to acknowledge the force of the case, but to say that it cannot be done.'

7 Flexing the system
Credit where it is due

Summary

This chapter addresses the question of how to make the whole system more flexible, so that people can take advantage of the entitlements we have just proposed. A coherent framework for building up learning credits is a central component of an overall system of lifelong learning. It is essential for flexibility, for progression and for bridging the divides between different types of learning, especially inside and outside work. We address some of the obstacles which have slowed down progress towards this. We also address the way financial incentives maintain the dominance of full-time study, especially in higher education.

What credit is

'It is a custom / More honoured in the breach than the observance'

(Hamlet, I. iv. 14)

In *The Learning Age: a renaissance for a new Britain*, the New Labour Government responded to three powerful reports which it received soon after taking office in 1997: Helena Kennedy's on further education (*Learning Works*), the Dearing report on Higher Education (*Higher Education in the Learning Society*), and Bob Fryer's on continuing education (*Learning in the 21st Century*).[1] One of the priorities distilled from all three and given a target by the new Government was that of a national system for credit accumulation and transfer (CATS), covering all levels and types of post-compulsory learning. The Government called for Records of Achievement (ROA) and a national CATS system to be in place 'by 2000'.[2]

The principles of credit accumulation and transfer are that learners should be able to earn and 'bank' independently-attested recognition of what they have achieved. In some cases this will stand alone, as part of their personal learning story, and be no less valuable for that. In other circumstances, it should be used to 'articulate' with other learning achievements, perhaps to build towards a qualification, or to

---

[1] Kennedy (1997); NCIHE (1997); Fryer (1997).
[2] DfEE (1998). Paragraphs 6.7 and 6.18.

demonstrate the ability to benefit from a programme of learning at a higher level. There should be clear and unambiguous recognition of the 'level' at which the achievements are set, and of the broad significance of the content. On the latter point, not all learning in a particular area will be able to be cashed in to assist progress towards qualifications in another area. Some parts of the credit earned will be 'general' (recognition of generic achievement at a particular level); others 'specific' (potential building blocks towards specific qualifications).

This is another area in which the promise of *The Learning Age* has been sadly unrealised. However, here the sectors have to shoulder most of the blame. Progress towards a simple, transparent, usable system has been feeble at best. A number of things have gone wrong:

- there has been a failure to agree on a single 'currency' for such credit, complicated by jurisdictional differences between education and training sectors, devolved administrations and the like;

- employers have been nervous about supporting a system wherein 'portability' of credit might lead to individuals being poached by others or demanding rewards for their educational and training progress;

- the hyper-complexity of the UK's pattern of qualifications has led to all sorts of anxieties about equivalence, notably between so-called 'academic' and 'vocational' awards;

- there have been all sorts of proxy battles around recognised credit and funding, ranging from attempts to secure public funding for particular programmes ('if it's accredited, it should be paid for') to concerns about who does the accrediting in these circumstances ('if we are paying for it we should be able to say what it is worth'); and most seriously

- individual institutions (especially in HE) have for various reasons (especially perceptions of relative status) been reluctant to accept the judgments of other institutions about the achievement of students and its relationship to that of those they have admitted to the beginning of their own courses.

Vested interests defended the status quo, and there was no single and public champion for the introduction of a new credit system. The outcome, crudely, is that injunctions like those in *The Learning Age* have led to a busy development of systems – designed to meet as many options as possible, and hence adding to the complexity of the field – but very disappointing levels of actual use. As a result, we now have the systems (although they could be much simpler), but hardly anybody is using them. We are in exactly the state described by the philosopher RG Collingwood when he said that a bicycle is not a bicycle unless someone is riding it.[3]

We explore several of these dilemmas, and what might be done about them. In summary, learners should be able to record their learning achievements through the award of credit, to build or accumulate these as and when they wish, and to move easily between different learning paths. A coherent framework for building up learning credits is a central component of an overall system of lifelong learning. It is essential for flexibility, for progression and for bridging the divides between different types of learning, especially inside and outside work. We focus here on credit as an enabling mechanism, i.e. as a means of encouraging demand for learning and allowing it to be recognised and accumulated.

We do not go into detail on how credit frameworks operate, as such accounts are already available. Proposals for credit frameworks exist at European level and nationally, but these do not always fit with each other, or with qualification systems. The European Qualifications Framework (EQF) is designed to 'function as a translation device making qualifications more readable. This will help learners and workers wishing to move between countries or change jobs or move educational institutions at home,'[4] but it is not integrated with the European Credit System. At national level, we have a Qualifications and Credit Framework (QCF) covering England, Wales and Northern Ireland, but there are also separate qualifications for Wales and Scotland, and it remains to be seen how well these fit together.

There are practical issues to be worked through; for example, how less formal types of learning might be given credit, and how an individual's record might be compiled (the development of a 'unique learner number' is important here), but our position is that the technical issues are not major obstacles. The key challenge is the political and institutional will to make constructive use of the systems that exist.

The Qualifications and Curriculum Authority (QCA) has recently completed a major project to establish and implement the Qualifications and Credit Framework (QCF). This is how they describe its progress.

---

[3] Collingwood (1946) p. 222.
[4] For more information see http://www.qca.org.uk/qca_19302.aspx

Qualifications and Credit Framework

QCA has a unique role to play in developing skills by introducing the new Qualifications and Credit Framework (QCF). The QCF embraces the culture of lifelong learning by recognising that everything learnt is valuable. All units of learning achieved in the QCF have a credit value. Credit allows individuals to take their learning achievements with them as they progress on a course and build these into qualifications. The framework is at the heart of a major vocational qualifications reform programme, designed to make the whole system simpler to understand, inclusive, relevant to the needs of employers and more flexible and accessible for learners.

QCA is tasked with co-ordinating capacity building across the sector and is committed to developing materials that will enable stakeholders to operate within the QCF. QCA is working with delivery partners, including the Federation of Awarding bodies (FAB), the Joint Council for Qualifications (JCQ), the Association of Learning Providers (ALP), the Association of Colleges (AoC), the UK Commission for Employment and Skills (UKCES), the Alliance of Sector Skills Councils (TASSC) and the Learning and Skills Improvement Service (LSIS), to deliver a QCF readiness programme for awarding organisations, learning providers, sector skills councils and standards-setting bodies.

It is anticipated that by December 2010 all vocational qualifications will be accredited in the QCF and the QCF will be the framework for all new vocational qualifications developed from 2011.

Current QCF progress is as follows:

- 1,300 live approved qualifications are available in the framework and individuals are being awarded credit as they progress through the qualifications.
- Over 200 organisations are applying for recognition in order to submit QCF units and/or qualifications.
- Over 650 providers have been involved since March 2009.
- Over 140,000 learners have been registered for QCF qualifications since March 2009.
- The majority of the current work is to ensure stakeholders are 'prepared' for this framework. Continuous communication and engagement activities will be delivered to ensure the full potential of the QCF is utilised.

Building credit: why it matters

In the film *Duck Soup*, Chico Marx describes how he and his intrepid fellow aviators flew across the Atlantic. On their first attempt, they made it 'half-a-way' over, but saw that fuel was low and turned back. As Chico tells it, subsequent sorties saw them get closer and closer to their New York destination, but each time they just didn't have enough in the tank to get them all the way and so had to abort the mission just a few miles out – and return all the way to London. The spectacular narration of the story disguised its lack of logic, almost but not quite fooling Chico's audience. In our current qualification system, the logic is better than Chico's, but still resembles it too closely. Too many people start on a qualification but are left stranded, unable to convert what they have learnt into recognised achievement unless they complete what can be a long journey on a single flight path, i.e. a full qualification achieved without interruption in a single institution. Their efforts sink sadly under the waves. This is true above all for those on the margins of the system.

At the other end of the spectrum, a lot of learning happens but does not gain recognition, especially in the workplace. Only 18 per cent of employer training carries some form of external recognition. Whilst it is understandable that much training does not need it from the employer viewpoint, the individuals concerned would often be helped (especially in a recession) if their learning was recognised by the award of credit. Accreditation can also help drive up quality.

As suggested above, the basic principle of a credit system is very simple. People should be able to gain credit for what they have learnt in quite small units, reflecting the fact that for practical reasons they may only be able to study for a quite limited time, or that the learning they need or wish to undertake is only quite short. Obviously there needs to be a minimum threshold (quantum of study) before credit can be given, but this should be low. Credits can build up into qualifications over time, according to the learner's motivation and circumstances. A credit system also allows people to transfer from one institution or workplace to another without having to start again *à la* Chico. This reduces failure rates, but it also greatly expands the choice available to learners. However, we recognise that in some cases there cannot be any or much choice – notably in qualifications that offer licence to practice.

Why is credit so central for a properly functioning system of lifelong learning? There are four main reasons, which all derive directly from the overall rationale we laid out in *Chapter 2*. They also address several of the flaws we identified in *Chapter 3*.

Bridging different types of learning

One of the weaknesses of the UK system is its deep divide between academic and vocational learning, accentuated by early specialisation and narrowness of study. This is not uniformly the case across all four nations – Scotland, for example, has historically had a broader school curriculum and less of a division. But, overall, we have sub-systems of education and training which go their own way, with little mutual recognition. This mutual shunning has been both reflected in and reinforced by class divides. The lack of a common system of credits is part of that divided story. Establishing such a system would help to make bridges that enable learners to pass between the different sectors. They could also pass more easily across different levels of the hierarchy, notably from FE colleges to universities (and vice versa).

This argument would hold even if we were not talking about lifelong learning, but only about initial education. Taking a lifelong perspective, though, gives it added salience. Adults have knowledge and skills that they acquire at work and in life, sometimes formally sometimes not. If these are not recognised by educational institutions, they can find themselves slithering down to the bottom of the ladder and having to start again – and as a result, often never get through the door in the first place.

Improving access, transparency and equality

Many of the particular inequalities we have noted earlier are exacerbated by a system still too reliant on full-time longer courses as its main currency. Potential students from poorer backgrounds often need to take small steps back into learning, and to have a goal in sight which is near enough to seem attainable. (The Open University's 'Openings' initiative, which offers a very small amount of credit [10 points] for highly structured introductory study, has proved highly successful). In particular, they need to be able to see where their study is leading, and what the further options are for progression. A flexible credit system delivers this, and in so doing helps combat inequalities.

Moreover, it offers the chance of doing so recurrently – precisely because it enables smaller units. In *Chapter 3* we argued that social mobility can only be satisfactorily addressed on a recurrent basis, through regularly available opportunities to move up. A credit system makes that more possible. Credit systems also widen opportunities by recognising 'small' achievements that are not cost-effective to recognise through a whole qualification.

This is not to argue against provision, which is continuous and long. Full immersion in study over time can be transformative in a way that shorter periods usually cannot. However, it is only one mode, and should not dominate the educational landscape as it does.

Extending choice

Choice is not the 'be-all and end-all' in education as elsewhere. Too much choice can perplex and dissatisfy.[5] However, a good range of options is needed if learners are to be fully motivated. This is significant both for equity reasons – encouraging those whose motivation might be weak – and for efficiency reasons: if people have made their own choice, they will be more committed and learn more effectively. Today, people are far more accustomed to exercising choice than they used to be, and there is no reason why this should not apply in education and training as elsewhere. A credit system allows a wider range to be offered, with many more permutations of options. This requires that good guidance is put in place, to make the choices as informed as possible – recognising that people must have 'the right to make the wrong choice.'

Credit and entitlement: a close link

There is one further, crucial, component to the rationale. In the previous chapter we outlined the case for a set of learning entitlements. For these to come about, a flexible system of credits needs to be in place. It is no good offering someone an entitlement to, say, ten weeks of learning if the only courses available are for a minimum of one year. Even with a system of learning leave, busy people will usually only be able to spare a short time away from work. However, many of them will want to accumulate their achievements over time, so the success of entitlements is very dependent on a proper credit framework being in place. These two bits of the system – a functioning credit system, and a set of entitlements to learn – are closely articulated.

The 'demand' for credit

A clear and flexible credit framework is, or should be, an integral part of a qualifications system, and the QCF makes this link. Indeed, without it, qualifications can obstruct as much as help, and credits would be left dangling in limbo. This is a central issue in the debate on training. The relationship between supply and

---

[5] Schwartz (2004).

demand for qualifications and skills is a complex one. We cannot sort it out here (see the IFLL Thematic Paper, *Work and Learning*, for further discussion),[6] but we can summarise the relevant issues in the following set of propositions:

- Qualification is not the same as skill. A certificate should indicate something about what has been learnt, but it may not say much about what the holder can do.
- Supply and demand interact, in relation to both qualifications and skills. There is a 'push-me/pull-you' effect. If more people appear with qualifications, the qualifications required for jobs will go up. If people with high skills take jobs with lower skill requirements, they are likely to affect the content of the job, pushing it upwards in the skill content.
- 'Demand' in this debate means at least two very different things: the demand by individuals for opportunities to gain qualifications/skills, and the demand by employers for qualifications/skills. Both are important.
- Employer demand itself has two faces. One is on recruitment: employing people who bring certain levels of skill/qualification. The other is on utilisation: how far these skills are actually put to effect in the jobs the employees are asked to do.

This last proposition is moving towards the centre of the debate. As the UK Commission for Employment and Skill has shown, we need to pay more attention to the demand side, and within that to how the skills and competencies which qualifications denote are actually used. This is a substantial shift from the Leitch analysis – and in our view a correct one to make.

The relevance of credit to this summary account is as follows. Employers and individuals often want short periods of training. Individuals are generally more keen than employers to have their learning certificated, since this gives them added options in the labour market if they choose to move jobs. Employers are more concerned about improving their productivity than meeting government qualifications targets. Therefore, the way to drive up demand is to provide the greater flexibility that a credit system provides. The Government has rightly introduced greater flexibility into the system (with an interesting uplift in demand resulting). The greater relevance of these shorter periods will give the skills greater purchase in the workplace. As credit develops, employers will change their expectations of what counts as learning as employees' access to learning increases. In short, a proper credit system is an important means of getting a better balance between supply and demand, in both its senses.

---

[6] Williams and Wilson (2009).

Again, the QCA has embarked on an important area of work: to ensure the appropriate recognition of key categories of employer-supported learning. Here is another progress report.

Employer Recognition Programme

The Employer Recognition Programme aims to get high-quality in-house employer training nationally recognised onto the Qualifications and Credit Framework (QCF).

There are a number of ways in which an employer can become involved:

- An employer becomes a recognised awarding organisation and provides the requisite standard of quality assurance to develop and award its own nationally recognised qualifications. Five employers have taken this route. For example, McDonald's became an awarding organisation in December 2007 and has one qualification accredited onto the QCF. It expects around 3,000 of its employees to have taken this qualification by the end of 2009.
- An employer works with an existing awarding organisation that designs and awards bespoke qualifications for the employer. Around 40 employers have so far chosen to go down this route. For example, B&Q has worked with City & Guilds to develop a Level 2 Award for its employees, 5,000 of whom are expected to have taken the qualification by the end of 2009.
- An employer works with a third party that becomes an awarding organisation or works with an existing awarding organisation. The third party may be a provider, trade organisation, higher education institute or a professional body. Three trade associations, one college and one training provider have chosen to take this route. For example, The Lift and Escalator Industry Association (LEIA) has worked with EMTA Awards Ltd (EAL) to develop a Level 4 Certificate for all 150 of its member organisations. One hundred and two learners are already taking this qualification with more expected in the coming year. In addition, City College Norwich became an awarding organisation in March 2008 and has worked with Norwich Union, Swiss Re and Marsh to develop two financial qualifications for their employees.

The scope of the programme has recently been widened in order to support the Government's emphasis on re-skilling the workforce; for instance, a more formal relationship with the National Employer Service (NES) has been established to strengthen the links with Train to Gain and apprenticeships. There will also be more encouragement given to employers to utilise existing qualifications and tailor units to fit their needs.

Credit crunches

Not everything is plain sailing. In *Chapter 4*, where we took stock of participation trends, we noted that the UK is at one extreme when it comes to the duration of learning episodes. The British, it seems, are more likely than most to take part in learning of some kind, but to do it for relatively short periods of time. It could be argued that a credit system will accentuate this. However, the fact that shorter units of learning are available should not mean that the individual cannot accumulate several of them. 'Bite-sized' does not mean one bite only.

Other concerns include excessive credentialism (valuing only learning that is assessed) and a perceived threat to institutional autonomy. Whatever their intrinsic merits, none of these arguments carries weight against the construction of a credit system. The details of the curriculum, the nature of assessment and the terms on which transfer operates can all be worked through. Some of them will be tricky; for example, assessment techniques will have to change, notably as new technologies encourage learning to become more of a collective, peer-to-peer, exercise. But we are clear that the obstacles to a better credit system are not primarily technical. There is no case against establishing a framework that gives greater opportunities for people to record what they have learnt in a systematic way.

The peculiar case of higher education: linking credit and mode[7]

In the IFLL paper on higher education, we concluded that 'our principal systemic failure is the lack of credit accumulation and transfer'.[8] According to the Higher Education Policy Institute (HEPI), in 2002–03, over 11,000 of the 300,000 students who entered HE institutions did so having been at a different institution in one of the preceding two years. The vast majority of these students received no credit for their previous studies.[9] This is in stark contrast to the United States, where several state systems have formal entitlements for progress (for example, from community colleges into universities), and over half of all students graduate from institutions other than the ones in which they start their higher education.[10]

---

[7] This section is another which mainly refers to England; many of the issues are very different in other parts of the UK, for instance in the relationship between FE and HE in Scotland.
[8] Watson (2009).
[9] Bekhradnia (2004).
[10] Weko (2004).

The IFLL paper goes on:

> *The flexibility that a proper credit framework brings will be needed all the more in the light of current economic turbulence and the effects this is having on employment. Large numbers of adults will be seeking to improve their qualifications without having to commit themselves to a long stretch of full-time education. This is not a technical issue: we have the systems. It is a cultural and moral issue: we fail to use these systems for reasons of conservatism, snobbery and lack of imagination.*

This is a serious indictment. A credit system enables flexibility. It is closely linked to the availability of learning opportunities in different modes: in intensive bursts, or part time over a longer period. This will become increasingly the case with technology-enabled learning. Yet we have witnessed a recent decline of part-time higher education, reversing a decade of growth. In 2007–8 both the overall numbers of part-time students and the full-time equivalent numbers decreased by 3 per cent compared to 2006–7, while the numbers of full-timers increased by 2 per cent. Within this figure, those who are not studying for any formal qualification dropped by around 30 per cent. The key to this is student support. Although their position has improved in recent years, part-time university students do not have automatic access to the same level of student support as full-timers do.

The National Union of Students sums up the position as follows:

> *The present system is inherently inflexible. It relies on units of funding measured in full-time equivalent (FTE) years, such as an annual fee payment or an annual loan for support. It is clear that, in many situations, taking amounts in annual units is useful and appropriate, but does make it more difficult to construct flexible funding mechanisms that can cope with the demands of those who want to study more flexibly. It is perhaps surprising that more use has not been made of academic credit as a measure and determinant in funding structures, given their near-ubiquity in determining the structure of courses and the quantity and level of learning that relates to particular outcomes.*[11]

Our proposition is very simple but radical. Financial support for lifelong learning should be distributed in a way that is neutral in respect of the form the learning takes. It should not favour full time over part time. This applies to funding for provision; i.e. to institutions to deliver courses; and to student support mechanisms, in the shape of grants or loans, for fees or maintenance. It does not mean that all courses should be funded at the same level: training doctors requires funding at

---

[11] National Union of Students (2009).

Figure 20: Full-time and part-time support

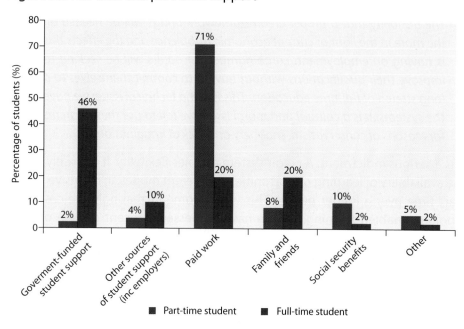

Source: calculations by Claire Callender from Johnson et al (2009)

a higher level than literature courses. However, full-time and part-time students should be treated alike.

Broadly speaking, more part time means more lifelong. It enables learners to combine study with work and family life; and, where students are following a job-related course, it can mean fruitful interaction between study and work, to the benefit of both. A lifelong learning system has room for full-time as well as part-time study. We are not suggesting that there should be a bias in favour of the latter. We are saying that there should not be a bias in favour of the former, and that we need to dethrone the full-time model from its current dominance. The obvious solution is to abolish the distinction between the two.

This could be seen as a matter of incentives (and disincentives). What we are trying to correct here is a system of incentives that rewards institutions for putting on courses in full-time rather than part-time mode; and which gives students who enrol on a full-time basis greater and more generous support than their part-time equivalents. In higher education at present, all full-time students but only ten per cent of part-time undergraduates receive government-funded student support.[12] This is clearly wrong.

----

[12] Johnson *et al.* (2009).

On efficiency grounds it is wrong because it penalises people who choose to carry on in employment and combine this with their studies. They therefore maintain their contribution to the economy. In addition, they will live at home (their own or parental) much more often than full-timers, and so reduce living costs.

It is also wrong on equity grounds. Although still heavily subsidised, university study carries costs. People from poorer backgrounds have fewer resources to draw on. Part-time study, which enables them to carry on earning, is therefore more likely to appeal to them – except if the incentives drive them either towards full-time study or, in effect, away from participating at all, as they currently do. For full-time students, eligibility for student support is primarily (but not exclusively) determined by financial need. For part-time students, eligibility for student support, as well as the funding they bring to the university, is determined by their previous qualifications and the number of hours they study.

Equity considerations include gender. As the National Skills Forum report on *Closing the Gender Skills Gap* pointed out, mature female students often prefer part-time study; it therefore recommends equalising funding arrangements as we propose.[13]

The effects of a shift to mode-free funding will be significant. It would have a major impact in the way institutions plan their provision: on the content and timetabling, but also on areas such as facilities and accommodation. The timescale for implementing this should therefore be quite long. However, the political need is for a commitment to do this to be made, so that the planning can begin. It is not good enough, as we have heard, for policy-makers to acknowledge the force of the case, but to say that it cannot be done. Maybe not within a single parliamentary term, but two should be enough.

Therefore, the distinction between full time and part time should disappear in England, as it largely has in Scotland, Wales and Northern Ireland. Until it does, 'mode-free' means that the system should be neutral between these two alternatives. Financial support, for institutions and students, is attached to a unit of credit, not to a mode. However, we need a point of reference for calculating the value of credit on a common and consistent basis. 120 is the magic number for the equivalent of a full-time year, because it divides so many ways. Therefore, a full-time semester gives 60 credits, a standard term 40 credits, a half semester 30 credits, and so on down to very small units.

We also need to distinguish support for institutions from support for individuals, especially in one respect: the minimum threshold required; i.e. the amount of

---

[13] National Skills Forum (2009), p.15.

time (as a proportion of a year) the course represents. The current funding system can in fact calculate institutional support down to a very small level of full-time equivalent (FTE). There will need to be a change in the way institutions record student participation, but in principle this should be manageable on a credit system. So the institution could receive funding for almost any student enrolled for credit, even if they were only doing, say, a course worth five credits. All these small units can be rolled up without too much difficulty in the institution's return.

On student support, the picture is different. If a student enrols for a very short course – of which there should be plenty – they cannot expect that the student funding system will be able to support them, at least in its current form. There has to be a minimum unit size for students to qualify for individual support, and we suggest 15 credit points – the equivalent of an eighth of a year as it is currently understood – is a reasonable threshold. If you are doing a course which yields 30 credits as learning achievement over the year, you should be entitled to 25 per cent of whatever the level of annual student support is for that type of course. The institution which is teaching you gets 25 per cent of the unit cost of a full-time student. (We leave aside here the question of whether funding should be conditional upon a student completing.)

In short, students should be entitled to support, and institutions should be funded, on a pro-rata basis. There should be no discrimination without justification. This will remove the distorting incentives that currently rigidify our system unnecessarily.

Why not a state scholarship for higher education?

One of the themes of our report is the unnecessary complexity of arrangements for supporting learning that have been put in place, added to, partially or radically reformed (usually without removing previous arrangements), and generally tinkered with. The motives for these developments are usually admirable, but the effects are invariably disappointing and sometimes dramatically unintended.

One such set of arrangements is that for supporting undergraduate students in higher education in England. Applicants face a bewildering array of types and amounts of support to meet both their tuition and maintenance costs. To over-simplify, for UK and EU-based students on full-time undergraduate courses these include:

- a variable fee loan;
- a subsidised maintenance loan;
- a maintenance loan;
- a small mandatory bursary; and

- discretionary bursaries and scholarships provided by institutions as a condition of being able to charge certain levels of fees.[14]

The first two of these are repayable once salaries reach a certain threshold, either through the Student Loan Company (SLC) or, in the case of the fee loan – also called the Graduate Contribution Scheme (GCS) – through the income tax system. The first is handled through a grant from the Department for Business, Innovation and Skills to institutions. The fourth is a mandatory and the fifth a 'negotiated' cost to institutions (overseen in England through the Office for Fair Access). The final four arrive in the form of cash payments. The middle three are means-tested, and the final one may be.

The transaction costs are huge, and the risks to public expenditure are significant. The Government itself estimates that as a combination of loan subsidy, inflation, non-eligibility to repay, discounting on the sale of the loan book to the private sector, absconding and administrative failure, up to 30 per cent of the public investment will have to be written off.

Nor does complexity bring fairness. The biggest casualties are part-time (and mixed-mode) students who in effect have no access to these means of support, despite the political commitment to a more flexible system. The excuse is the cost. A significant divergence has also emerged between the countries of the UK, with, for example, Scotland not charging fees and having wound up their version of the GCS.

Unwinding these arrangements would also be highly costly, not least because of the long-term commitments which are now built into public expenditure. It would also take time. However, in the spirit of our longer-term vision we propose a radical alternative.

We suggest that all of these sources of public and institutional support are consolidated into a single fund, to be disbursed on a means-tested basis by a reformed Student Loan Company to students to support both tuition and living costs. Eligibility should be 'mode-free' (that is, part-time and mixed-mode students should have the same access on a pro-rata basis).

We further propose that (echoing the US's 'Pell grants') these scholarships should be called 'Dearing grants' after Ron Dearing (1930–2009) whose report in 1996 established the principle that students should make a contribution to the costs of their initial higher education, and whose record of service to the policy-making of governments of both major political parties is unrivalled.

Sir David Watson, Chair of the Commission

[14] Callender and Heller (2009).

Going further: HE and FE

The logic applies to sectors as well as modes. Just as full-time and part-time students should in principle be treated equally, so should students in different types of institutions, unless there is justification for the difference. There is currently a huge difference in the treatment of higher education and further education. Table 13, from Mick Fletcher's analysis, sums these up for England.

It is not our role here to redesign the post-compulsory sector in its entirety. We look at the issue from the perspective of lifelong learning, and how this may be properly reflected in the sector's organisation. Further and higher education have been collaborating increasingly over the past number of years, with better progression paths for students to follow between them. However, colleges and universities have different missions. We argue in *Chapter 9* that lifelong learning should be firmly included in both, but it is arguably even more central to colleges than to universities. A far higher proportion of FE students are part time and adult, though the proportion of adults in colleges has dropped dramatically in the last few years – a serious unbalancing of the system. Giving part-timers their due will strengthen support for further education, and rightly so.

To what extent does a systemic commitment to lifelong learning entail a different and more equal distribution of unit funding between the two sectors? We believe that differences in mission should be respected, but the system should be

Table 13: Financial support summary

Category	Type of support	HE[a]	FE
Fees	Fee loans	£1,060 million	
	Fee grant	£160 million	
	Fee remission		£140 million
Maintenance	Maintenance loans	£2,740 million	£20 million
	Maintenance grants	£800 million	£35 million
Hardship	Institutional bursaries	£300 million	
	Hardship and childcare	£50 million	£100 million
Total		**£5,110 million**	**£295 million**
Total £/FTE		**£4,482**	**£468**

[a]*This excludes the extra £400 million announced by the Secretary of State in July 2007.*

Source: Fletcher (2008).

adjusted over time to give a better balance in the support it offers to institutions and students across the two sectors. For FE students, wider access to Education Maintenance Allowances (in parallel with our suggestion of a 'Dearing grant' for higher education) would be a big step. As with the shift to mode-free funding within sectors, this is something which would only happen over a reasonably long time-span. It will be much more complex than the adjustment to unit-based funding. It should not be done in a way that will weaken the quality or global standing of British universities. However, a coherent system requires a more consistent treatment of students, especially adult students, across the two sectors.

Relevance to the themes of the Inquiry

A credit system is not just a matter of internal educational engineering. It cuts across a number of the Inquiry's main themes.

Learning at work

We have already pointed out that a credit system is an important way of helping people at work gain better access to learning, and build up their learning achievements into qualifications that will improve their employment prospects. It opens up avenues for further progression, if working people can accumulate credit through their learning at work, which they can then transfer into an academic institution, and vice versa.

Migration

Increased mobility generates stresses at personal and community level. As people move around, within and across national boundaries, more flexibility is needed so that they can carry on learning in their new surroundings. Without this, drop-out rates will rise and their human capital will just seep away. The recognition of qualifications from other countries is addressed by the QCF.[15]

Crime

Better progression routes are an important part of improving offender learning. At first sight, prisoners might seem to be full-time students *par excellence*, but in fact their learning is often interrupted, as they can be moved to another prison

---

[15] This relates directly to one of the Public Service Agreements, PSA 3 on Migration.

without notice. The learning entitlement we proposed for the passage from prison to probation and release is more likely to succeed if a flexible credit system is in place. In any case, many offenders have very poor initial education, and are better served by small units of learning.

Technology

New technologies are changing the way we learn. We need frameworks which enable people to capture their learning (if they wish). However, technology also dramatically affects the administration of learning systems. In relation to credit, electronic records are now available in a way that would not have been possible even a few years ago, enormously lightening the bureaucratic costs. This is a huge advantage (see *Chapter 6* on Learning FuturesCards).

Recommendations

- We should *move quickly* to a *coherent system of credits* as the basis for organising post-compulsory learning. The system should be broad and flexible. It should allow students and trainees to accumulate credits as a matter of choice. It should enable them to transfer between institutions and across sectors. It should encourage bridges to be built between different types of learning, notably between learning at work and in educational institutions.

- The funding for learning should be *mode-free*. In other words, it *should not discriminate against part-time provision or part-time students*. Institutions – colleges and universities – should be funded for part-time students on the same basis pro rata as full-time students. Student financial support should similarly be even-handed.

- The *funding should be credit-based*; i.e. it should attach to chunks of learning that are an identifiable part of a course, but which are not themselves necessarily a qualification.

- Employers should be encouraged to *integrate the training they offer into a credit framework*; this should form part of their reporting requirement in return for receipt of corporation tax relief on training expenditure.

- We propose the eventual *abolition of the distinction between full-time and part-time study*, just as we see the disappearance of the distinction between full-time and part-time work. The distinctions are unhelpful and anyway inaccurate.

- In the light of the arguments above, we wish to see much *greater consistency and fairness* in the support for further and higher education.

'Citizenship as an inclusive term means that everyone should have opportunities to take part in different spheres of activity: work, civic activity, and cultural and community life... A citizens' curriculum should be interpreted in very different ways in different contexts and locales, but a common framework should reinforce some sense of common belonging.'

'Intermediaries are the key to driving up demand for learning because they can do it both directly and surreptitiously; they can take the issue head-on, or they can insinuate learning into people's lives without them realising.'

8 Capabilities and capacity

Summary

We turn now to topics that are perhaps more recognisably the flesh and blood of learning: the content of what is learnt, and the contribution of those involved in delivering learning opportunities, in whatever role.

We propose simply a general framework for what we call a citizens' curriculum. The rationale for it derives directly from the vision we spelled out in *Chapter 1*: of learning as an essential component of freedom of choice, personal well-being, respect for others and democratic life, as well as prosperity. Preconditions for this include enabling all citizens[1] to have the basic skills of literacy, language and numeracy, and the minimum qualification we proposed as entitlements in *Chapter 6*.

Against that background we define four broad capabilities: civic, health, financial and digital. This framework is to be interpreted locally in many different ways and at different levels. Our use of capability draws its inspiration from the work of Nobel laureate Amartya Sen, and of the cultural critic Raymond Williams. It makes a strong link to the essential role of lifelong learning as empowering people to take control of their lives. We discuss each of the four capabilities briefly. There is already policy interest and much practical experience in each of the areas. Our aim is to set them in a common context.

We then turn to the capacity of the system to deliver learning: the skills of those involved as teachers, trainers and tutors, but also as guides, advisers and mentors. We include here learning intermediaries who would not think of themselves as part of the lifelong learning workforce, but who have the potential to contribute significantly to raising our learning levels.

---

[1] We include in this category all those living in the UK, whether or not they have formal citizenship.

Curriculum and capabilities

The Inquiry's remit has been very broad. Our nine themes (see *Preface* for details) cover an enormous range of policy areas, and they speak to very different audiences – teachers at every level in the system, workplace trainers, learners themselves, and policy-makers and professionals in many different sectors. Given this breadth, it would be absurd to attempt detailed prescription on the content of what is learnt. Our aim, as elsewhere in this report, is to provide a framework which enables a more consistent and accessible system to grow in the future. We have selected four principal 'capabilities' for such a framework – civic, financial, health and digital – but placed them in a broader context of employability and of cultural fulfilment. Any list of this kind will instantly provoke cries of 'how could you leave out x, y and z?' One overview assembles no fewer than 24 separate examples of lists presented as 'key skills', 'essential competences' and so on.[2] We compile our set by using the Nobel laureate Amartya Sen's work as a springboard to draw on the specific discussions within the Inquiry itself.[3]

Sen has a lifelong preoccupation with inequality on a global scale, and with how we can use our individual and collective potentials. The combination of these drives his notion of capability. Reduced to their simplest terms, 'capabilities' constitute *the capacity to achieve well-being*. His approach is distinct from other approaches to well-being, which concentrate for example on primary goods, or on resources. What makes it particularly relevant to our concerns is the notion that we should pay attention to the human potential that is there to be mobilised. All individuals and groups should have the opportunity, not only to realise their full potential, but also to raise the level they aspire to achieve. Sen's deep concern with reducing inequalities in societies stresses the obstacles to achieving capability which different individuals and groups encounter.[4]

This poses an ambitious challenge to our standards of what people can attain. Sen's approach gives us the edge needed to go beyond current potential, with the challenge of recurrently uncovering and developing further potential. His perspective links capabilities directly to freedom. Aspiration is a part of freedom, and will take very diverse forms. All of these resonate with our own approach.

---

[2] Lucas and Claxton (2009).

[3] Sen (1992, 2009).

[4] An IFLL-commissioned analysis of the implications of the 2009 Equalities Bill shows the relevance of Sen to legal interpretations of equality: 'The public sector duty does not just contain a need to 'eliminate discrimination' without any intelligent thought about what that means. It truly embraces Sen's capability-based model of equality. Public authorities are required to address their minds to all barriers to participation from disadvantaged groups.' (Mountfield, 2009).

This may appear to be philosophical abstraction, but it speaks directly to the evidence and experience contributed to the Inquiry. There is splendid work being done on the ground, in a host of different contexts, which aims to realise potential, raise aspirations and reduce inequalities. We have tried to give these a simple common structure, to enhance our sense of common capability.

We also draw on Raymond Williams' analysis of the roles of lifelong learning in a period of rapid change, as a relevant counterpart to Sen's capability concept. Williams identifies three key and different ways in which learning helps people:

- *to make sense of change*, by acquiring information, ideas, knowledge and a critical and challenging mind;
- *to adapt to change*, by making the most of it, capturing and applying knowledge;
- *to shape* change, being authors of change rather than its victims, navigating risk and uncertainty as part of the democratic project.[5]

The combination of these three fits well with the notion of capability as something that enables agency and action as well as understanding. We apply these across the four capabilities.

A citizens' curriculum

We turn now to the four capabilities which could form the basis of a citizens' curriculum – or, as one of our colleagues put it, a 'C21 survival kit'. When we began to put these forward to audiences as part of the consultation process, one response was that they seem very instrumental, and ignore the more intrinsic values of learning. We have no intention of subordinating these values, let alone excluding them. Our selection is of capabilities which enhance people's ability to exercise a degree of control over their own lives; to take part with others in decisions that affect the contexts of their lives; and to envisage alternative futures for themselves and their families. They open up space for the creative, the aesthetic, the spiritual and other essential dimensions of personal development and growth. They are both instrumental and intrinsic.

Three points by way of introduction. First, this set is not derived from any extensive theory. It has emerged from the submissions to the Inquiry and the discussions which these provoked. We are in no doubt that there are alternatives which deserve equal consideration, but we base our conclusions mainly on the work of the Inquiry itself.

---

[5] Williams (1990).

Secondly, we do not go into any detail on the content of learning – on what should be included and how it should be taught or learnt. There is already a mass of experience and research which can provide the basis for this. Within the Inquiry, work on it is continuing, and this will add flesh to the bones. In particular, we shall be tapping the experience of learners and teachers in response to the proposals. Our goal here is, once again, to provide an overall framework for further development.

Thirdly, we have drawn on Sen's notion of capability because of its breadth and ambition. 'Literacy' was an alternative option – terms such as 'health literacy' have an established currency. We preferred 'capability' because of its sense of agency, but also because it has no sense of the basic or elementary about it. Perhaps unfairly, 'literacy' has this, at least in one reading. It suggests something remedial, especially when linked with adults. All of the capabilities listed can be developed to high levels – and however competent you may be in them, there is always the challenge to develop further. Often, though, we could comfortably interchange 'literacy' and 'capability', as will be obvious from some of the definitional discussion.

We call our set of capabilities a 'citizens' curriculum' because citizenship is something almost all of us share, across the social and geographical divides. Citizenship as an inclusive term means that everyone should have opportunities to take part in different spheres of activity: work, civic activity, and cultural and community life – and in our sense it extends to those living in the UK who do not have formal citizenship. A citizens' curriculum should be interpreted in very different ways in different contexts and locales, but a common framework should reinforce some sense of common belonging.

In summary, capabilities are 'combinations of doings and beings' that a person might achieve, even if they have not yet done so. Learning, of different forms, is the means of converting potential into actual. Capability as a notion makes us go back a pace, to take into account the potential as well as the actual. This is the best way of raising our game, individually and collectively.[6]

---

[6] In the 1980s the Royal Society of Arts (RSA) conducted a major programme, 'Education for Capability', devoted to reforming education and training on these lines. Although the RSA campaign was driven more by the needs of employment than Sen's broader societal conception, it did acknowledge that there was much more to the school curriculum than the reproduction of traditional knowledge and skills.

Digital capability

> ### 'It started completely by accident...'
>
> The four part-time workers who make up the Wordsley School Cleaners Group are very clear about how they got into adult learning: 'It started completely by accident. Just as she was leaving work one day, the Head of Learning4Life – Kath Tunnicliffe – overheard one of us saying that she would never be able to use a computer. We had a bit of a laugh with Kath, but she was quite adamant that we would be able to learn. We decided to develop our skills to challenge the idea people have that cleaners are "thick"', they say. 'We felt a little embarrassed because we work in an establishment where literally thousands of adults have been taught to overcome their initial fears and gain access to the world of technology... We really felt we had no choice in the end!'
>
> Since coming together in 2005, the group has learned how to operate computers, access their training materials online, manipulate and input text, and to form, print and save documents. Having completed word processing courses, two members of the group are now studying a course in electronic communications and the other two are learning about computer art. 'We've learned to support one another... We rarely need a tutor anymore; we now laugh and enjoy our sessions. When anyone needs help, there's always someone in the group who can either help or be there to work out how to solve the problem together.'
>
> And the rewards are tangible: 'Chris gained promotion to housekeeper. The site management spotted her newly acquired skills and she now provides technical support by inputting data into the [...] IT system at Wordsley School for staff contracts and stocktaking supplies... Denise has a new-found relationship with two-year-old Charlie Lee, the youngest of her ten grandchildren: she no longer just watches, she's actually with her on the computer... Helen believes in herself: she knows she doesn't lack intelligence and she has the confidence to achieve further success. Tracy is changing her family's opportunities... Her family is able to benefit from buying holidays on the net and snapping up bargains from eBay. Computing is [...] so popular in Chris's household that a second laptop is being purchased so that her son hasn't got to share the computer with his mum.'

We live in a world saturated with information, but not everyone knows how to squeeze it out. *Digital Britain*'s estimate is that 11.6 million people in the UK fall into the category of 'digitally excluded'.[7] The 'digital divide' is a contested phrase, but there can be no doubt about the inequalities which exist. People who have low access to new technologies are very likely not to participate in learning at all. This reduces their employability, but it also reduces their chances of taking part in other spheres: cultural, civic and social.[8] Ufi/learndirect alone now provides more than 600 different programmes of study and, since opening, more than 2.5 million people have followed almost 7 million courses with the service. However, in spite of their very considerable efforts, many are still excluded.

What do we mean by 'digital capability'? The Digital Britain Media Literacy Working Group (DBMLWG) proposes three components of what they call 'digital engagement' (the capacity of people to participate in the digital world). *Digital inclusion* ensures that no community of citizens is prevented from access to broadband. *Digital life skills* are those needed for employment and beyond – this is the term used by the former Secretary for Education (and ex-teacher), Estelle Morris in her recent report. *Digital media literacy* is 'the ability to use, understand and create digital media and communications'.[9] Our understanding of digital capability combines the last two, leaving digital inclusion as a necessary condition for the capability to exist and be used.

Raymond Williams' learning purposes, listed above, fit readily here. Digital capability enables people to *make sense* of change, notably through the access it provides to information and ideas, and the links it provides to their fellow citizens. It enables them to *adapt to* change, as a key skill for managing their lives as well as for employability. Increasingly, it allows at least some people to take part in *shaping* change, in their professional lives, but also in the civic and political sphere. Digital capability has to include capacity to exercise critical judgment: this is crucial if people are to sort useful and valid information from the mounds of poor quality quasi-information which pours out by the minute.

Digital capability is the fastest-changing one of our four capabilities. This is, obviously, mainly because the technologies underlying it are evolving so quickly. With our long-term horizon, this conveniently excuses us from being more specific. However, the pace of change affects the way the curriculum will be adapted to the needs of different ages. We stress that there is no automatic read-off of people's capability from their chronological age. Most people in the fourth stage will

---

[7] BIS and DCMS (2009).
[8] Selwyn, Gorard and Furlong (2005).
[9] Morris (2009), p.9.

have a relatively low technical grasp, while the opposite is true of the first stage. (Please note the qualifiers: 'most' and 'relatively'.) Yet the importance and the potential to the individual can be the same. Your level of digital competence does not determine its significance for you – even a modest level can be enormously important.

For older people, digital capability is increasingly important for staying in touch – with friends, family and the outside world. Limited personal mobility raises the value of it. People who cannot easily travel, even small distances, benefit enormously from the enhanced communication it offers. The same is true for younger people who are not fully mobile. Keeping in touch with friends and family around the world – staying connected – is essential to well-being. Digital capability will be an increasingly central component of family and intergenerational learning.

For those in the first three stages, digital capability will often be a prerequisite for employment, or a major asset in the job, if they are working. We should not equate increased use of ICT with increased skill; but for individuals without such competences, fewer jobs will be available. Recent comparative analysis[10] shows how complex the relationship between digital capability and employment is; for example, it appears that ICT is linked to progression in employment for men, but to getting a job for women. The overall conclusion, though, is clear: the absence of capability increases the likelihood of marginalisation and exclusion.

For all ages, but perhaps particularly for young people, digital capability is a key way of developing their potential and of opening up new avenues of interest. It is also socially almost a prerequisite. The DBMLWG sums up the position very well, as shown in Table 14.

Each of these needs can be met at different levels, from basic use, through understanding, to the ability to create digital material. The competences can be developed directly through the job, or informally through other activities, or through a range of education and training. However, a key component of capability is the ability to make some kind of critical evaluation of the massive range of information (and misinformation) which new technologies give access to. This, arguably, is what distinguishes technical competence from capability.

Finally, we need to return to Sen's point about potential and aspiration. The scope of digital capability is changing very rapidly, as we have said. Young people today will move forward in life with an easy familiarity with current competences. However, there is no guarantee – if anything, the reverse – that, even with this platform established so early, they will continue to keep up with developments.

---

[10] Reding and Bynner (2009).

Table 14: People's digital life skills often relate to the needs associated with their life stages

Life stage	Needs
Young people	Develop their educational potential
	Develop social networks
	Gain new knowledge and networks
Adults	Look for and develop employment
	Look after their families (health, education)
	Save time, money, inconvenience
Older people	Overcome the risk of social isolation
	Stay healthy
	Remain independent

Source: Digital Britain Media Literacy Working Group, 2009 (Table 2, p.18.)

We simply cannot tell if those now in the first stage will experience the same kind of difficulty in even understanding the terminology as the older people who today think of a mouse as something with whiskers and a tail. The aspiration must be to prevent this from happening – at any age and stage.

Health capability

> **Diagnosed by Yahoo**
>
> 'Being in my sixties, I'm likely in the future to have to find out much more about the NHS and health problems. The internet has opened up the world. I am on two email lists relating to a neurological condition I have and as the research is more advanced in the USA, it's very useful to be in instant contact with other people across the world who have the condition. We all have a joke that we were 'diagnosed by Yahoo', since without the internet to identify subjects, the research probably would not have taken place.'
>
> *Richard, participant in NIACE seminar, 2009*

Maintaining health is a fundamental challenge to all of us. It combines individuals looking after themselves, in the lifestyles they adopt and in the use they make of health services; policy-makers devising policies which encourage healthy lifestyles and ensure good health services; employers ensuring healthy work environments; and citizens taking part in shaping a political climate which makes all this happen. It therefore involves personal and professional learning, and the link with civic capability is immediately obvious. Our focus here is on the personal side.

The demographic trends which are a recurring theme in this report are a major driving factor. An ageing society need not be overall a less healthy society. However, the steepness with which demands on health services climb as people get older is dramatic: dementia costs the health and social care economy more than cancer, heart disease and stroke combined. Other trends are almost as powerful. Drug and alcohol abuse destroy individuals and families, and drag down a society's level of well-being. Obesity trends, especially amongst young people, have serious long-term consequences. Mental ill-health is now the most prevalent form of illness, and impacts on economic performance as well as personal happiness.[11] Education can only do so much (even in Finland, with its outstanding education performance, mental ill-health is sadly prevalent). However, a well-balanced system could surely do more to contain and reverse these depressing trends.

In health above all, inequalities are at the heart of the issue. Poverty is directly associated with poor health, and with disability. Poor people live in less healthy neighbourhoods, with less access to good food and higher rates of crime and stress. However, the equality argument has specific force in relation to health. *The Spirit Level* shows that this direct relationship between poverty and ill-health is only part of the story.[12] Its truly original finding is that the health of all, even of those who are better off, is adversely affected in an unequal society. The uncomfortable truth is that education can often accentuate rather than reduce that inequality; that, after all, is one of the lessons of our account of participation and expenditure in *Chapter 4*. Achieving greater equality in both health and education is something which would benefit everyone, not just those at the lower end of the scale.

So the challenge is a daunting one. Applying Raymond Williams' purposes to health capability means it can be defined as follows:

- ability to understand one's own physical and mental health, and to translate that understanding into action to maintain and improve it;
- ability to make effective use of existing health services, and to contribute to their improvement, as a consumer and a citizen; and

---

[11] Government Office for Science (2008).
[12] Wilkinson and Pickett (2009).

- ability to understand the circumstances which generate good and poor health, and to formulate a positive response to those circumstances.

Once again, the capacity to evaluate critically is central: for individuals faced with huge choices of treatments (drugs or services), but also in the wider sense of understanding how and why ill-health is generated and how to act to change that. The overlap with civic capability is patent.

Some of this involves learning which relates directly to health issues. For example, the notion of 'expert patients' is now well established, aiming to make self-management as accessible as possible for the 17 million people living with long-term conditions in England, and their carers.[13] This gives them more control over their lives, and reduces the length of hospital stays, benefiting everyone. However, much of the impact of learning on health is indirect. Analysis carried out for the Inquiry using longitudinal data on over 5,000 people over 50 shows how participation in evening classes improves well-being as well as quality of life.[14] It raises people's levels of self-esteem (identity capital), and through this improves their health. It is also about norms and values; learning helps people be part of networks that sustain healthy lifestyles (social capital). Capabilities have a collective as well as individual form.

Health capability also encourages new relations between providers and consumers of health (and related) services. 'Co-production' is the fashionable term to describe a more equal partnership between professionals and clients: the involvement of people in the design and delivery of services. At the most basic level, if people cannot understand the labels on drug bottles, or the instructions the doctor has just given them, the whole performance is a charade. However, this goes up through many different levels, as people join in improving the services and environment which shape our health. Patients and clients give more constructive feedback, and come forward with proposals for improvement, or new ideas. They are involved in service design, on a small or large scale.

A crucial component is the parallel development of health staff, especially those with fewest qualifications. There is massive inequality in the distribution of training investment in the NHS, between highly qualified professionals and the rest.[15] If co-production is to develop, the service providers must themselves be given the relevant opportunities to learn and develop.

---

[13] For more information see www.expertpatients.co.uk
[14] Jenkins (2009).
[15] Fryer (2005). See also the submission to the Inquiry by Knox, F. (2007). *Differential policy and implementation discourses on lifelong learning in the NHS.*

Health capability requirements vary over the life course. People's attitudes to, and preoccupation with, their personal health change, as does their relationship with the health of their families and more broadly. People in the time-squeezed second stage tend to suffer from the stress this causes; they also do not tend to have time to use health services (a factor in men's relatively high levels of mortality from cancer). Some need to learn to manage their own or others' chronic illnesses. Often, there will be a strong intergenerational dimension: health capability includes the need to understand the health of other ages and the implications for their lives and well-being. The growth of eldercare is a major feature of modern life. In other words, most of us need to understand and deal with both our own health needs and those of others around us; and this generates a shifting mix of preferences and needs, which changes constantly as we grow older. Health capability is learning to manage the mix.

Finally, Sen's linking of capability to aspiration signals the link between learning and an ambition to improve the overall conception of health. As one of the submissions to the Inquiry put it: '[we need to] challenge the widespread defeatism which leads people to believe that mental health problems are an inevitable part of growing old.'[16]

Financial capability

A springboard from redundancy

The withdrawal of UK military operations in Cornwall led to an outplacement programme for civilian personnel at RAF St Mawgan in 2008. Thanks to a partnership between the HR Department, Cornwall County Council and Unionlearn, 1,300 administrators, firefighters, cooks, engineering technicians, maintenance staff, cleaners, waitresses and drivers were offered personal finance courses to help them decide, for example, the best use of the lump sum redundancy payment – whether to pay off mortgages or invest the money in starting a small business. The course proved to be a springboard: some have gone on to develop skills for self-employment; those approaching retirement have attended a two-day in-house retirement training course, with spouses invited to attend too, covering subjects including inheritance tax and investment.

From *Basic Skills Agency (2008)*.

---

[16] See the Submission to the Inquiry from Lee, M. (2007). *'Improving services and support for older people with mental health problems'* and *'Promoting mental health and well being in later life'*, UK Inquiry into Mental Health and Well-Being in Later Life, Age Concern England.

Financial capability may seem a strange choice for a central place in a citizens' curriculum. Yet, arguably a sense of control over one's finances is an essential precondition for broader participation and well-being – never more so than in a period of economic turbulence and uncertainty such as we are currently experiencing. Note that we say a sense of control – not the maximisation of financial returns. Without such control, lives can slip into chaos, even where income or wealth is actually quite high. One stark indicator is the fact that the Citizens Advice Bureau deals with around 2 million people annually with debt problems; these can drastically undermine personal and professional confidence and well-being.

The term 'financial capability' has been brought into public usage by the Financial Services Authority (FSA). The FSA was given a statutory remit in the Financial Services and Markets Act 2000 to increase public understanding of the financial system. Prior to this, the term most in use by policy-makers and professionals had been 'financial literacy', defined as follows: 'the ability to make informed judgments and to take effective decisions regarding the use and management of money.' The new term stresses an active, skills-based approach to personal finances rather than the importance of knowledge on its own.

In its submission to the Inquiry,[17] the FSA said that it planned to reach 4 million employees with written material, and deliver seminars or disk-based information to 500,000. Competence on all of these dimensions is clearly important. However, this stops short of including the broader perspective that makes this a part of a citizens' curriculum. This would embrace a critical understanding of how personal finances fit (or do not fit) within the wider economic context. Since an impressively large majority of professional economists failed to understand the system well enough to foresee the credit crunch of 2008, this seems a tall order for citizens generally. It's possible, indeed, that a little knowledge is a highly dangerous thing in the financial world; certainly, it's not the case that the more you know the more secure and in control you will feel. However, this is precisely why Sen's capability notion is so challenging: it sustains the aspiration to understand and engage, on our own behalf and as part of wider society.

If the technical details are the preserve of the few, the moral dimension is certainly not. The consumer role is a vital part of empowerment. However, this role is not confined to selecting the best deal for oneself. It means having the ability to locate one's financial needs in a wider context, relating material needs to other factors. We include in this environmental considerations. We do not think that the

---

[17] See the Submission to the Inquiry from FSA (2007) *The Future Of Lifelong Learning – Response To Call For Evidence Around Learning In The Workplace.*

current crisis will transform us abruptly into a less materialist society. However, the conjuncture of a very sudden economic rupture and a slow-burning awareness of the significance of climate change is having an impact on the way people seek to manage their lives, and the part consumption plays in it. Financial capability in our understanding includes that growing awareness of matching consumption more accurately to need.[18]

Are we suggesting that we should all spend hours every week carefully calculating our finances like some Dickensian clerk? Hardly. Many have to watch pennies very carefully, but good financial capability can take some of the stress away and free them for other more fruitful things. It may seem curious to think of financial capability as an essential liberating force, but it has a strong claim.

Finally, as with other capabilities, the profile of financial capability will vary significantly over the life course. The skills needed to make things work at the age of 25 differ from those required at 50 or 75 – but only to a degree. Younger people typically have concerns about mortgages, holidays and the cost of child-rearing. Older people also think about these, but they will be concerned too with pension arrangements, whilst their adult children may be worrying about eldercare. People have different concerns at different stages, but there are common threads. The market in financial products responds to these to some extent, but only very partially. The pensions crisis has shown how difficult people find it to begin early enough to save adequately for retirement. A coherent citizens' curriculum should address these common issues. Our proposal for key 'staging-post' reviews (*Chapter 5*) is intended to include the stocktake needed to meet these varying financial challenges.

Civic capability

Local people challenge and change their community from within

Twenty members of the Community Experts group – all local residents from the South Leeds area – responded to a volunteering campaign led by Leeds Voice, which was searching for local adults to take part in training and community research in 2006. Since then, the group has taken part in an intensive course in 'participatory appraisal' – a community research method – and produced 'honest perceptions' studies of disadvantaged neighbourhoods using the new research skills they have acquired. Eleven local areas have been covered

---

[18] We welcome the commitment in the new *Skills for Life* Strategy 'Changing Lives' (DIUS, 2009b) to expand family finance courses.

in the group's findings, and have affected directly how a £500,000 funding pot allocated to the locality by Leeds City Council should be spent.

Rather than employing 'professional' consultancy companies to conduct research and generate community priorities, this project turned that approach on its head. Using local people provided many opportunities to elicit honest comments from the public, and has demonstrated to the council and other statutory agencies that local people are the 'professional experts' and are more than capable of being commissioned to undertake research.

Bringing together community members from different neighbourhoods to learn together, has broken down historical barriers and helped people to better understand other communities' issues and problems. With the skills and experience to take on other pieces of commissioned work, the options open to group members have increased. As they themselves say, 'by doing this project, we have increased people's awareness of how local people can change the community from within… We lacked confidence to speak to strangers… [In the future we want] to do more community work, mostly for [our] children, and hopefully start to look for work. We have the confidence to do that now.'

This book is being written at a time (June 2009) when the UK parliament's reputation is at almost an all-time low. The possible responses include cynicism; apathy; and withdrawal from all forms of political engagement. The sour political mood may pass, but it should not obscure the wider picture of civic activity. Lifelong learning encourages scepticism but not cynicism; promotes wider forms of civic activity which go beyond conventional politics; and enables people to maintain the norms which uphold both representative democracy and direct participation. Citizens feel more in control of their lives if there is a thriving civil society alongside a political democracy in which they have trust. Disengagement and cynicism undermine that feeling.[19]

Civic capability for us includes making sense of and shaping one's own and other cultures. We do not seek to pin down culture, so this is broad indeed. But remember Sen's sense of agency, and Williams' notion of shaping change, and apply this to the aesthetic, the spiritual, the intellectual, the sporting. It extends to the public understanding of science, of literature, and of history. Promoting capability means inviting people to play a role themselves in cultural activity,

---

[19] See also the work of the Carnegie Inquiry into the Future of Civil Society, http://democracy.carnegieuktrust.org.uk/civil_society

whatever form that may take. They may be spectators only, but active spectators, or they may themselves be involved directly as participants. We are not here stepping into the minefield of what counts as 'good' cultural activity; our point is that making positive choices about what you do in the cultural field is almost always a good thing, and learning helps you do that.

As with the other capabilities, civic capability can be developed through both formal and informal modes of learning. Evidence submitted to the Inquiry on the part played by cultural institutions such as museums or libraries in fostering civic engagement illustrates this breadth. As one submission put it, '…the values of a democratic society rest on information, understanding and engagement. The public library service, a free, accessible and non-judgmental service reaching into the heart of every local community, espouses all of those ideals.'[20] Several submissions stressed the role of libraries and museums in enabling marginal groups such as refugees or asylum-seekers to find their way into civic activity, and other initiatives are worth noting, especially as they come from departments which are not 'educational'. For instance, the Office of the Third Sector is promoting volunteering opportunities for disabled people, and the Department for Work and Pensions is exploring how those on benefits can be supported if they engage in civic activity.

As one of the Inquiry Commissioners, Bob Fryer, notes in his Thematic Paper on Citizenship and Belonging, in the 1990s the reports by Sir Bernard Crick on citizenship in school (especially) and then for young people over 16 generated an enormous surge of energy in the system.[21] We have taken a rather wider view of 'citizenship' in our scoping of a citizens' curriculum, but the essence of Crick's work applies directly to our notion of civic capability.

The second Crick report defines a number of different roles as part of the citizens' repertoire: consumer, community member, family member, taxpayer, voter, worker – and lifelong learner. These are crossed with a list of actions and competences to form an extensive matrix of 70 cells into which competences for civic capability can be mapped. (They include financial capability, which just goes to show how many different ways the capability cake can be cut.) The competences are:

- demonstrating an understanding of the rights and responsibilities associated with a particular role;
- applying a framework of moral values relevant to a particular situation;

---

[20] See the Submission to the Inquiry from Derbyshire County Council (2008). *Submission to the Inquiry around Citizenship and Belonging.*
[21] Fryer (2009); Crick (1998, 2000).

- demonstrating an understanding of, and respect for, cultural, gender, religious, ethnic and community diversities, both nationally and globally;
- combating prejudice and discrimination;
- critically appraising information sources (advertising, media, pressure group, political parties);
- managing financial affairs;
- assessing risk and uncertainty when making a decision or choice;
- initiating, responding to, and managing change;
- selecting the appropriate mechanisms or institutions for dealing with particular issues; and
- identifying the social, resource and environmental consequences of particular courses of action.

This list retains its validity, and ties in well to the conceptual frameworks we have borrowed from Sen and Williams.

There is now a growing range of specific methods for encouraging wider civic participation. They include citizens' juries, user panels, participatory appraisals, future searches and open space technologies.[22] These techniques have different purposes, appropriate for different groups and contexts. The point here is that all these will work better, the greater the capabilities of those involved – and learning comes from doing. Just as employment fosters digital capability, so participatory activity fosters civic capability.

Citizenship and lifelong learning

Arrangements need to be in place – organisation, opportunity, funding and support – for learning throughout life and active citizenship increasingly to become mutually influential, each strengthening and enriching the other. Both have at their heart the objectives of enhancing people's autonomy, developing their sense of themselves and their identity, enabling them to contribute with confidence to a wide range of personal and shared goals and both to dream imaginatively and act decisively for improvement in their own lives and in those of their loved ones and the wider communities in which they live and work. Stronger, independent-minded citizens, engaged in lifelong learning, will contribute to better, more accountable government, will be able to review more critically and creatively the values and workings of society, will cherish mutual tolerance of diversity and difference, will exercise more control

---

[22] Involve (2005).

over the unfolding of their own lives, including, importantly, their health and well-being, and will be able to deploy knowledge and understanding to their own benefit and to that of their fellow citizens, in both this country and internationally.

Professor Bob Fryer, IFLL Commissioner and
former Chief Learning Advisor, Department of Health

Both inequalities of power and the broad diversity of our society mean that there are very different notions of participation. It is not a question of just including more groups in a fixed process. At the Inquiry seminar on citizenship we heard about the development of gender-related civic capabilities, through the Women Take Part initiative. This involves both individual journeys (from 'getting there' to 'staying there'; i.e. levels of involvement) and organisational change, towards a different culture which validates women's experience.[23] The same would apply, as other historically disempowered groups gain a greater purchase on their rights. The act of civic participation transforms the process itself. This is the force of the capability approach, with its accent on freedom and potential.

Is it the case, as it is with the other capabilities, that the application of civic capability changes over the life course? On this one, it is not so evident. One of the glories of a flourishing civic society is its ability to bring together people from different generations. Naturally, the particular interest groups and societies that people join will vary by age, and there is some evidence of how political attitudes change as people get older. However, we suspect that civic capability shows the least variation across the life course of all our four capabilities.

Finally, perhaps the biggest challenge facing citizens of any nation is that of climate change. The looming scale of this demands that civic capability is developed within a systems framework that connects local participation with global responsibility. The ability to deal creatively and constructively with situations of complexity, uncertainty and risk will be essential attributes for citizens to survive and thrive in the twenty-first century. The science of climate change and global warming; renewable energy; wildlife conservation; and eco-tourism: these are all issues which we might aim to understand as citizens, and act on, but which might also be embedded in employability programmes. However, as society struggles to understand and respond to the enormous implications of climate change, it

---

[23] See the paper presented at the Inquiry Expert Seminar on Citizenship and Belonging: Woman Take Part Framework (2008) *'Moving on up': the role of lifelong learning in women's journeys to active citizenship.*

is all too easy for people to feel disengaged, bewildered and powerless to make a difference. The persistence of what has been termed the 'value-action' gap indicates that, even among those who recognise the problem, behaviour change can be hard to put into practice. Sustainable development needs that gap to be bridged – the move from understanding and adaptation to shaping change.[24]

---

90 years ago!

'In a modern community, voluntary organisations must always occupy a prominent place. The free association of individuals is a normal process in civilised society, and one which arises from the inevitable inadequacy of state and municipal organisation. It is not primarily a result of defective public organisation; it grows out of the existence of human needs which the State and municipality cannot satisfy. Voluntary organisations, whatever their purpose, are fundamentally similar in their nature, in that they unite for a defined end people with a common interest. There is, therefore, in a voluntary body a definite point of view, a common outlook, and a common purpose which give it a corporate spirit of its own. This corporate spirit is, perhaps, the most valuable basis for group study.'[25]

Conclusion: the capabilities overlap

We stress the overlaps between the different capabilities. Digital and civic capabilities coincide in the example just mentioned, where library staff pride themselves on training members of the public in developing ICT skills, which helps to engender a sense of active belonging.[26] The Open University, in addition to specific initiatives related to volunteering (for example, on school governors), has an online presence which publicises volunteering opportunities across the country.[27]

Other evidence submitted to the Inquiry demonstrated how better health leads to strong community involvement, and vice versa.[28] Evidence presented at the seminar on poverty illustrated strongly how debt problems paralyse people,

---

[24] See Plant and Ward (forthcoming, 2009).

[25] British Ministry of Reconstruction, Adult Education Committee (1919), para 205.

[26] Libraries and Information East Midlands (2008) *Submission to the Inquiry on Lifelong learning, Citizenship and Belonging.*

[27] The Open University (2008) *Submission to the Inquiry on Lifelong Learning, Citizenship and Belonging.*

[28] Blackburn with Darwen Borough Council (2008) *Submission to the Inquiry on the Impact of Lifelong Learning on Happiness and Well-being.*

almost literally, so that learning now to manage your finances is part of learning how to improve your health and well-being.

We have been able to give only an outline of the capabilities and how they are learnt. Our chief proposition in this chapter is that we should look at these as forming some kind of unity. In *Chapter 9* we take this further, through the idea of a local minimum guarantee, which would mean that wherever you are in the country you would have access to some form of learning encompassing at least this set of capabilities. How capabilities are interpreted will vary across groups, and across the life course. However, the opportunity to learn this capability in a general sense should be open to all, on an equal basis.

Capability and employability

We began the chapter by locating the citizens' curriculum in a broader context, of cultural aspiration. We finish this section by linking it to employability. Employability skills are the set of essential skills that equip people to undertake work, progress within work and transfer between different types of work. The UKCES report, *The Employability Challenge*, defines them as:

- skills relating to the foundation of a positive approach; i.e. being ready to participate, make suggestions, accept new ideas and constructive criticism and take responsibility for outcomes;
- functional skills; i.e. using numbers effectively, using language effectively and using IT effectively (digital life skills); and
- personal skills; i.e. self-management, thinking and problem solving, working together and understanding the business.[29]

Employability skills, at the appropriate level, equip a person not just for one role but also to progress within their chosen, or to a different, occupation or field. These skills are equally relevant to people involved in different forms of work such as self-employment, volunteering and informal work.[30]

Most people will need to earn their living, either working for themselves or for someone else (we include self-employment as part of employability). Without this, other aspirations are unlikely to succeed. However, in the current employment context, employability has a different sense to that which prevailed when the labour market was tight and jobs were not hard to come by. Sen's thinking helps

---

[29] UKCES (2009b).
[30] See NIACE (forthcoming).

us relate capability to employability, moving away from the narrow concept of employability as concerned exclusively with job skills.[31]

There are two key points here. First, employability involves personal attributes which go well beyond technical or professional skills. Resilience is essential: it is the attribute which enables you to persevere, and to draw on the resources available to you, whether in yourself or with others. It means, literally, bouncing back, but has a more active connotation than just rebounding from adversity. It means absorbing stresses and strains, and turning them to advantage. Resilience should help you to gain employment; most importantly, it helps you maintain your confidence and competence. This will be increasingly decisive in enabling people to maintain contact with a turbulent labour market, whether or not they are actually in employment.

Secondly, the capabilities discussed above are not self-evidently employment-related, other perhaps than digital capability. The other three – civic, health and financial – seem at first sight to relate more to personal, community or domestic concerns. Yet all these different types of capability underpin employability, directly or indirectly. They pervade people's lives, affecting their basic level of self-control, and therefore their ability to seek, find and maintain employment. Someone who cannot manage their personal finances will often carry that stress into work, to the detriment of their performance there. That in turn will affect their health. Participation in civic activity helps reinforce people's sense of identity and well-being, which helps them maintain their links to the labour market. In this way our three capitals – human, social and indentity – interact.

The capacity of the lifelong learning workforce: teaching, training, tutoring, designing, guiding, enthusing

'We need a well-trained professional workforce to deliver high quality learning.' Cliché? 'Adult educators are too often in marginal employment, with no security or continuity.' Universally agreed. Now try these. 'Volunteers play a vital role in many forms of lifelong learning', and 'Adult education has to be demand-led and learner-centred.'

---

[31] Kenway and Blanden, make an interesting distinction between 'incentive-building', which assumes people are rational individual agents, and 'capability-building' approaches, which aim 'to make people better equipped to flourish in the environment they find themselves.' (2009, p.56). This explains well why we favour the latter.

We endorse all of the above. Either this makes us illogical or the issue of how to provide the right kind of workforce poses some complex questions (possibly both; as the physicist Niels Bohr once admonished a student: 'You are not thinking. You are just being logical.'). Those working in lifelong learning are often hugely committed to their students and skilful in their teaching. It is no disrespect to say that we need a higher level of capacity. As a participant in our online debate on learning infrastructures observed: 'workforce development for practitioners surrounding "pedagogy" is the key.' This means some new thinking on how we conceive of the lifelong learning workforce, and how it should be developed. Once again, we confine ourselves to an outline framework.

From our perspective there are four strategic issues, beyond the material ones of pay and conditions. These are issues which, if dealt with creatively, should help to make the system an intelligent one – reflecting somewhat the principles outlined. We deal with them only illustratively – each could be the subject of an entire chapter.

Experience and background

First, a brief overview of what is a very varied field. There are over one million individuals working in lifelong learning across the UK, including people working in career guidance, community learning and development, further education, higher education, libraries, archives and information services, and work-based learning. (Lifelong Learning UK – LLUK – is the employer-led sector skills council covering this field.) As the list would suggest, the profile of the lifelong learning workforce is very diverse. This has notable strength, for instance, in its variety of background and experience. The question is how far to go in driving up professional requirements and bringing diverse fields together. As a de-schooler who saw professions as disabling, the dissident Ivan Illich would have warned strenuously against development of this kind (and dissented from the first proposition at the start of this section).[32] We are neither de-schoolers nor anti-professions, but the issue of how far professionalisation should be taken and in which direction is a real one.

Evidence submitted to the Inquiry on this topic included a 'Declaration on Learning' from a group of people experienced in working on effective learning. They affirm learning as 'the only source of sustainable development' and as 'reinforcing the informed, conscious and discriminating choices that underpin democracy', so they are in tune with the Inquiry's own orientation. However,

[32] Illich *et al* (1977).

> they have a specific set of challenges to teachers, trainers and developers, which include the following:
>
> '● Be role models for effective learning.
> ● Encourage *everyone* to have learning goals and development plans.
> ● Respond to both the complexity of situations and the diversity of learners.
> ● Support people through the discomfort and uncertainty sometime associated with learning.
> ● Empower others to take responsibility for their own learning.'[33]

Identifying the right staff and enabling them to develop the right experience are crucial. The criteria here are not just formal qualifications. Adult learners who have themselves come through a non-traditional path are often best equipped to engage other adults as learners. Professionals with direct experience of specific professional fields should be present in our colleges and universities in greater numbers. This is all common sense; it needs flexibility and initiative to make it happen. The Institute for Learning (IfL), the professional body for all teachers and trainers across further education and skills, promotes just such a varied approach to continuing professional development (CPD). Teachers and trainers are dual professionals – as experts in their subject or vocational area and in teaching methods for really effective learning.

In some fields the profile of the staff has not caught up with changes in the student population. There is no case for an absolute matching of the two on any specific social characteristic. However, to take just one example, the ethnic composition of FE staff is a very long way from reflecting that of FE students. In 2006–07, 16.8 per cent of learners were from black and minority ethnic groups compared with only 7.7 per cent of staff. In addition, the proportion of learners from black and minority ethnic groups is increasing at a faster rate than that in the staff population.[34] The Commission for Disabled Staff in Lifelong Learning[35] called for a culture of disability equality for disabled staff, as well as learners, and this has yet to be heeded.

---

[33] Submission to the Inquiry from Cunningham, I. *et al* (2008) *A Declaration on Learning: How do you Respond?*

[34] LLUK (2008).

[35] Commission for Disabled Staff in Lifelong Learning (2008).

Obviously the right staff profile will vary according to the type of learning in question. Our point is simply that the strategic goal should be to make sure that formal credentials are in balance with appropriate experience. A relatively large part of the FE workforce could retire in the next few years, which offers both challenge and opportunity. This extends to staff development: it should entail an appropriate balance between experience and formal study. There are lessons to be learnt from past training of teachers in achieving this balance.

Technological implications

The IFLL Thematic Paper on Technology underlines how pervasive technology is becoming – it is not an optional add-on. We are careful to avoid the message – heavily broadcast at about ten-yearly intervals over the last half-century – that technology is about to transform the entire education system.[36] However, it certainly looks likely to change substantially the relationship learners and teachers have with time and space, and with each other. This has implications for staff, and not only for teaching staff. *Digital Britain*[37] identified a significant shortage of teachers of IT, at every level. Our conclusions here are drawn directly from the evidence submitted, but also from the online consultation held by the Inquiry as part of its work on learning infrastructures.

Online training, interactive video and audio communication, global asynchronous or real-time exchanges, electronic performance support systems – these are just some of the new technologies for learning. Some of the implications for 'teaching' are clear, at least at a general level. People will expect to learn in many different ways, especially through combinations of different media, and of different media with face-to-face teaching. There will be less direct instruction and more guidance, as well as more self-directed learning. The traditional divisions between teaching and support staff will dissolve, and new kinds of staff will be needed, with different professional boundaries then emerging.

Some of the possible implications are less obvious. Many more of the 'teaching' or 'training' staff will be doing other kinds of work, combining a teaching function with applying the skills they are teaching. In a way, this harks back to the master-craftsman role. One question this raises is how will professionalism in teaching be developed and assured. Another is what this will do for the collective spirit of the teaching profession, or equivalent professional groups. There will be far

---

[36] At the Inquiry's seminar on Technological Change, speaker after speaker, all technologically-oriented, confirmed the importance of location in learning. There is no sense that we are, or should be, heading for a space-free future.
[37] BIS and DCMS (2009), p.177.

more emphasis on enabling teachers to form networks helping each other as professional communities of practice.

Learners will also be producers. This is the same 'co-production' theme as we saw with health capability above, but writ large. We can assent to this quite easily as a principle, but the implications for the workforce are not at all clear. Learners rather than organisations will come to define learning environments rather than the other way around – indeed, this is already happening. Who and what will be able to contain, manage and communicate information will become far more unpredictable, as inanimate objects become actively 'informational', providing information unprompted. Being able to predict who at any given time has access to what will become more difficult as people will carry around the means of accessing 'information clouds'.[38]

Assessment will become a particular issue. There is the practical but important issue of authenticity: bogus courses and fake qualifications are bound to become a more persistent challenge. More interesting from the educational point of view is the challenge of providing assessment when much of the learning has been so thoroughly collaborative, through shared media tools, that it is impossible to distinguish who has contributed what.

In conclusion, though, there is a fundamental message: whatever the technology, learners will still often need to talk and meet each other. They will usually want, and need, to spend time in physical spaces together. Teachers and trainers will need to become skilled in enabling these direct interactions to be as fruitful as possible. Managing physical and social spaces will be a central skill.

Representatives, champions and intermediaries

It is time to salute one of the most unambiguously successful initiatives in the recent history of lifelong learning: the introduction of union learning representatives (ULRs). Since the ULR scheme was introduced, some 22,000 representatives have been trained, helping hundreds of thousands of learners to learn. Their functions are to motivate and support employees to take part in learning, in or out of the workplace; to inspire their belief in their own capabilities. The trade union Unison alone has trained over 3,000 ULRs, using them to combine with employers to create a culture of learning at work).[39]

---

[38] Mauger (2009).
[39] Submission to the Inquiry from Unison (2007) *Learning and Organising in the 21st Century. The trade union role.*

The current government plans to expand the number of ULRs. They reach people who are often quite distant from formal learning prospects; they carry trust; and they combine support for individual progress with a spirit of collective advancement. They should, of course, be backed up by colleges and other institutions which respond to what the ULRs tell them about workers' needs. Making effective use of such intermediaries for the design of new initiatives would be a strong indication of a system that values experimentation and reflection.

Less well established, but promising, are 'learning champions'.[40] These are people selected to promote learning amongst their community. For example, they will visit schools to encourage parents to engage in learning, or shopping centres to encourage consumers to sign up. One of the biggest barriers to learning is the fact that many people do not appreciate the benefits it brings, and part of the learning champions' job is to make sure this changes. They inject energy into the system.

Both union learning reps and learning champions have 'learning' in their titles. They are, as it were, paid-up members of the LLUK workforce. There are many para-professionals, such as teaching assistants, learning support staff and technicians who also figure, and who have great potential for further development. However, there are many, many others who would not recognise themselves as belonging in this way, but who have or could have a major influence on our learning. We call these learning intermediaries. Intermediary roles can help stimulate participation and/or support teaching and learning. Examples include Citizens Advice Bureau advisers, probation officers and health visitors,[41] but many more could be added to the list. Intermediaries may be volunteers or professionals at different levels. The common characteristic is that they are in a position to guide people towards learning opportunities at a time when the potential learner is at something of a transition point – in other words, just when they may be most open to the idea of learning.

Intermediaries can:

● provide information on opportunities, and on where and from whom to find out more;
● encourage participation, and point the way to progression;
● influence their environment so that it encourages learning; and
● help colleagues to help learners, even when they might not think it part of their job.

---

[40] Submission to the Inquiry from The Scarman Trust (2005) *Analysis of Community Champions Programme – Award winners 2002 and 2003*.
[41] Submission to the Inquiry from Cardiff University (2008) *Learning as Work: Teaching and Learning Processes in Contemporary Work Organisations*.

Why are all these intermediaries so important? Because we essentially have a demand-side problem. Put another way, our learning aspirations are too low. People need stimulus, encouragement and the example of others to go for learning. If possible, they also need the approval of their peers. All this adds up to cultural change. Even where people have the motivation, they often do not know quite where to look to satisfy it. Intermediaries are the key to driving up demand for learning because they can do it both directly and surreptitiously; they can take the issue head-on, or they can insinuate learning into people's lives without them realising. They operate where people are, physically and mentally.

Army wives discover learning is a force for good

The Blandford Camp Learning Champions are a group of nine women, all of whom have husbands serving in the Army and live 'behind the fences' at the base in Dorset. A partnership between the Army Families Federation Employment Advisory Service, the Army Welfare Service and the Learning Champions Project allowed a Learning Champions course to be offered, which the women signed up for enthusiastically, undertaking an OCN Accessing Lifelong Learning qualification at Level 2.

Many of the participants felt uncertain about their ability to achieve in learning and the nature of life on the camp – where people come and go, and stay for varying periods of time – means that it can be difficult to build up friendships and a sense of community before moving on again. However, by coming together in a supportive group atmosphere, the women were able, not only to give each other confidence, but also the motivation to work through the course and achieve the qualification.

Now, as fully trained learning champions, members of the group are well-equipped to support and signpost others towards learning opportunities within their wider community. As members of the group say, 'moving around to different camps and to different countries is a huge barrier to learning but, luckily, the course was only seven weeks long so this fitted in well for all of us… We all feel a sense of pride and achievement, and we all now have personal goals and plans for the future. Learning as adults has been fun, challenging, yet also life-changing, as we now all know what we can do next. [In the future we plan] to carry on learning – no matter where we end up'.

Developing capacity

Lifelong learning reaches into all corners of society, or should do. The range of professional and para-professionals involved is already large. The addition of intermediaries extends even further the range of personnel for whom high-quality support should be available. Whether volunteer or paid, they need to be supported to build their capacity through initial training and regular continuing professional development.

Good progress has been made in providing training where often little or none existed. A great deal of training is already done, led by the Institute for Learning. FE staff now have a requirement to undertake a minimum of 30 hours professional development per year for full-time teachers and trainers (pro-rata for those who work part time, with a minimum of six hours). This progress needs to be consolidated.

A major source of support will be FE colleges, whose role we discuss in the next chapter as the institutional backbone of local lifelong learning. In her IFLL Sector Paper, Ursula Howard defines an ambitious role for them in adult pedagogy. They should, she argues, take the lead on:

- pedagogy for personalisation; i.e. with initial and diagnostic assessment based on what learners know and want to know, building on their existing knowledge, expertise and skills;
- the development of pedagogies for flexible, ICT enhanced learning;
- enabling advanced FE learners to take on roles as assistant teachers, mentors, coaches and learning support;
- developing good practice in learning outside the classroom, including online communities of interest;
- the development of pedagogies for workplace learning; and
- new pedagogies for learning from recognising and building on people's existing knowledge and experience.[42]

There are plenty of other sources beyond the colleges, but it is important for this agenda to be tackled. To develop capacity more generally, there should be a suite of easily accessible materials and training modules that can be used by all those involved. The repository of materials should be open to contributions from the full spectrum of those involved in supporting and delivering learning. There is already a mass of experience to be drawn on. However, there is a significant question as to whether there are core competences and skills needed for working with people

---

[42] Howard (2009).

to help them learn. What unites the youth worker, the FE teacher, the workplace trainer, the adult tutor, the community worker, and so on? This needs some debate on feasibility and desirability. It would certainly help individual workers to transfer from one context or specialism more easily and would aid career progression.

The adult advancement and careers service is due to bring much of this together. The UKCES is recommending a simplification of the training system, which will be a crucial step in enabling support to be delivered in a transparent and accessible way. In the next chapter we discuss the potential of libraries and colleges to act as key focal points for the delivery of information and guidance; and we propose that Local Learning Exchanges be established, perhaps in those institutions, to enable learners to join with each other in extending the range of opportunities. All of these are part of an emerging network of support for the lifelong learning system.

Recommendations

- We propose a national debate around the idea of a citizens' curriculum with a common set of identified capabilities, locally interpreted to meet diverse needs.
- Our proposal is for a set of four capabilities as the initial core of the citizens' curriculum: digital, health, financial and civic. These relate closely to employability and to wider cultural development.
- We recommend that there should be a minimum local offer which guarantees access to learning in relation to these.
- Significant support for workforce development is needed, with a broad definition of who makes up the lifelong learning workforce.
- We strongly endorse the support already given to ULRs and learning champions. Their experience should be drawn on and disseminated. Other learning intermediaries should be identified and supported. These will be in both voluntary and professional capacities.
- We recommend the establishment of an online repository of materials available to all those involved in the design, delivery and use of learning opportunities.

'The concept of "an affordable college education for all", universally understood in the US, should become a key concept for policy in the UK, supporting adults' social and economic aspirations.'

'All of this points to Lifelong Learning Exchanges as a means of enabling peers to come together and help each other learn – building a collective capability to complement the individual capabilities sketched in the previous chapter. By enabling mutual contact and support, they would help people to develop their own services and solutions, complementing state and private services.'

9 Organising locally
Governance and institutions

Summary

In this chapter we look at how the system is organised to deliver, primarily viewed from the local level. We declare in favour of stronger local powers, without wanting merely to push back the pendulum from its current highly centralised position. A system needs to be properly, but not rigidly, articulated: its different parts should be related, but in a way which allows them all to function properly, and to change. This is why the degree of centralisation which currently exists in England is so counter-productive: it actually makes change harder. The contrast with wider trends towards greater devolution is striking.

We suggest that local authorities should have a different and more strategic role, ensuring a broad local infrastructure to improve access to learning. Further education colleges are central to this, but they need to be linked well with many other players; we briefly summarise the roles of the different stakeholders, including local employers. We put forward the idea of Local Learning Exchanges. These would act as nodes in the system, combining the functions of information, mutual help and social space for learning.

Higher education institutions have a major role to play as partners in this local system. They have a wider range of functions, but lifelong learning should figure explicitly as part of their mission.

Finally, we look at the connections between these parts of the learning system and the wider policy framework. If we can't work out how learning is encouraged or discouraged by what is done elsewhere – for example, in social security or employment policy, the prospects for success will be seriously limited. We therefore give some examples where articulation with external policies is needed, and we suggest a mechanism for driving the whole enterprise forward, at central level.

In this chapter particularly, the variation within the UK is great. Much of what follows applies to England only; the degree of centralisation is far less in Scotland, Wales and Northern Ireland, which themselves differ significantly in the extent to which local authorities have responsibility. Many of the ideas may nevertheless have value for prompting debate across the UK.

A new local landscape

Governance relates to the way power is exercised. We are particularly concerned with how powers are used to shape expectations and offer opportunity in some kind of consistent way and at an appropriate level. We focus particularly on the local, but of course there are regional and sub-regional levels which need to be taken into account also. We repeat the earlier message that the position in the devolved administrations is quite different.

Ecology and articulation

The Inquiry did not call for evidence specifically on governance, but as we looked at the implications for different sectors of a move to a genuine lifelong learning system, there were very strong messages about the need to change from the degree and type of central control currently exercised. Those arguing for decentralisation envisaged new forms of local control, not a mere swing back of the pendulum to previous formats. We therefore need a fresh look at the landscape. The Inquiry could not redesign the political map, in any case, but the notion of a 'local learning ecology' emerged as a very fruitful metaphor. Ecological perspectives provide a useful critique of top-down performance management and of markets as the mode of governance of lifelong learning. They help practitioner, policy and researcher communities to move away from mechanistic engineering metaphors. Local ecologies also have an important horizontal dimension spanning health, social services, the environment and economic development, as well as education services.[1]

The challenge from the ecological metaphor to policy and practice is clear: how to sustain a system which can develop and grow organically. We support the UKCES drive to simplify the training and qualification system. However, simplification should not result in excessive tidiness, which goes against local initiative, experimentation and the ability to change. Simplicity should not rigidify the system. If the model is not of a single body at the top dictating strategy to all the local players, then success depends on constantly evolving links and relationships that allow both flexibility and coherence – a tricky combination. From a systemic perspective, we might call this loose articulation.

The decline of local powers has had grave consequences. It has accompanied a sharp decline in local learning opportunities. Figures published by the Learning and Skills Council (LSC) at the end of 2008 showed a fall of 86,400 in the number of adult learners since 2006–07, bringing the number of adult learning places lost

---

[1] Hodgson and Spours (2009).

Table 15: Participation in LSC-funded courses by learners aged 19+ (FE and skills participation – learner volumes), 2004–05 to 2007–08 (England)

Learner numbers				Change in learner numbers		
2004/05*	2005/06	2006/07	2007/08	04/05–07/08	05/06–07/08	06/07–07/08
4,547,100	3,854,000	3,181,800	3,095,400	−31.93%	−19.68%	−2.70%

Source: LSC (2008)

from all publicly funded learning over the past three years to nearly 1.5 million (see Table 15).

Behind this overall decline there is much evidence that communities and groups are losing access to learning. Two large examples to make the point: on gender and age – which clearly interconnect. Women are particularly active users of local provision, making up 77 per cent of the participants in adult and community learning. Faced by its disappearance, some of them – primarily, the better off and better educated – will have found their way to other opportunities, but many will not. Older people, less interested in qualification-bearing provision, have also been hit hard. Again, some have been able to compensate, by joining 'Universities of the Third Age' (U3As), but U3As cannot cater for all.[2]

Beyond favouring greater local autonomy as a general approach, what are our specific suggestions on how this might work? They are as follows:

- see the local authority as the strategy-maker for local collaboration and as guarantor of a minimum local offer;
- treat FE colleges as an institutional backbone for lifelong learning, with greater autonomy combined with an obligation to collaborate with other providers and voluntary and community organisations;
- strengthen local employer networks, to foster a culture of workplace learning;
- strongly promote the role of libraries, museums, galleries and sports facilities as learning institutions;
- ensure that national initiatives on education and training have a significant component of their budgets allocated to relevant local bodies;

---

[2] We are currently exploring the implications of the 2009 Equality Bill in relation to the impact on the age profile of learners. At first glance, there appears to be a strong case for thinking that it entitles older people to press for more equal treatment, based on the fact that, as a group, they have benefited less than others from educational services (Mountfield, 2009).

- give high priority to family learning, especially through early childhood services; and
- develop Local Learning Exchanges as nodes for information and advice, spaces for social learning, and channels for the matching of demand and supply at individual level.

We develop these below. We do not cover the entire range of bodies which currently have some stake in local provision: regional development agencies, government offices of the regions, sub-regional groups and so on.[3] We cannot redesign the entire government system or anticipate what the future will bring on that front. The analysis and proposals refer to the bodies which are most likely to endure, if not necessarily in their current shape, or to new initiatives.

The local authority as local strategy-maker

Here we are to some extent second-guessing political developments, since we cannot predict how future governments will treat local government. We do not exclude local authorities as direct providers of adult education, but their primary role will be different, and more strategic.

This strategic role applies to all four stages of the life course. The immediate implication is that educational services must be linked to other functions and services, notably health (primary care trusts), but also cultural activities, sustainable economic development and the voluntary and community sectors. It will often be at this level that effective coordination can be genuinely achieved, as distinct from lines on a central planning board, to provide services for all ages. Local authorities are best placed to plan for an integrated set of services for each stage. They should have the powers to coordinate the engagement of all partners and providers in making lifelong learning opportunities available that can meet identified needs and support community well-being. This leadership role and the importance of lifelong learning to all community partners could, as the New Opportunities White Paper suggested in January 2009, be given 'bite' through the new area inspection regime. The new local landscape should be clearly mapped and signposted.[4]

---

[3] The complexity is pithily illustrated by a recent Parliamentary Question from Annette Brooke MP: 'To ask the Secretary of State for Children, Schools and Families what role *(a)* local authorities, *(b)* sub-regional groups of local authorities, *(c)* Government offices of the regions, *(d)* regional planning groups, *(e)* the Young People's Learning Agency, *(f)* regional development agencies and *(g)* his Department will have in (i) funding and (ii) commissioning education and training required for 16 to 19-year-olds in (A) schools, (B) academies, (C) sixth-form colleges and (D) further education colleges.' (5/5/09).
[4] Cabinet Office (2009).

For specific recommendations we draw here on the formulation by Tim Brighouse in his IFLL Sector Paper, that the local authority role should include the following:

- define lifelong learning broadly and see it as a means of complementing economic regeneration with the creation of social capital;
- build lifelong learning into the various different and overarching common identities of its community (for example, the learning city, town village or community);[5]
- ensure that cabinet portfolio holders and executive directors all have a role to play in delivering lifelong learning with one person holding lead responsibility for it;
- review progress every three or four years through its Scrutiny Committee;
- include 'lifelong learning' entitlements and responsibilities in all council job descriptions and encourage similar practice by other employers;
- run an 'annual awards' ceremony and secure the support of the local media both for it and as key promoters of lifelong learning; and
- secure (and provide) resources for lifelong learning, especially innovative practices in lifelong learning and in overcoming social exclusion.[6]

Along with Brighouse, we would stress that how a local authority interprets these tasks will vary according to its context and tradition. This is wholly in line with our general approach, providing a common framework for local interpretation.

A particular issue for local authorities should be to ensure that when decisions about planning and funding are taken, public funding is allocated according to community need. This also relates to access to facilities; for example, there are often perverse incentives that deprive adult learners of access to buildings for no good reason at all. Local authorities should seek to minimise these.

FE colleges as an institutional backbone

FE colleges have historically catered for the widest range of learners, with the widest curriculum offer, of any of our institutions. They are the most comprehensive component in the system, an all-purpose player that performs on very different terrains. One of the dangerous current trends is the narrowing of this range, with a sharp shift towards youth.

---

[5] The 'learning city' concept is further elaborated by Ian Sandbrook in his IFLL paper (Sandbrook, 2009). He puts particular emphasis on the celebratory function, i.e. the visible valuing of learning in all its forms. As Brighouse implies, 'city' stands for any political unit or authority with a relevant remit for learning.
[6] Brighouse (2009).

The concept of 'an affordable college education for all', universally understood in the US, should become a key concept for policy in the UK, supporting adults' social and economic aspirations. Colleges are overwhelmingly the largest local provider of learning. They can offer the necessary blend of vocational, academic and general education with the size and capability to perform a dual role of leadership and support.

The essential recommendations on what is needed to achieve that goal are taken from Ursula Howard's IFLL Sector Paper:[7]

Colleges' values and mission should be inclusive and pluralistic, offering a 'comprehensive' and diverse curriculum for a diverse adult population

A single model will not do. Complex and diverse missions are the only realistic approach to colleges' roles, given the needs and demands of the individuals, families, communities and the range of employers and their staff which they serve. Their employment-facing work goes hand in hand with working for social inclusion and catering for those with the greatest learning needs, at pre-entry and entry level; those with 'spiky profiles', and those who have already achieved educationally, but need or want to change direction.

Colleges should be first and foremost local organisations, except where specifically validated to play a wider role in specialist areas

We argue below for greater autonomy, but colleges should be focused on their local community and economy; this is a restriction on their autonomy, which should be part of national strategy. The local focus should be their primary concern. Of course, this itself will vary: 'local' will mean something different in a rural area, a town, or a slice of a large city. Colleges would work in partnership and cooperation with others, including local authorities, employers, training providers, universities and the voluntary sector, to create and sustain a thriving local ecology of lifelong learning.

Vocational education, including work-based training and professional development from Level 1 to post-graduate should remain central to colleges' mission

Colleges should remain the mainstay and leading sector for vocational education. They should offer a fully rounded vocational education as well as academic learning, rather than a narrow knowledge-poor approach to skills and training. This means a twenty-first century rendering of general and liberal studies: 'habits

---

[7] Howard (2009).

of reflection, independent study and free inquiry' because 'we cannot afford either to fall behind in technical accomplishments or to neglect spiritual and human values'.[8]

Colleges should have a significantly greater degree of autonomy

This applies to all key areas of strategy and operations, with new models of governance and lines of accountability. Greater autonomy for colleges should include more flexibility in their funding so that they can be locally responsive; and more powers to award qualifications, within the proposed unit-based credit system.

Strengthen local employer networks: building social capital to grow human capital

A culture of learning depends on people subscribing to common norms – that is, they should demonstrably value learning. Norms are most effectively enforced through repeated social interactions: it is much harder to transgress if you meet the people you offend against, face to face and on a regular basis. Put this fact alongside the view that British employers are particularly concerned about poaching – if they invest in training, their fellows do not and use the money saved to offer higher wages and entice the trained person away. Evidence on this is a little sketchy, but there is no doubt that a major mechanism for boosting demand for training is to foster an employer culture where it is the norm. This requires leadership from the centre, but the effective channel for it will be local as well as sectoral.

We therefore support the encouragement of local employer networks as a mechanism for raising training standards and commitment – a line of thinking currently pursued by UKCES. Local Chambers of Commerce are an obvious vehicle for taking this forward with their Chambers Skills Networks. This will be particularly helpful for the millions of small and medium-sized enterprises (SMEs), where access to ideas and encouragement from peers can play a big part in encouraging them to take training seriously. This includes the implementation of regulatory frameworks, and the monitoring of licences to practice. In other words, for large parts of the UK, good practice can be developed and spread through effective local employer work.

This may also apply to skills development in some industrial sectors, though not all. Where an industry is particularly prominent in a local area, it makes sense for that sector's approach to be tailored to fit with the local authority's more general strategy.

---

[8] Unwin (2009).

Learning difficulties/disabilities

The case of people with learning difficulties and/or disabilities illustrates the need for local leadership in building links between education and employment. To achieve seamless pathways for students to move from formal education to sustainable employment, different agencies and providers need to commit to a process which encompasses all the necessary stages of transition, from formal education and training to sustainable employment. Job coaching is key to this. Some colleges do it already, but either need to grow this expertise further themselves or form partnerships with supported employment organisations (who are already expert in job coaching and engaging with employers).

Local authorities have an important role to play in prioritising and aligning resources for key elements, particularly when the current LSC local partnership capacity disappears. Key elements include:

- ensuring adequate resources exist for job coaching and effective benefits advice;
- commitment from partner organisations for staff to give sufficient time and energy to person-centred planning as the first step in ensuring that services meet people's requirements; and
- developing and coordinating programmes to raise expectations amongst professionals, parents and carers about people's potential for open, paid employment.

More local budget autonomy

We have already referred to this when discussing FE colleges. We fully accept the need for accountability – this is part of any serious strategy – but accountability means allowing people to take responsibility, within clearly defined parameters, and then checking on how well they performed. It means allowing risks to be taken; this in turn entails the possibility of failure. All of this makes genuine accountability potentially uncomfortable for a central government, especially in a media culture that focuses its energies on seeking out bad news.

However, stronger localism must mean more decentralised budgets without sacrificing accountability. This opens up big questions of public finance which go beyond the Inquiry's competence. However, to make this more than fine words, we suggest a simple rule of thumb to apply to central initiatives: at least 20 per cent of the budget allocated should be devolved to local level (whatever that might be in the relevant context).

The information flow should be a two-way process. Central authorities should learn from the lessons of local experience, as well as local authorities being able to draw on expertise accumulated at the centre. Such a measure is, in fact, an essential part of an 'intelligent system', as it encourages experimentation. We return to this in our discussion of measurement.

A recognised role for cultural institutions and voluntary organisations in the lifelong learning system

We received very positive indications of the willingness of institutions such as libraries, museums and galleries to play a front-line role in lifelong learning. Of course, the people who made these arguments are not a representative sample, but we were very encouraged by the innovative spirit showed. Most libraries are predominantly local in focus; many museums are too, but more will also have a national outlook. (At present, museums in particular are frustrated by perverse incentives, which reward them only for work which relates to the school curriculum.)

Natasha Innocent's IFLL Sector Paper gives detail on the role and potential of cultural institutions.[9] Libraries already operate the People's Network, with 30,000 free or low-cost internet-enabled PCs, available in every public library, giving them a vital role in reducing digital exclusion. As we noted in *Chapter 8*, many of them actively seek to include marginal groups in a process of civic engagement. They are a crucial part of any system. We would like to see stronger links between local libraries and schools and colleges, including the possibility of co-location (as we saw with one example under Building Schools for the Future).[10]

One obvious partnership is between an FE college and local library as the basic axis for local provision. This could operate almost as the default model; i.e. one that would be expected to be in place as a major feature of the local infrastructure unless local circumstances dictated otherwise. A partnership of this kind would combine the formal and the informal, including family units, as well as individual students, with natural access to books, IT and other information sources.

Under this heading also come sports facilities of all kinds. Once again, the link between learning and health is central, at different stages. IFLL analysis shows a very strong benefit to older people's mental health from involvement in gym classes; and local sports facilities are a key asset for schools which may not have their own.

---

[9] Innocent (2009).
[10] DfES (2007).

Museums also have their part to play. At a national level, museums can inspire huge interest in topics which can then be taken up locally. They are a natural venue for family and group learning.

The Inquiry also received very powerful testimony from a range of voluntary organisations with a primary or secondary interest in lifelong learning. Foremost amongst these is the Workers' Educational Association (WEA), which embodies many of the principles and values we support, and has done so for a long time. Another, with a different provenance, is the Women's Institute (WI). For both, the organisation is its membership, and the individual and collective benefits of membership are immense, if not always captured by contemporary methods of assessment. The programmes of the WEA and the WI are living examples of the citizens' curriculum, with local activity flourishing within a national framework of explicit values – different in both cases, certainly, but each building social and human capital. This is not to ignore the mass ranks of local voluntary and community organisations working up and down the land – on our estimate over 35,000 organisations in the UK with over 680,000 paid workers and over 15 million volunteers.[11] The training and learning implications of such a workforce are themselves significant. However, in addition, over 60 per cent of voluntary organisations in England and Scotland report their most frequent area of activity is providing learning and training opportunities to the community.[12]

All of these forms of cultural and voluntary activity are major sources of the learning intermediaries which we identified in the previous chapter as a major potential resource. Volunteers and front-line staff can play a vital role in encouraging individuals and families to benefit from the resources offered in their institutions, but also point them towards wider learning opportunities where they can take further the interests which their visits inspire.[13]

---

[11] MakesFive (2009) *Investment in LL: Scoping the Third Sector*, research for IFLL.
[12] Clark (2007); SCVO (2008).
[13] An interesting example of how 'capacity' can be built in more than one sense comes from the Science Museum, which is about to celebrate its centenary. Recently, all senior staff were required to shadow members of the public as they moved around the gallery, observing how they interacted with the exhibits and used the space. This was part of an innovative approach to the development of spaces and resources based on observation of how people interact and use them – an approach that could be more widely adopted.

Everyone has a story to tell

Tell Us Your Story is a story-telling project developed and delivered in the North West through a partnership between the BBC, local adult learning services and voluntary and community sector organisations and the Learning and Skills Council. Story-telling is used as the catalyst to engage with vulnerable individuals and groups who have traditionally been reluctant to engage in formal learning. Nearly 100 learners from over 12 different countries have participated since 2004, developing confidence and literacy skills along the way to discovering hidden talents.

Learners' stories have been produced for broadcast; one participant is writing a book; others have written a drama production for radio; whilst others still have joined creative writing workshops. Everyone has a story to tell, but not everyone is given the opportunity and support to do so. This approach engages adult learners by harnessing the facilities and expertise of the BBC, the influence and resource of the LSC… and the reach and support of trusted local voluntary and community organisations.

Early years, schools and family learning

Learning as a family has a powerful contribution to make to lifelong learning: it crosses policy areas and provides many of the critical building blocks for long-term changes in aspirations and learning practices. This combines national strategy and local implementation. The following recommendations come from the IFLL Sector Paper by Penny Lamb and Carol Taylor:

- the introduction of a lead learning practitioner at a local level to advocate on behalf of learning in families for both parents and children;
- a recognition across government departments of the critical interaction between parenting support and learning as a family;
- the integration of family learning into parenting support strategies;
- support for the introduction of the new family learning practitioner qualifications; and
- the introduction of the units on family learning into initial teacher training and training of other relevant practitioners.[14]

---

[14] Lamb and Taylor (2009).

Early childhood provision has been a major focus of educational policy over the last decade. The introduction of Sure Start has been one of the biggest initiatives in decades, linking education with wider social support at local level. The setting up of Children's Centres has massively improved the facilities available. It is the area where the mutual benefits of intergenerational learning are seen most clearly. Margaret Lochrie in her IFLL Sector Paper argues that adequately funded lifelong learning could make a particularly decisive contribution, both to early childhood development and family well-being. Among her key recommendations are:

- a new education and skills deal for all parents;
- a broader definition of *Skills for Life*, including skills related to parenting and the care and education of children, financial and health literacy; and
- a qualified and appropriately structured early years workforce.[15]

As with early years learning, schools have a dual role in respect of lifelong learning:

- for children they lay the foundations for learning throughout the life course; and
- they can involve adults, especially parents, as participants in this process, and as learners themselves.

In their IFLL Sector paper on schools, Guy Claxton and Bill Lucas call for a significant reorientation of teaching in schools, in order to foster curiosity, imagination and reflection amongst school students, so that schooling becomes an 'epistemic apprenticeship': the key task is instilling a love of learning, giving students the tools, attitudes, courage and discipline to make this effective.[16] They argue for major change, therefore, in the way teachers are trained and school leaders developed. School governors are another category with a role to play; they themselves need access to training to help them envisage and realise the potential that schools have for lifelong learning. Developments such as the extended school are definitely a step in this direction.

In short, the recognised institutions of education all have a part to play in the system. For them to work together in a genuinely systemic way requires some basic principles (e.g. information should be shared) and practice (e.g. good leadership). However, above all, it needs much higher levels of trust than we have: in professionals, between sectors and between levels. Trust is the most effective way of getting people to work together and, once it is in place, the most efficient.

---

[15] Lochrie (2009).
[16] Claxton and Lucas (2009).

As a former college principal and a passionate advocate of the further education sector's capacity to change for the better the lives of individuals, I believe that colleges, more than any other educational organisation, bring together people from different backgrounds, with different needs and aspirations. However, sometimes colleges succeed in spite of, rather than because of, the systems and procedures in place. Therefore, the key challenges I identify for the Inquiry to have an impact are as follows: colleges need greater autonomy to work with their communities; they need a qualification and funding system which recognises credit-based units which may or may not lead to full qualifications, allowing adults at any stage of their lives to build up a portfolio of skills, recognising individual circumstances, including the worth of programmes which go beyond current recognised qualifications. All the above should be wrapped in a re-energised culture that learning pays for the individual, the community and the country.

Dr Helen Gilchrist, IFLL Commissioner and former Principal at Bury College

Local Learning Exchanges

Most of the above has been about strengthening current features of the different institutional players who will foster lifelong learning at local level. We turn now to a novel proposal, which links our emphasis on localism with some of the ideas in previous chapters. We suggest that Local Learning Exchanges (LLEs) be developed. The Exchanges would:

- encourage and enable people to *offer themselves as teachers, trainers, mentors and guides, as well as learners.* The idea is very simple: you want to learn something, but also feel that you have a skill or competence to offer to others. The LLE would register this, and act as a node or broker to put people in touch with each other. A typical example might be people helping each other to reach a certain level of digital competence, without enrolling formally in a course, or immigrants (temporary or permanent) who want to offer their language in return for learning English;
- provide a *physical venue* for people to meet, explore opportunities, and run their own courses. This is the spirit of *The Learning Revolution*'s recommendations on the use of premises. Fifty libraries have recently opened new community spaces. The University of the Third Age (U3A) is a classic example of how both these first two functions can operate: there are approximately 730 U3As in the UK, with over 200,000 members, sometimes just needing a physical space to be able to learn from and teach each other (see www.u3a.org.uk);

- enable the *sharing of technology and digital content*. This could be done virtually, to make effective use of high-spec technology in colleges, universities and even businesses, linking with schools, community centres, technology at home and on the person; and
- facilitate the *pooling of entitlements*. Learning Accounts and other entitlements should not be seen in a wholly individual context. Raising demand and increasing choice – their primary goal – will not happen if we think this way. We therefore need mechanisms that will enable individuals to get together to combine their personal entitlements with some form of collective demand. The Exchange could offer this – a local learning 'bank', but run on a mutual basis.

All of this points to LLEs as a means of enabling peers to come together and help each other learn – building a collective capability to complement the individual capabilities sketched in the previous chapter. By enabling mutual contact and support, they would help people to develop their own services and solutions, complementing state and private services. The LLEs might be initiated by the local authority, but then be given an arm's length status, for they might flourish most when drawing on a mix of local resources, as a kind of mutual organisation. They could be the location for the adult advancement and careers service; maintain a single local learning portal; provide a home for learning champions. They could be the local host for national initiatives such as learndirect and UK Online, making technology further available to the community and building digital capability. They need not require any major building programme – indeed, they would be better located in places where people are already used to going.[17] An obvious place would be in a library or college, especially if these were operating in partnership, as suggested above, and had a strong outreach record.

The idea is simple, but the model needs elaboration. That – elaborating, to suit the context – is what should be done at local level.

---

[17] As the Vice-Minister for Education in the People's Republic of China recently observed, we should mobilise idle resources: 'For instance, Confucius temples around the country can be used as a centre for lifelong learning. Many marginalised groups can communicate with each other on these sites.' (Zhang Xinsheng, 2009) We could have a good debate on what is our equivalent of Confucian temples.

Long before I became Chief Executive in Islington, I was a community education worker there, working with local groups to connect education with the needs of the locality. I could see how adult education was a lifeline to thousands of elderly people, and to people with disabilities and mental health difficulties – providing them with the means to maintain social contact and to keep physically and mentally active. It made an important contribution to musical and artistic developments locally, and was strongly linked to regeneration and community development activities.

Local government's ambitions – for a more active citizenship, for the social and economic regeneration of communities, and for better support for families and older people – should also be the ambitions for lifelong learning. In the past, this was much better understood and councils were encouraged to develop educational and social provision for adults which, in the words of the former Ministry of Education, was designed to enable people 'to deal competently and democratically with the complex questions of our time, or to develop those interests and activities which go to the making of a full and satisfying life… and a civilised community'.

Aspirations for learning have become progressively narrower in recent times and funding for local authority adult learning has been all but squeezed out of existence. While to some extent this work was revived in the early twenty-first century through initiatives such as Neighbourhood Renewal and New Deal for Communities, sustainable funding and structures which would make learning central to meeting the needs of local communities is far from being fully recognised in policy.

We believe that lifelong learning should once again have a much stronger local focus, and be better integrated into the work of local government and other services such as health. This is not to say that local authorities need to be big providers themselves, but they do have an important leadership role to play in ensuring that learning opportunities are available in their area which can support the well-being of their communities. Currently, Government shapes too much of the adult education curriculum, making it difficult to respond to local community needs. Providers need more local discretion over their budgets, and local authorities should have the powers to coordinate all partners, such as libraries, health and social care agencies, to make learning opportunities available that meet local needs and support community cohesion.

Leisha Fullick, IFLL Commissioner and Pro-Director, Institute of Education,
University of London

The university contribution

Most UK universities operate at several different levels: local, national and international, with varying degrees of emphasis on the different levels. They have different traditions, shaped in part by their history as national or regional institutions. We support universities' autonomy, and this includes the capacity to define for themselves the balance they choose between these levels. There should be no single model for university engagement with lifelong learning. They may combine extramural provision for local communities, in-service training for national professionals, and opportunities for adult students from all over the world. In the governance context, our main recommendation is that universities make explicit, in their missions, the nature of their particular commitment to lifelong learning; and included in this is the nature of their service to the local community and economy.

Compared to the counterparts in many other countries, UK universities are already a much stronger part of the lifelong learning system. They provide multiple access points for adults to return to learning, and many have a proud tradition of serving the local community. However, this has happened largely independently of, or even in spite of, public policy. Ensuring that they form part of an overall system requires further thought and effort, from those inside the institutions (staff and leaders) and those responsible for their funding.

The Open University (OU) was founded in 1965 as 'the university of the air'. Its charter (granted in 1969) prescribed not only a special duty of 'promoting the educational well-being of the community generally', but also pedagogical innovation: 'the advancement and dissemination of knowledge by teaching and research by a diversity of means, such as broadcasting and technological devices appropriate to higher education, by correspondence tuition, residential courses and seminars and in other relevant ways.' Critically, it revolutionised the British system by requiring no prior qualifications for entry. The goal of this innovation was clearly social justice. Over time, the founders' confidence in the abilities of 'new' types of student – without traditional qualifications, without family or surrounding community experience of higher education, and, significantly, with disabilities – that would make conventional study patterns difficult or impossible – has been amply justified.

We envisage the main systemic contributions from the university sector as follows:

- active support for and participation in a comprehensive credit system, as discussed in *Chapter 7*;
- promotion of more flexible part-time provision. The introduction of mode-free funding is a challenging but fundamental condition for this;
- linking with colleges and other providers in local and regional learning federations. These would turn around the key issues of access, transition and progression;
- sustaining a commitment to liberal adult education;
- developing public engagement;[18]
- making available their facilities to local communities; and
- using their research capacity to build a strong knowledge basis across all forms of learning, including the development of human, social and identity capital.

In doing so, universities will often be returning to their historical roots. Until the advent of company or for-profit universities in the late twentieth century, all university institutions grew in some way from the communities that originally sponsored them. It is revealing, for example, to look at the charters of the Victorian and Edwardian 'civics' (where local and regional themes abound). In this context, the familiar image of a university as somewhat separate from its community – as, for example, an ivory tower – is curiously unfaithful to the historical record.

Today, no self-respecting university or college would dare to lack a civic and community mission. However, in some important respects, universities are relinquishing their involvement in lifelong learning. Pressure to compete as research institutions can weaken their commitment to the 'third leg'; that is, community-oriented activity. Financial incentives can deter them from engaging in activities which are not properly recognised by funding bodies. Most noticeably, more and more universities are currently dismantling their departments of adult and continuing education. These departments were the major providers of part-time opportunities, at all levels. Their disappearance is a major issue. It is a systemic loss, for these descendants of the old extra-mural departments were, and are, change agents within the university sector. They have consistently pioneered change and innovation, reaching out to adult students and forging links with the community. We are in grave danger of losing this valuable leavening agent.

---

[18] See for example the Beacons for Public Engagement project. 'This aims to build partnerships between universities and a host of other organisations including museums, community organisations and broadcasters. Each is committed to trailing new approaches to public engagement, and to unlocking the huge potential of universities within the communities they serve.' For more information go to www.publicengagement.ac.uk/project/default.htm

In summary, there are three key ways in which higher education institutions should play a part in the future of lifelong learning:

- build into their missions an explicit commitment to lifelong learning, accompanied by a statement of how they interpret this in practical terms;
- commit themselves to joining in local strategies for lifelong learning, so that they figure on the local landscape; and
- revive and reinterpret the tradition of commitment to making publicly supported research knowledge available to the wider public.

At a different level, it is up to the HE Funding Councils across the UK to ensure that these several types of contribution are given positive incentives, and not the reverse.

Local and national responsibilities

We have put the emphasis in this chapter on the local. However, as the ecological metaphor suggests, levels are interdependent. Insulated, water-tight compartments do not sit well with this metaphor. Links between different parts of the system cannot be very tidy either. In particular, people's motivation to learn, and their ability to take advantage of learning opportunities, are often dependent on factors which have nothing to do with education. There need to be good articulations between the local and the national, and across boundaries.

National responsibilities

However flourishing the partnerships are locally, we need strong impetus at the central level – not determining how things will be done, but ensuring that progress is being made, and that lessons are being learnt on how to do things better. This needs:

- clear lead responsibility;
- a mechanism for linking strategy to expenditure; and
- a body independent of those immediately responsible, which can check on progress and offer strategic advice.

On the first, a mainstream government department should have responsibility (as is broadly the case in Scotland). However, because of the range of lifelong learning's applications across all four stages of the life course, a specific Cabinet Committee should be set up to oversee the cross-departmental links.

On the second, we need a technical cross-departmental committee to focus specifically on the interactive effects of lifelong learning. In other words, to what extent do the pay-offs we have described in the rationale and elsewhere actually occur, how might they be best assessed and recorded, and what are the implications for collaboration across departmental and professional boundaries?

Thirdly, we need a body that is capable of taking an independent overview of the system as a whole. It should be able to adjudicate between different constituencies, point to gaps and take clear positions on priorities for the system as a whole. There are a number of possible options here. One is for a parliamentary Select Committee to exercise this oversight. Another is for an independent Standing Commission on Lifelong Learning, bringing parliamentarians together with employer, union, media and civic society representatives. A third option would be to give the role to an authoritative body with strong experience of monitoring policy, such as the National Audit Office.

Policy coherence

Other policies need to support not obstruct learning policy. One of the best-known obstacles to participation in learning for some groups has been the actual or feared loss of welfare benefits. A major example has been the 16-hour rule which meant that people were excluded from many courses because they should be available for work. Another has been the loss of housing benefit which could in the past result from someone going onto a training course, getting a job, but then losing the job and not being able to get back onto housing benefit. These have been major deterrents; it is good that the policies have now been adjusted, although the perceptions may take time to adjust in response.

We return to people with learning impairments for a different example: there is a large group of people with disabilities or long-term health conditions that are out of work and have been falling through a void between Jobcentre Plus services (because they have not been actively seeking work) and local authority day services (because they do not have 'critical and substantial needs'). These crevasses may be narrow, but also very deep for those that fall into them.

This goes beyond material benefits. We know that volunteering is a major benefit to individual well-being. It also helps people develop new skills, or apply existing ones. We have argued that there are likely to be new mixes of paid and unpaid work, notably in the expanding ranks of Third Agers. However, faced with high and possibly lasting unemployment, do Jobcentres adequately inform people of where they can go to engage in volunteering activity? Here is a major link needed to preserve human capital, as well as resilience and decent lives. More generally, linking the work of Jobcentre Plus to employability skills of the kind we described in the previous chapter will be a crucial part of any move to economic recovery. Jobcentre Plus staff could be enormously influential as one of the learning intermediaries we identified in the previous chapter.

We refer back to our discussion of ESOL as part of the general basic skills entitlement discussed in *Chapter 6*. This is a prime case for local coordination, as the recent DIUS document on *Skills for Life* observes: 'To foster integration and community cohesion, a new partnership approach is needed which targets English language provision at local need. Local authorities are well placed to lead these partnerships to ensure ESOL is focused on priority groups. The new approach will involve ESOL needs being considered as part of wider local planning arrangements such as Local Area Agreements and city strategies. This will involve a range of partners – local authorities, the Learning and Skills Council (LSC), Jobcentre Plus, colleges and other key planning and delivery partners, including the voluntary sector.'[19]

The associations between education and health are well known, and the potential pay-offs for closer collaboration are very large. Co-locating health and education facilities is a natural option. Initiatives such as Health Prescriptions, where doctors prescribed classes rather than drugs, are a good example of how links can be made to work, though they face professional and institutional barriers.[20] Education's role in preventing ill-health, delaying dependency and enabling patient self-management is an area which will grow hugely in significance as the population ages. The White Paper on *Building a society for all ages,* for example, cites the estimate that 'improving healthy life expectancy by just one year each decade, could generate a 14 per cent saving in spending on health care and an 11 per cent saving in spending on benefits between 2007 and 2025.'[21] It is an area ripe for more broad and systematic cost–benefit analysis. Indeed, carrying out such analysis and discussing the result and implications are potentially powerful ways of making connections across departmental and service divides.

The Offender Management System was intended to manage offenders' learning journeys throughout their term. The principle is correct. Whatever the record on that, our proposal for a transition entitlement that guarantees offenders a place in a course when they leave prison or very soon thereafter will demand strong links between the prison and probation services, the prison education service and outside providers.

---

[19] DIUS (2009b), paragraph 2.4.
[20] James (2001).
[21] Department for Work and Pensions (2009).

In economic development terms, regions or sub-regions can be the natural points of coherence for skills development. Specialist vocational centres in further education colleges or new university colleges are necessarily situated in their localities, but their reach extends to learners and employers across a wider area. In short, at almost every angle or bend of our system there is a link to be made with other parts of our lives, and pulling on one bit affects the rest.

Recommendations

National frameworks

These links need to be forged and strengthened at national and local level. Coordination is not enough: it too easily results in administrative rather than cultural links. We believe that at the national level, the Government should:

- Confirm a lead role for a single government department in promoting lifelong learning nationally, targeting support and ensuring coherence and collaboration. Its objective should be to nurture a sustainable healthy system based on trust, transparency and innovation. The department's work should be supported by a new Cabinet Committee responsible for devising, monitoring and delivering new cross-government targets for lifelong learning across the four stages of the life course identified in this report.

- Initiate as part of the next Comprehensive Spending Review, a cross-departmental expenditure study. This should be aimed at identifying cost efficiencies to be gained through the promotion of lifelong learning, and reviewing priorities for spending across the four stages. This work should seek to ensure that incentives (financial or other) in one part of the system do not operate against the objectives of another part.

- Establish an authoritative body to oversee and scrutinise the development of the national system of lifelong learning, with suitable arrangements in the devolved administrations. Options include a new Select Committee in Parliament (possibly a joint Committee of both Houses); an independent Standing Commission, with representation from politics, the world of work and civic society; or the National Audit Office.

A governance system closer to the ground

- Local authorities should act as strategy-makers at local level, promoting lifelong learning across their territories, targeting support and ensuring coherence and collaboration. (This remit fits with that defined for them in *The Learning Revolution*, paragraph 4.5.)

- FE colleges, as an institutional backbone for local lifelong learning, should have a predominantly local focus. They should not be forced into a single mould but encouraged in their diversity. They should regard vocational training as central to their mission but within a comprehensive offer.

- Local strategies should include cultural institutions, sports facilities and voluntary organisations, that are often best suited to reach specific groups for whom the barriers to learning are highest.

- A partnership between a college and a library should be the default model for the foundation for local collaboration. Other models are possible, but these two institutions bring together the formal and the informal in ways which make it particularly appropriate.

- Local employer networks should be supported, as part of strengthening a culture of learning in and out of work. Local Chambers of Commerce are the natural vehicle.

- As a general principle, budgets for national initiatives on education and training should have built in a component for local discretion, amounting to perhaps 20 per cent.

- Universities should build lifelong learning into their missions, interpreting it in a way that matches their particular profile. Their contribution to local learning should be made explicit as part of a strengthened 'third leg'; ie in addition to research and the teaching of undergraduates and postgraduates.

- Models for Local Learning Exchanges should be developed. These would enable people to connect as potential teachers as well as learners; provide a focal point for advocacy, advice and information, including on how entitlements might be used, individually or collectively; and provide physical space for local groups to engage in learning, with suitable access to technological infrastructure. LLEs could well be located in libraries or colleges.

'The UK can take the lead in demonstrating how learning can be properly integrated into this new mosaic of time, enabling individuals and communities to take greater control of their lives. Developing and sustaining a wider range of capabilities across the life course is the key to this.'

10 Lifelong learning for a change
Summary and recommendations

A recapitulation

It's time to remind ourselves of the direction we're travelling. Our horizon is medium to long term, which is why we have not gone in depth into current policies. That does not mean we have taken a blank sheet; as we said in sketching out the vision in *Chapter 1*, our approach is both radical and incremental, building on what exists. Some of what we propose involves quite major change; some of it is more in the nature of a tweak. (Readers may of course differ on which of our proposals falls into which of these categories.)

In this concluding chapter we first summarise the main lines of argument that we have already put forward. We then assemble our main recommendations, and use the opportunity to comment also on issues where there was no place in earlier chapters.

We began from the premise that the *right to learn throughout life is a human right*. The Inquiry's goal is to present a broad vision of how learning links with freedom of choice, with well-being and democratic tolerance, as well as with productivity and prosperity, and with local and global solidarity and responsibility. Integral to this is a commitment to greater equality and fairness, seen as a challenge which recurs across people's lifetimes and not just as a matter of equalising initial opportunity.

The Inquiry's scope has been extremely broad. It covers learning from cradle to grave, but with a primary focus on adult learning. It includes formal education and training, but embraces also more informal modes of learning. It covers learning for personal growth, for professional competence and for community development. It also links with a whole range of policy areas outside education and training, such as health and well-being, migration, crime, poverty and sustainable development. This breadth explains why our analysis and our recommendations do not fit tidily into familiar compartments. Our ambition is to address a range of audiences in such a way that they can find common ground for looking at the system as a whole.

Our central argument is for a *rebalancing of the system*, based on a new approach which is genuinely lifelong. We develop in *Chapter 5* a *four-stage model* which divides the life course broadly into quarters: up to 25, 25–50, 50–75 and 75+. This allows us to get a grip on the overall distribution of opportunities and resources, within and between these stages. The system has been particularly unresponsive to gradual but massive demographic trends. Such responses as there have been to these trends have often pointed in the wrong direction. The system has been more reactive to faster-moving shifts in the labour market, but without coherence. The patterns of working and living are changing gradually with the impact of female labour market participation, and more suddenly with the unemployment crisis, in ways which call for a new approach to time. This should be developed steadily but with real momentum. The UK can take the lead in demonstrating how learning can be properly integrated into this new mosaic of time, enabling individuals and communities to take greater control of their lives. Developing and sustaining a wider range of capabilities across the life course is the key to this.

Our analysis of overall expenditure in *Chapter 4* reveals that a total of approximately £55 billion is spent annually on learning after compulsory schooling, from public, private and individual sources. But the resource distribution is still heavily skewed towards the initial post-compulsory phase of education and training, and the mindset which accompanies most discussion of learning is similarly skewed. We have spelt out the case for a new model of the learning life course. If this takes root, it will mark a major shift in the way we think about the distribution of opportunity. Materially, it opens the way for a better balance in resources across the ages and stages of the life course, and for addressing inequalities. It will also mean changes in the way we gather information, building a better knowledge base for policy and practice in education and training. None of these shifts is trivial; taken together, they would produce a radically better balance in our system.

Our second principal argument is for *a set of entitlements* to encourage latent demand for learning and enable everyone to benefit. Entitlements are a primary instrument for giving people more choice and encouragement, not just as consumers of learning, but as more powerful partners in the whole process. We propose a small set of general entitlements of different kinds: a legal one to literacy and numeracy; a financial one to a qualification giving the competences required to function in tomorrow's global society; and a 'good practice' entitlement to learning leave as an integral part of mainstream employment conditions. We link entitlements also to certain key transitions where learning can have a lasting impact in setting people on new paths to personal and professional fulfilment.

We put forward proposals for a general system of *Learning Accounts*, as a vehicle for state, employers and individuals to invest in learning, in a variety of permutations. This should promote the principle of co-financing or mutual investment, which we see as an essential driver. Most entitlements could be channelled through the Learning Accounts.

We do not expect all of these entitlements to be brought into effect directly and in full. Some should be developed on a universal basis, applying across the country; others are very much to be tailored to local or specific circumstances, and to the state of public and private finances. So there will be considerable variation, but the framework provides a means of achieving over time a better balance. Since entitlements can be geared to disadvantaged groups they are a key instrument for building greater equality into the system.

As *infrastructure* for the entitlements, we call for two guarantees of universal access: to a comprehensive advice and guidance service, independent and free; and to a suitable contemporary level of digital technology – currently meaning broadband at 2Mbps, but changing as the technological context changes.

We underline the need for *rapid progress with a credit system*, enabling learners to accumulate recognition for what they have learnt, in different contexts. Our complementary, and more contentious, argument is for linking the funding of education and training to credit – mode-free, so that the discrimination against part-time study is abolished. This is a powerful mechanism for achieving a better balance. We point also to the need for more consistency and fairness between funding for the higher and the further education sectors.

We advocate a *citizens' curriculum* as a set of capabilities, and propose four core capabilities as a framework: digital, health, financial and civic, linked with employability. This should provide a common structure for a minimum offer of adult education wherever you are in the country, but encouraging local variation on this. We are quite ready to see the specific set of capabilities that we propose modified; the key proposal is for the idea of a common framework, universal but locally interpreted. We link this with the important challenge of building workforce capacity within the system; this includes the training of teachers at all levels, from pre-school to post-school, and of a wide range of intermediaries who can support learning in all its diversity.

We address governance – how the system is, or could be, run. Diversity within the UK is particularly marked under this heading, and we focus primarily on England. We address particularly the local level, recommending *a strategic role for local authorities*, a strong local focus for colleges and places for cultural institutions, universities and voluntary organisations within the local strategy. We develop the notion of Local Learning Exchanges as spaces for people to come together to explore the local potential for learning and teaching. But we say repeatedly that any system – especially a system of lifelong learning – involves complex interaction between different levels and across boundaries.

We link the local with the national with recommendations for *greater coherence at national level* (in devolved administrations as well as the UK): a single department to take lead responsibility for lifelong learning; a cross-departmental expenditure review; and a high-level body to take on the monitoring function on a regular basis, as a way of embedding progress into the machinery of power. We include in *Annexe A* proposals for strengthening the knowledge base further. A central proposal there is for a regular triennial *State of Learning* report which assesses progress across a range of individual and organisational measures; and a stronger research base, with broader longitudinal and evaluative analysis.

The recommendations below summarise our drawing together of the different strands in this volume, but we emphasise that the Inquiry has built a very broad knowledge base. There are thematic, sectoral and other reports published as part of the Inquiry's work. These contain a wealth of conclusions and proposals specific to the theme or sector. It would have been incoherent to assemble all of these into a long string of recommendations, tempting though it was. Readers are referred to the Inquiry's website from where the reports are downloadable.

Recommendations

Our recommendations are quite diverse in type, as well as broad. Some of them are very specific; others will seem abstract. The key test we ask you as a reader to apply is this: do they, in combination, open up the way for envisaging and fashioning a better system for all learners?

1. Basing lifelong learning policy on a new four-stage model

Our case for rethinking the educational life course is based on two key factors: demographic change, especially the ageing of the population; and social and labour market change, especially the extended fuzziness of the transitions people make into and out of employment, at both ends of their working lives. These have massive implications which our current system does not adequately engage with. The model implies major revision: to our attitudes and mindsets; to our policies and practice; and to our approaches to fairness and opportunity.

The model proposes that the educational life course should be thought of as falling into four broad stages: up to 25, 25–50, 50–75 and 75+. There are all kinds of sub-divisions and overlaps[1]; but this simple structure will help us fashion a system of lifelong learning which better reflects the massive demographic and

---

[1] Within the first stage there are many such sub-divisions possible, for example at age 3, 5, 11, 14 and 16. We need particularly to draw a line to mark the passage from compulsory education. Eighteen is the most logical age for this.

labour market changes. It will also help us to sweep away some of the constraints of current age-based divisions.

We need to be clear: the model is to help us adjust our overall thinking, policies and practice. It is not an account of how everyone actually behaves, or how they should behave. It is a reflection of major trends which shape the overall patterns of most people's lives. There is a huge amount of diversity within these patterns –and so there should be.

The patterns of today's working lives are in turbulent flux. At the same time, ageing resculpts the shape of the population, slowly but massively. The combination of these two forces for change means that there will rarely be a better time for fresh thinking about a more sensible, fairer and better spread of paid and unpaid work and learning time across the life course.

We recommend:

a) A four-stage model should be used as the basis for a *coherent systemic approach to lifelong learning*. All those with a stake in any form of education and training (policy-makers, social partners, practitioners) should directly address the implications of extended lives, and of extended entry into and exit from employment. More generally, *official information-gathering* should use the four-stage model as a framework, as appropriate.

b) The first stage (up to 25, but starting at 18 for our practical purposes as people move into the post-compulsory phase) should be looked at as a whole – a very diverse group, but a group nevertheless, with all of its members having claims to *learning and development as young people*. This is a fundamental change of perspective from the current approach, which constantly divides and re-divides young people.

c) Learning in the second stage (25–50) should be seen, not only as a key measure for sustaining productivity, prosperity and strong family lives, but as part of a *new mosaic of time*, exhibiting different mixes of paid and unpaid work and learning time. Ironically, the unemployment crisis opens up scope for the UK to move away from the current second stage time squeeze, where career and family responsibilities result in huge pressures that reduce well-being.

d) The Third Age[2] is central (50–75): more people need and want to work longer, and consequently to carry on learning at work. *Training and education opportunities should be greatly enhanced for those over 50*. Policy, including learning policy,

---

[2] We use the title Third Age as this is already common currency for this stage. The same does not apply to the other stages.

should treat 75 as the normal upper age limit for economic activity, replacing the outmoded 60/65. This will unblock a better general distribution of working time across the life course. This is not a call for everyone to work to 75, but a recognition that 'retirement' will increasingly become a gradual and uneven process lasting several years.

e) The implications of demographic trends for the *content of lifelong learning* should be explored systematically and creatively (these two not being in opposition). In particular, the emergence of the fourth stage (aged 75 and over) means that we urgently need to develop an authentic *curriculum offer in later life.*

f) *25, 50 and 75* should be identified and used as *key transition points*. Of course people do not make the transition at the same age or in the same way, but focusing on these points gives a useful structure, for personal development and for policy. Special information and guidance arrangements should be in place for those making the transition to enable them – if they so wish – to review what part learning might play in their lives.

2. Rebalancing resources fairly and sensibly across the life course

We have assembled for the first time an overall picture of the way public, employer and private resources are spent on all forms of learning. We estimate the annual current total at around £55 billion, excluding the value of time (opportunity costs). We have shown the trends of participation in education and training at different ages, and across different social categories, and combined this with estimates of how long people spend in learning. This enables us to demonstrate the gross imbalances in resource distribution across the life course. We calculated that per capita expenditure on formal and informal learning is around £8,045 for those in the first stage (18–24), £283 for those in the second, £86 for those in the third, and £60 for those in the fourth (see *Chapter 5*). Any independent observer would have to say that this is a strange way of matching resource to need, given the current and (even more so) the future shape of the population, as well as the pace of change in knowledge and technology.

The same analysis shows how unfairly opportunity is distributed across social groups, as advantage and disadvantage accumulate over time. This applies inside and outside the workplace. Age is not the only or even the dominant factor shaping this, but a life course approach enables us to get a handle on many of the other key factors which determine people's access to learning.

This is the foundation of our case for a better balance. Arguing for a life course approach in this way does not for one moment imply that we recommend age segregation. To the contrary: we argue for much stronger awareness of the benefits of learning across age boundaries.

We also argue for a more conscious approach to solidarity between the generations. This means recognising how different generations contribute through public and private transfers, and supporting these to make the most of mutually beneficial investments in learning. All generations benefit from each other's learning, and could do so more. We put forward a simple model to show this.

Financial resources are only part of the picture, but understanding them is an essential condition for moving to a system which better represents our vision, and gives body to the values we spelt out in *Chapter 1*.

We recommend:

a) Public agreement on the *criteria for fair and effective allocation of resources for learning across the life course*. The debate should include both efficiency and equity: what do we need to do to make sure that resources have maximum impact, and how are they used to include all segments of society? Current policy discussions are still rooted in investment in education as an initial phase. They should be framed around the interdependence of generations, so that investment in learning for all ages benefits all other ages.

b) As a starting point, we propose the very broad goal of shifting from the current *86: 11: 2.5: 0.5* allocation across the four quarters, to approximately *80: 15: 4: 1* by 2020. If total expenditure remained the same this would mean an increase in investment in learning in the second stage from around £6.1 billion to £8.2 billion; in the third stage from around £1.4 billion to £2.2 billion; and in the fourth stage from a broad estimate of £285 million to around £550 million. The adjustment should be seen not so much as a specific target as a collective aspiration for a fairer spread.

c) To counter any sense that we favour age segregation, we recommend redoubling efforts in support of *family and intergenerational learning*. Investing in families, broadly understood, is an absolute win-win strategy, and an outstanding way of breaking the cycle of disadvantage.

3. Building a set of learning entitlements

We argue for a strategy to increase learning built upon clear entitlements. We began by referring to education throughout life as a human right; entitlements of various kinds, universal or tailored to particular groups or circumstances, are a way of giving practical application to this right. They enhance motivation and choice – not on their own, but if linked to responsive provision.

Entitlements need not be contribution-based, but we see them as part of an implicit contract. The contributions will come in various combinations: finance from the employer, and time from the individual, for example. Entitlements are a means of enabling everyone to participate – and people who participate in learning contribute more, economically and socially. They can be supported from public or from private resources, or from both; the basic assumption is that they are in the mutual interest.

We envisage two main categories of entitlements. First, a set of *general entitlements*: to literacy and numeracy, as basic skills; a financial one to a level of competence adequate for future economic and social participation; and a 'good practice' entitlement to learning leave as a mainstream feature of employment. The second set is of *specific 'transition' entitlements*, designed to help people learn their way through periods of their life which pose particular challenges; for example, moving to a new area, leaving prison, or becoming 50.

Underpinning these entitlements should be an infrastructure with two main components: a universal advice and guidance service, independent and free; and universal access to a minimum digital technology (currently broadband at 2Mbps, though this will change over time).

The list of possible entitlements is quite long (and could easily be longer). Are we signing off blank cheques, watermarked 'idealism'? No. We do not attempt to cost the entitlements precisely because for it is up to those involved (government, employers, individuals) to decide on what the range, goals and generosity of the entitlements should be. This will be a matter of negotiation and priorities. There will be both direct and indirect costs – and direct and indirect benefits. [3] What we provide is a framework for all parties to judge what kinds of entitlement are to be supported, and how.

---

[3] Time is the biggest issue. Our resource analysis shows the importance of the cost of time (measured through the income or output lost because someone is away from their work, learning but not producing). We cannot ignore this, but valuing people's time is enormously difficult to do in a meaningful way. Market-based wage rates are a very poor proxy, and when growing numbers of people are outside or beyond employment, wage rates become weaker still as an estimating tool. Time is an asset as well as a cost. (You could even say that the whole point of lifelong learning is to transform it from the latter to the former, by giving people the power to use it well.) Measuring the benefits of learning is equally difficult, but equally, if not more, important; we have given some simple examples in *Chapter 2*. This all adds up to an urgent need for more and broader analyses of the benefits and costs of learning.

We recommend a *clear overall framework* be adopted for developing a set of learning entitlements. We propose two key categories for this framework:

a) *General entitlements*

- A *legal* entitlement of free access for all that need it to *basic skills*, i.e. *literacy and numeracy*, currently for all levels of provision up to and including Level 1, but revising this as circumstances change. This should not be restricted to those currently defined as 'of working age'; it should extend to all, regardless of age. We also recommend extending free access to English language tuition to asylum-seekers and spouses.

- A *financial* entitlement to education for a qualification judged to be the appropriate minimum platform for the competencies needed in the future; the standard for this is currently Level 2, but is pushing upwards and outwards. The current entitlement to a full Level 2 qualification should be able to be achieved via a unitised credit route, so that access is on a much more flexible basis than has been in the past. The future level should be set around the current level 3, but very openly interpreted. This too should extend to all ages.

- A '*good practice*' entitlement to *learning leave,* an occupational benefit to be developed flexibly and over time as part of mainstream employment conditions in the second and third stages. This is best developed incrementally, tailored to the context of the sector or organisation. Publication of learning leave arrangements should be part of public information on investment in training by all organisations. Reserve powers should be held for legislation to encourage all employers to make progress on access to learning, including through learning leave.

b) *Specific 'transition' entitlements* These are designed to help people make potentially difficult transitions, notably from institutions. The recommendations below are for possible candidates; others could be added and/or given higher priority.

- *Big birthday bonus*. A simple but powerful entitlement would be for the individual's Learning Account to receive an additional contribution every time they start a new decade, i.e. at 30, 40, 50 and so on. An initial step would be to introduce it at 50, signalling the continuing potential for learning of those moving into the Third Age. It could be universal or means-tested, e.g. according to whether people had already benefited from publicly supported higher education.

- *Release from prison.* A guarantee of a place on a course outside would give offenders a goal, an identity and a social context where they stand a far better chance of establishing a new life and avoiding return to prison. The entitlement should include pre-release preparation.
- *E-learning entitlement for parents of young children.*[4] Parents of young children will often find it difficult to leave home. An e-learning entitlement would give them access to learning from home.
- *Leaving care and other institutions.* The transition out of a care institution can be traumatic, even if the quality of the care may not have been high. A strongly supported entitlement to participation in learning would give a lifeline to this very disadvantaged group.
- *Moving places: a welcome entitlement.* Any incomer to a local authority should be entitled to a free welcome course. This would apply both to internal migrants, i.e. those changing homes within the UK, and to those migrating here from a different country. The entitlement would encourage integration and community cohesion, and help people to see being a 'learner' as part of their new identity in their new home. In all these cases, the entitlement will necessarily be limited, though it may be more generous in some cases than others, in the scope of learning or level of financial assistance offered.

c) These entitlements should be underpinned by *infrastructure guarantees*: universal access to advice and guidance (currently being developed in the adult advancement and careers service), and to a minimal level of digital technology (broadband, as with the current commitment to universal access to 2Mbps by 2012, or its future equivalent). Infrastructure guarantees should be the responsibility of government (national or local), whereas responsibility for entitlements should be more widely distributed across employers and individuals.

d) The main vehicle for channelling the entitlements should be a *national system of Learning Accounts*, drawing on the current experience of Skills Accounts and the Scottish Individual Learning Accounts, and the past experience of Individual Learning Accounts in England. The goal should be a comprehensive, flexible system which will enable and encourage all stakeholders to increase their investment in learning. Technology should make this easy: the technical form could be a Learning Futurescard (see *Chapter 6*).

- The Learning Accounts should be set up by the State for people reaching their twenty-fifth birthday. We recommend that consideration be given to

---

[4] Taken from the National Skills Forum paper, *Closing the Gender Skills Gap (2009)*.

channelling 50 per cent of the public contribution to the Child Trust Fund to this, as a far better investment in the young person's future than handing over a lump sum in cash at age 18. The Learning Account will then be a vehicle for regular co-investment from interested parties, from grandparents through to employers.

- We would wish to see collective forms of entitlement developed, building on the experience of Group Training Accounts and Collective Learning Funds.

e) The universal advice service should give particular emphasis to Staging Post reviews, at or around 25, 50 and 75. These would offer comprehensive and impartial advice across a range of areas, enabling individuals to explore what their learning needs might be, and what support would be available to them for this, for instance in their Learning Accounts.

f) A system of personal portfolios ('MyFutures Folders') would be set up, on a voluntary basis, enabling the individual to hold information which will help them make social or professional plans, and to carry a record of their learning and other achievements.

4. Engineering flexibility: a system of credit and encouraging part-timers

The logic of flexibility implies moving the system away from being geared towards long qualifications, especially where these are full time. We welcome recent shifts in this direction, especially in the way the Train to Gain budget is used. They should be extended further. It is particularly important for working people, especially those at lower levels, who wish to improve their employment chances and can best do so through the accumulation of credit.

It is also in the logic of more complex living and working patterns that most learning will be part time. In fact, the division between full time and part time is itself unhelpful, since part time is really only a meaningful category when opposed to full-time.

Whether or not a flexible and coherent system of accumulating credits exists is an acid test for whether a system is learner-centred or not. If the system cannot manage to organise itself so that different parts of it recognise learning that has been carried out elsewhere, it's the learner that suffers. A straightforward credit system is essential for choice, and so a necessary complement to the entitlements framework we have sketched above.

Within the UK nations there is divergence in the way things are developing, with different qualification frameworks; they should be designed at least to be highly compatible with each other.

We recommend:

a) *Moving quickly to a coherent system of credits* as the basis for organising post-compulsory learning. The system should be broad and flexible. It should allow students and trainees to transfer between institutions. It should encourage bridges to be built between different types of learning, notably between learning at work and in educational institutions.

b) The credit system should *allow lateral as well as vertical progression*, especially as qualifications become outdated. The recent withdrawal of financial support for 'equivalent level qualifications', depriving many people of the chance to retrain in alternative careers, should be reversed.

c) Employers should be encouraged and incentivised to *integrate the training they offer into a credit framework*; this should form part of their reporting requirement in return for receipt of corporation tax relief on training expenditure.

d) The *funding for learning (both fees and student support) should be mode-free*: it should not discriminate against part-time provision or part-time students. Institutions – colleges and universities – should be funded for part-time students on the same basis pro rata as full-time students (with appropriate adjustment for the fixed costs). Student financial support should similarly be even-handed.

e) The *funding should be credit-based*, i.e. it should attach to chunks of learning which are an identifiable part of a course, but which are not themselves necessarily a qualification.

f) The distinction between full-time and part-time study should eventually disappear.

g) In the light of the arguments above, there should be *much greater fairness and consistency in the funding of further and higher education.*

5. Improving the quality of work[5]

The debate around skills and qualifications is very extensive. Recently, we have seen a quantum shift occurring. In England, the Leitch report set ambitious targets

---

[5] This section does not correspond directly to a chapter in the book. It draws on recurrent discussions throughout the Inquiry, especially the thematic work around workplace learning.

for driving up qualification levels. We do not dissent from that as an aspiration, but it is increasingly revealed as a one-sided analysis. The evidence is that how skills are actually used is as much, if not more, the central issue as the overall supply of qualified people.

This is particularly the case if we look at regional variations in the match between supply and demand. The debate over 'over-qualification' and similar terms is a charged one. However, it is clear that in many parts of the UK, beyond London and the south-east, there is no shortage of highly qualified workers. In Wales, Scotland and some of the English regions there are more low-skilled jobs than low-qualified workers. This stands in stark contrast to the rhetoric of knowledge economies. Recent international evidence confirms that UK employers favour 'lean' rather than 'discretionary' work, i.e. work which is closely monitored and targeted, as opposed to work which allows staff to exercise judgement and autonomy. If the overall goal is to move to a more high-skill economy, the emphasis should equally be on how skills are utilised. This does not detract from the persistent need to improve the supply of skills. It poses an even more complex set of problems: how to make sure that people with skills work in environments which make good use of those skills.

In Scotland, this debate has taken firmer root than elsewhere in the UK but there is no easy way of addressing the issue. (Scotland has a higher-qualifications but lower-productivity economy.) The answer is likely to lie in a combination of:

- integrating training with broader business strategies;
- raising capital investment geared to high-performing workplaces;
- raising leadership and management skills designed to make best use of workforce skills; and
- changing the basis for the evaluation of organisational performance, to recognise investment in, and utilisation of, human capital.

It is very welcome that the UKCES is taking a fresh look and a firm grip on the issue of skills utilisation. Their recent report, *Ambition 2020*, provides a powerful analysis of the situation, and in our view points in the right direction.[6] We need a better balance between the simple development and certification of skills, and strategies to ensure their effective deployment. The case for raising overall levels of skills and qualifications remains a compelling one.

Several of our recommendations under other headings relate closely to this issue; for example, the better integration of learning at work with learning outside through an integrated credit system, and the promotion of learning leave.

---

[6] UKCES (2009a).

Necessarily, though, our focus is on improving learning levels, inside and outside work: the wider demand for learning, rather than the narrower demand for skills simply relating to work.

We recommend:

a) Abandonment of crude notions of 'demand-led' provision which conflate different kinds of demand and which divert attention away from the complexities of the interaction. Work should be done on a *much deeper understanding of 'expansive' work environments* which encourage formal and informal learning as a means of raising performance and productivity.

b) Thresholds or *standards to be set for public and private employers' engagement with learning*, using indicators of participation in training and progress in raising qualification levels. Performance on these indicators should be linked to receipt of corporation tax relief on training expenditure. If, collectively, employers do not reach this standard, there should be recourse to stronger measures, including the possibility of legislation, to drive up employer performance on enabling access to learning.

c) *Greater transparency in training performance and expenditure*, including learning leave arrangements: relevant data should be published in organisations' annual accounts.

d) Stronger forms of *licence to practice*, which extend requirements into more sectors/occupations to raise the levels and use of skills.

e) The use of *procurement as an instrument of public policy* to drive up levels of human capital investment throughout the supply chain.

6. Constructing a framework for a citizens' curriculum

We have said repeatedly that the Inquiry's goal is to provide overall frameworks, within which people will develop their own initiatives and variants. Here we propose the development of an agreed set of kinds of learning which should be available to every citizen. Our aim is to ensure that every citizen has access to opportunities to acquire the skills, knowledge and understanding to take control over their lives.

We draw on Amartya Sen's work on capabilities, because it deals with potential and aspiration, and not only with current competences, and because it focuses on equalising people's chances of realising their potential.[7]

---

[7] Sen (1985, 2009).

All citizens should have access to opportunities to develop their capabilities in four key areas:

- digital;
- health;
- financial; and
- civic.

These are plausible candidates for enabling people to navigate through the turbulence of their daily lives in order to achieve that goal. We link these specific capabilities to a broad definition of employability. We emphasise that the capabilities include the ability to understand the wider context of the relevant issues in each case (for example, health) in order to be a critical as well as an engaged citizen, in a global society.

Other capabilities could well be supported. Environmental capability – enabling people to live sustainably and to understand the wider, infinitely complex, issues of climate change and the interdependence of nations – is one such candidate (currently subsumed under civic capability).

We recommend:

a) A national debate around *the framework for a citizens' curriculum with a common set of identified capabilities*. These should be locally interpreted to meet diverse needs. A set of four capabilities should be the initial core: digital, health, financial and civic, linked to a broad understanding of employability and cultural fulfilment.

b) In every area, there should be *a minimum local offer* which guarantees access to the citizens' curriculum.

7. Broadening and strengthening the capacity of the lifelong learning workforce

Any system will depend for its success on the quality of those who work in it. The breadth of the Inquiry means that we take a similarly broad view of how this should be interpreted.

If the goal is for a more coherent system, this implies that people working in different parts of the system should as far as possible be aware of how their work fits with and relates to that of others. This means that there should be clear and accessible information on this. It also suggests that movement between different parts of the system should be encouraged. This includes movement between the formal sector and voluntary organisations.

We recommend:

a) Significant support should be given to workforce development, with *a broad definition of who makes up the lifelong learning workforce.* In particular, this should include careers and advice staff, support staff and paraprofessionals such as teaching assistants, and voluntary facilitators of informal learning.

b) *School teachers and early years practitioners should be included* in the discussion of workforce development. If schools are to lay the foundation for lifelong learning, the training of teachers should give serious consideration to the implications.

c) The work of *union learning representatives and learning champions* should be further promoted and disseminated.

d) Other *learning 'intermediaries'* should be identified and supported, in 'non-educational' fields such as health, probation or citizens advice. These will be in both voluntary and professional capacities, as guides, informants and animateurs.

e) An *online repository of materials* should be established and made available to all those involved in the design, delivery and use of learning opportunities.

8.   Reviving local responsibility....[8]

We share the widespread feeling that there is too great a degree of centralisation, with excessive levels of top-down micro-management. This should not lead to a mirror image preoccupation with the local level. We need a sophisticated approach to making sure that the different levels in the system interact with each other fruitfully, not on a mechanical basis (the metaphor of learning ecologies is helpful in this respect). The system as a whole needs to be loosely articulated, leaving full room for initiative, innovation and experimentation.

A first step needed is a clear mapping of the institutional landscape – who is doing what in the world of learning, especially, though not only, in a local context. We mean this in a literal sense: there should be an easily accessible picture of who offers what, and this should go well beyond the formal system, including employment-related learning, voluntary organisations and cultural institutions. Local maps should include the broader background, i.e. opportunities provided by national bodies which are locally available – most obviously, through new learning technologies.

---

[8] This issue applies primarily to England; the position in the devolved administrations is significantly different.

However, governance is not only about local institutions. We include, notably, higher education which has a national and international focus, and employers who may also be national or international. Their arrangements for taking responsibility for their share in the overall system are part of the picture.

As an overview, we see three key elements of governance in the system as a whole, if it is to be coherent, responsive and effective:

- explicit inclusion of lifelong learning in the mission or function of all the relevant bodies, to be interpreted by them in ways which match their own priorities – going with the grain;

- commitment to collaborate appropriately with other institutions or parts of the system, formally or informally; and

- accountability procedures which make maximum use of trust, but which generate momentum for innovation.

We recommend:

a) *Local authorities*, as the key democratic agencies responsible for the welfare of local communities, should act as the *key strategy-makers at local level*, promoting lifelong learning across their territories, targeting support and ensuring coherence and collaboration.

b) *FE colleges*, as an institutional backbone for local lifelong learning, should have a *predominantly local focus*. They require greater autonomy, with accountability. They should not be forced into a single mould, but encouraged in their diversity. They should regard vocational training as central to their mission but as part of a comprehensive offer.

c) *Local strategies should include voluntary organisations and cultural institutions*, who are often best suited to reach specific groups for whom the barriers to learning are highest.

d) A partnership between *a college and a public library* should be the default model as the main axis for local collaboration. Other models are possible, but these two institutions bring together the formal and the informal in ways which make it particularly appropriate.

e) *Local employer networks* should be promoted, as part of strengthening a culture of learning in and out of work. Local Chambers of Commerce are a natural basis for this.

f) As a general principle, budgets for national initiatives on education and training should have built in a component for *local discretion*, amounting to perhaps 20 per cent of the total, subject to certain guidelines (for example on promoting equality).

g) Models for *Local Learning Exchanges* should be developed. These would: enable people to connect as potential teachers as well as learners; provide a focal point for advocacy, advice and information, including on how entitlements might be used, individually or collectively; and provide physical space for local groups to engage in learning, with suitable access to technological infrastructure. LLEs could well be located in libraries or colleges.

h) *Higher education institutions* should:
- build into their missions an explicit commitment to lifelong learning, accompanied by a statement of how they interpret this in practical terms (this is likely to go beyond the local);
- commit themselves to joining in local strategies for lifelong learning, so that they figure on the local landscape; and
- revive and reinterpret the tradition of commitment to disseminating their research knowledge to the community.

9. … within national frameworks

A genuine strategy needs links at national and local level. Coordination is not enough: it too easily results in administrative rather than cultural linkage.

We recommend:

a) A *lead role for a single department* in promoting lifelong learning nationally (at UK level and within devolved administrations), targeting support and ensuring coherence and collaboration. This should be supported by a new Cabinet Committee responsible for devising, monitoring and delivering new cross-government targets for lifelong learning across the four stages of the life course identified in this report.

b) As part of the next Comprehensive Spending Review, a *cross-departmental expenditure study* aimed at identifying cost efficiencies through the promotion of lifelong learning, and reviewing priorities for spending across the four stages. This work should seek to ensure that incentives (financial or other) in one part of the system do not operate against the objectives of another part.

c) The establishment of an *authoritative body to oversee and scrutinise* the development of the national system of lifelong learning, with suitable arrangements in the devolved administrations. Possible options include: a new Select Committee in Parliament (maybe a joint Committee of both Houses); a Standing Commission, including parliamentarians, but also wider representation from the world of work and civic society; or attributing the role to the National Audit Office.

10. Making the system intelligent

An intelligent system needs a compass, a good set of measures to know whether it is making progress in the right direction. It needs a diet of constant and varied feedback to nourish it.

A constructive monitoring system should have several different components, operating at different levels. It should be heavily formative, providing information of a kind and in a process which are helpful to those in the system. It should draw on sound research, again of different kinds, including both quantitative and qualitative data and with a particular emphasis on longitudinal and biographical research. It also requires a consistent and independent source of 'hard' data, a key role for the Office of National Statistics.

External benchmarks are available from a number of international sources: from the very broad Human Development Index to OECD's statistics and the EU's data on progress to the Lisbon targets. These international rankings are a useful prompt to more detailed internal debate.

We recommend:

a) A *State of Learning* report should be published every three years, covering major trends and issues. The core should be regular statistics on participation, expenditure and achievement, together with information on innovation and capacity. This should be linked to revised Public Service Agreements.

b) Routine use of *external comparators*, including a benchmark group of countries; and a one-off OECD review of the UK's lifelong learning strategy. A revision of current survey work is needed to provide more policy-relevant and robust information.

c) New capability to be developed for the *benefit-cost analysis* of lifelong learning, and systematic experimentation (especially for evaluation), with particular emphasis on longitudinal research in a life-course context.

d) Regular use of *peer review and of inspections*, extended to cover learning beyond the education sector, and of 'learner voices'.

References

Alakeson, V. (2005) *Too Much, Too Late: Life chances and spending on education and training.* London: Social Market Foundation.

Aldridge, F. and Tuckett, A. (2008) *Counting the Cost: The NIACE survey on adult participation in learning 2008.* Leicester: NIACE.

Aldridge, F. and Tuckett, A. (2009) *Narrowing Participation: The NIACE survey on Adult Participation in Learning 2009.* Leicester: NIACE.

Aldridge, F., Lamb, H. and Tuckett, A. (2008) *Closing the Gap? A NIACE briefing on participation in adult learning by minority ethnic adults.* Leicester: NIACE.

Atwood, M. (2008) *Payback: Debt and the Shadow of Wealth.* London: Bloomsbury Publishing.

Basic Skills Agency (2008) *Financial Literacy with Trade Unions in the Workplace.* Leicester: NIACE.

Bauman, Z. (2006) *Liquid Times: Living in an age of uncertainty.* Cambridge: Polity Press.

Bekhradnia, B. (2004) *Credit Accumulation and Transfer, and the Bologna Process: An overview.* Oxford: HEPI.

Biesta, G. *et al.* (2008) 'Learning lives: Learning, identity and agency in the life course'. TLRP Research Briefing 51. London: TLRP.

Blackburn with Darwen Borough Council (2008) Evidence submitted to the Inquiry. (See www.lifelonglearninginquiry.org.uk)

Blakemore, S. J. and Frith, U. (2005) *The Learning Brain: Lessons for education.* Oxford: Blackwell.

Brassett-Grundy, A. (2004) 'Family life illustrated: transitions, responsibilities and attitudes', in Tom Schuller *et al.*, *The Benefits of Learning*, London: Routledge Falmer, pp.99–118.

Brighouse, T. (2009) *A Lifelong Learning Authority: IFLL Sector Paper 6.* Leicester: NIACE.

British Ministry of Reconstruction, Adult Education Committee (1919) *Final Report* (Chaired by Arthur L. Smith and commonly known as 'The 1919 Report') Cmnd 321 (1919), London: HMSO.

Cabinet Office (2000) *Winning the Generation Game.* London: The Stationery Office. p.47.

Cabinet Office (2009) *New Opportunities: Fair chances for the future.* London: The Stationery Office.

Callender, C. and Heller, D. (2009) 'The future of student funding in England', in Withers, K. (ed.) *First Class? Challenges and opportunities for the UK's university sector.* London: IPPR.

Cardiff University (2008) *Learning as Work: Teaching and learning processes in contemporary work organisations.* Evidence submitted to the Inquiry. (See www.lifelonglearninginquiry.org.uk)

Chevalier, A. and Feinstein, L. (2006) *Sheepskin or Prozac? The causal effect of education on mental health.* Centre for Economics of Education, London School of Economics.

Clancy, G. (2009) 'Labour demand: the need for workers.' Featured in *Economic and Labour Market Review.* Vol 3. No 2. February 2009. London: ONS.

Clark, J. (2007) *Voluntary Sector Skills Survey 2007.* London: UK Workforce Hub.

Claxton, G. and Lucas, B. (2009) *School as a Foundation for Lifelong Learning: The implications of a lifelong learning perspective for the re-imagining of school-age education: IFLL Sector Paper 1.* Leicester: NIACE.

Coats, D., and Lehki, R. (2008) *'Good Work': Job quality in a changing economy.* London: The Work Foundation.

Collingwood, R. G. (1946) 'Human nature and human history.' pp. 204–231 in *The Idea of History.* Oxford: Oxford University Press.

Commission for Disabled Staff in Lifelong Learning (2008) *From Compliance to Culture Change: Disabled staff working in lifelong learning – Final Report.* Leicester: NIACE.

Corney, M., Brown, N. and Fletcher, M. for Campaign for Learning (2008) *Higher Education and the Cuckoo in the Nest: Getting beyond the fixation with full-time study by young people.* London: Campaign for Learning.

Crick, B. (1998), *Education for Citizenship and the Teaching of Democracy in Schools.* London: QCA.

Crick, B. (2000) *Citizenship for 16-19-year-olds in Education and Training.* London: Further Education Funding Council.

Cunningham, I. *et al.* (2008) *A Declaration on Learning: How do you Respond?* Evidence submitted to the Inquiry. (See www.lifelonglearninginquiry.org.uk)

De Coulon, A., Marcenaro-Gutierrez, O. and Vignoles, A. (2007) *The Value of Basic Skills in the British Labour Market.* London: Centre for Economics of Education, Discussion Paper 77.

Dearden, L. *et al.* (2000) *Who Gains When Workers Train?* London: Institute for Fiscal Studies.

Dearing, R. (1997) *Higher Education in the Learning Society.* London: National Committee of Inquiry into Higher Education.

Department for Business, Enterprise and Regulatory Reform (BERR) (2009) *Building Britain's Future: New industry, new jobs.* London: BERR.

Department for Business, Innovation and Skills (BIS) and the Department for Culture, Media and Sport (DCMS) (2009) *Digital Britain: Final Report.* London: The Stationery Office.

Department for Education and Employment (DfEE) (1998) *The Learning Age: Renaissance for a new Britain.* Sheffield: DfEE.

Department for Education and Skills (DfES) (2007) *Designing Schools for Extended Services.* London: DfES, p.117.

Department for Innovation, Universities and Skills (DIUS) (2009a) *The Learning Revolution.* London: The Stationery Office.

Department for Innovation, Universities and Skills (DIUS) (2009b) *Skills for Life: Changing lives,* para 2.4. London: DIUS.

Department for Work and Pensions (DWP) (2009) *Building a Society for All Ages.* London: The Stationery Office.

Derbyshire County Council (2008). Evidence submitted to the Inquiry. (See www.lifelonglearninginquiry.org.uk)

Digital Britain Media Literacy Working Group (2009) *Report of the Digital Britain Media Literacy Working Group.* London: Digital Britain Media Literacy Working Group.

Eagleton, T. (2008) *The Meaning of Life.* Oxford: Oxford University Press.

Esping-Andersen, G. (1999) *The Social Foundations of Postindustrial Economies.* Oxford University Press.

European Foundation for the Improvement of Living and Working Conditions (2006) *Working Time and Work–Life Balance: A policy dilemma?* Dublin: European Foundation for the Improvement of Living and Working Conditions.

Eurostat (2008) *Adult Education Survey.* Featured in Boateng, S.K (2009) 'Population and social conditions,' *Eurostat Statistics in Focus,* 44/2009.

Feinstein, L. and Duckworth, K. (2006) *Are There Effects of Mothers' Post-16 Education on the Next Generation? Effects on children's development and mothers' parenting.* Centre for Research on the Wider Benefits of Learning, Institute of Education.

Feinstein, L. *et al.* (2008a) *The Social and Personal Benefits of Learning: A summary of key research findings.* Centre for Research on the Wider Benefits of Learning, Institute of Education.

Feinstein, L. *et al.* (2008b) *Foresight Mental Capital and Well-being Project. Learning through life: future challenges.* London: The Government Office for Science.

Felstead, A. *et al.* (2007) *Skills at Work, 1986 to 2006.* University of Oxford: SKOPE.

Felstead, A. (2009) 'Are jobs in Wales high skilled and high quality? Baselining the One Wales vision and tracking recent trends.' *Contemporary Wales,* 21(1).

Field, J. (2009) *Well-being and Happiness: IFLL Thematic Paper 4.* Leicester: NIACE.

Fletcher, M. (2008) *Mind the Gap: Funding adults in further and higher education.* London: National Skills Forum.

Fryer, B. (1997) *Learning in the 21st Century: First report of the National Advisory Group for Continuing Education and Lifelong Learning.* London: National Advisory Group for Continuing Education and Lifelong Learning.

Fryer, B. (2009, forthcoming) *Citizenship, Belonging and Lifelong Learning: IFLL Thematic Paper 8.* Leicester: NIACE.

FSA (2007) *The Future Of Lifelong Learning – Response to call for evidence around learning in the workplace.* Evidence submitted to the Inquiry. (See www.lifelonglearninginquiry.org.uk)

Fullick, L. (2009) *Poverty Reduction and Lifelong Learning: IFLL Thematic Paper 6.* Leicester: NIACE.

Furlong, A., Cartmel, F., Biggart, A., Sweeting, H. and West, P. (2003) *Youth Transitions: Patterns of vulnerability and processes of social inclusion.* Edinburgh: Scottish Executive.

Gosling, M. (2009) *Where Now for the Unskilled and the Low Paid? Positioning paper.* London: City & Guilds Centre for Skills Development.

Government Equalities Office (2009) *Flexible Working: Benefits and Barriers: Perceptions of working parents*. London: Government Equalities Office.

Government Office for Science (2008) *Foresight Mental Capital and Wellbeing Project: Final project report*, London: GOS.

Green, A. *et al.* (2008) *Education, Equality and Social Cohesion: A comparative analysis*. London: Palgrave Macmillan.

Hammond, C. and Feinstein, L. (2006) *Are Those Who Flourished at School Healthier Adults? What role for adult education?* Centre for Research on the Wider Benefits of Learning, Institute of Education.

Harper, S. (2009) *Demographic Change, Generations and the Life Course*. Oxford: Oxford Institute of Ageing, p.7.

Higher Education Policy Institute (HEPI) (2009) *Male and Female Participation and Progression in HE*. Oxford: HEPI.

Hirsch, F. (1976) *The Social Limits to Growth*. London: Routledge & Kegan Paul.

HM Government (2009). *Building a Society for all Ages*. Cm 7655. London: The Stationery Office.

HM Treasury (2003) *The Green Book: Appraisal and evaluation in central government*. London: The Stationery Office.

Hodgson, A. and Spours K. (2009) *Collaborative Local Learning Ecologies: Reflections on the governance of lifelong learning in England: IFLL Sector Paper 6*. Leicester: NIACE.

Howard, U. (2009) *FE Colleges in a New Culture of Adult and Lifelong Learning: IFLL Sector Paper 7*. Leicester: NIACE.

Illich, I., *et al.* (1977) *Disabling Professions*. London: Marion Boyars.

Innocent, N. (2009) *How Museums, Libraries and Archives Contribute to Lifelong Learning: IFLL Sector Paper 10*. Leicester: NIACE.

International Commission on Education for the Twenty-first Century (1996) *Learning: The Treasure Within. Report to UNESCO of the International Commission on Education for the Twenty-first Century*. Paris: UNESCO Publishing.

Involve (2005) *People & Participation: How to put citizens at the heart of decision-making*. London: Involve.

James, K. (2001) *Prescribing Learning*. Leicester: NIACE.

Jenkins, A. (2009) *Mental Health and Well-being in Older Adults: IFLL Public Value Paper 5*. Leicester: NIACE.

Johnson C. *et al.* (2009) *Student Income and Expenditure Survey 2007/08: English-domiciled students*, DIUS Research Report 09 05. London: DIUS.

Kallen, D. and Bengtsson, J. (1973) *Recurrent Education: A strategy for lifelong learning*. Paris: Centre for Educational Research and Innovation, OECD.

Keep, E., Mayhew, K., and Payne, J. (2006). 'From skills revolution to productivity miracle – not as easy as it sounds?' *Oxford Review of Economic Policy*, 22, 4, 539–559.

Kennedy, H. (1997) *Learning Works: Widening participation in education*. Coventry: FEFC.

Kenway, P. and Blanden, J. (2009) 'Poverty, inequality and social mobility', in Uberoi, V. *et al.* (eds.) *Options for a New Britain*. London: Macmillan. pp.51–71.

Kirkwood, T. *et al.* (2009) *Mental Capital and Well-being: Making the most of ourselves in the 21st century*. London: The Government Office for Science.

Knox, F. (2007). *Differential Policy and Implementation Discourses on Lifelong Learning in the NHS*. Evidence submitted to the Inquiry.

Kuh, D. and Ben-Shlomo, Y. (eds) (2004) *A Life Course Approach to Chronic Disease Epidemiology*. New York: Oxford University Press.

Lamb, P. and Taylor, C. (2009) *The Impact of Learning as a Family: A model for the 21st Century: IFLL Sector Paper 9*. Leicester: NIACE.

Lamb, P. *et al.* (2009) *Providing the Evidence: The impact of wider family learning*. Leicester: NIACE.

Layard, R. (2005) *Happiness: Lessons from a new science*. London: Penguin.

Layard, R. and Dunn, J. (2009) *A Good Childhood: Searching for values in a competitive age*. London: Penguin.

Leadbeater, C., Bartlett, J. and Gallagher, N. (2008) *Making it Personal*. London: Demos.

Lee, M. (2007) *Improving Services and Support for Older People with Mental Health Problems* and *Promoting Mental Health and Well-being in Later Life*, UK Inquiry into Mental Health and Well-Being in Later Life, Age Concern England. Evidence submitted to the Inquiry. (See www.lifelonglearninginquiry.org.uk)

Leitch Review of Skills (2006) *Prosperity for All in the Global Economy: World class skills*. London: The Stationery Office.

Libraries and Information East Midlands (2008) Evidence submitted to the Inquiry. (See www.lifelonglearninginquiry.org.uk)

LLUK (2008) *Annual Workforce Diversity Profile 2006/07*. London: LLUK.

Lochrie, M. (2009) *Lifelong Learning and the Early Years: IFLL Sector Paper 3*. Leicester: NIACE.

LSC (2007) *National Employer Skills Survey 2007: Main report*. Coventry: LSC.

LSC (2008) *Post-16 Education: Learner participation and outcomes in England 2007/08*. London: LSC.

Lucas, B. and Claxton, G. (2009) *Wider Skills for Learning*. Paper for National Endowment for Science, Technology and the Arts (NESTA). London: NESTA.

Matrix Knowledge Group (2009a) *Lifelong Learning and Crime: An analysis of the cost-effectiveness of in-prison educational and vocational interventions: IFLL Public Value Paper 2*. Leicester: NIACE.

Matrix Knowledge Group (2009b) *Lifelong Learning and Well-being: An analysis of the relationship between adult learning and subjective well-being: IFLL Public Value Paper 3*. Leicester: NIACE.

Mauger, S. (2009) *Technological Change: IFLL Thematic Paper 2*. Leicester: NIACE.

McNair, S. (2009a) *Demography and Lifelong Learning: IFLL Thematic Paper 1*. Leicester: NIACE.

McNair, S. (2009b) *Migration, Communities and Lifelong Learning: IFLL Thematic Paper 3*. Leicester: NIACE.

Milburn, A. (2009) *Unleashing Aspiration*. London: Cabinet Office.

Morris, E. (2009) *Independent Review of ICT User Skills*. London: DIUS.

Moser, C. (1999) *A Fresh Start: Improving literacy and numeracy*. Sheffield: DfEE.

Mountfield, H. (2009) *Age Discrimination and Education: A legal briefing paper*. Leicester: NIACE.

Moynagh. M. and Worsley, R. (2009) *Changing Lives, Changing Business: Seven life stages in the 21st Century*. London: A & C Black.

National Committee of Inquiry into Higher Education (1997) *Higher Education in the Learning Society (Dearing Report)*. DfEE: London.

National Skills Forum (2009) *Closing the Gender Skills Gap*. London: National Skills Forum.

National Union of Students (2009) *Five Foundations for an Alternative Higher Education Funding System for England*. London: NUS.

NIACE (forthcoming) *Education for Employability and Employability Skills*. Leicester: NIACE.

Nordic Network for Adult Learning (2007) *Future Competencies. A report from The Think Tank on Future Competencies.* Nordic Network for Adult Learning, p.6.

OECD (1973) *Recurrent Education: A strategy for lifelong learning.* Paris: OECD.

OECD (1975) *Educational Leave of Absence: A six-country study.* Paris: Centre for Educational Research and Innovation, OECD.

OECD (2007) *Evidence in Education: Linking research and policy.* Paris: OECD.

OECD (2008) *Growing Unequal? Income distribution and poverty in OECD Countries.* Paris: OECD.

OECD (2009) *Highlights from Education at a Glance 2008.* Paris: OECD.

ONS (2000) *UK Time Use Survey 2000.* London: HMSO.

ONS (2005). *Focus on Older People. (2005 Edition).* Basingstoke: Palgrave Macmillan.

ONS (2008a) *First Release: Internet access 2008: Households and individuals.* London: HMSO.

ONS (2008b) *Labour Force Survey.* London: HMSO.

The Open University (2008) Evidence submitted to the Inquiry. (See www.lifelonglearninginquiry.org.uk)

Plant, H. and Ward, J. (2009, forthcoming) *Lifelong Learning and Sustainable Development: IFLL Thematic Paper 9.* Leicester: NIACE.

Reder, S. and Bynner, J. (2009) (Eds.) *Tracking Adult Literacy and Numeracy Skills: Findings from longitudinal research.* Oxford: Routledge.

Sabates, R. *et al.* (2006) *Determination and Pathways of Progression to Level 2 Qualifications: Evidence from the NCDS and BHPS.* Centre for Research on the Wider Benefits of Learning, Institute of Education.

Sainsbury Centre (2008) *Short-changed: Spending on prison mental health care.* London: Sainsbury Centre for Mental Health.

Sandbrook, I. (2009) *A Learning City Perspective: IFLL Sector Paper 5.* Leicester: NIACE.

The Scarman Trust (2005) *Analysis of Community Champions Programme – Award winners 2002 and 2003.* Evidence submitted to the Inquiry.

Schuller, T. (2009) *Crime and Lifelong Learning: IFLL Thematic Paper 5.* Leicester: NIACE.

Schuller, T. and Field, J. (2000) 'Networks, norms and trust: explaining patterns of lifelong learning in Scotland and Northern Ireland', in Frank Coffield (ed.) *Differing visions of a Learning Society*, Vol 2, Bristol: Policy Press, pp. 95–118.

Schwartz, B. (2004) *The Paradox of Choice: Why more is less*. New York: Ecco/HarperCollins.

SCVO (2008) *Voluntary Sector Skills Survey 2007 – Scotland*. Edinburgh: Scottish Council for Voluntary Organisations (unpublished).

Selwyn, N. *et al.* (2005) *Adult Learning in the Digital Age*. London: Routledge.

Sen, A.K. (1985) *Commodities and Capabilities*. Amsterdam: North Holland.

Sen, A.K. (1992) *Inequality Re-examined*. Cambridge (Mass): Harvard University Press.

Sen, A.K. (2009) *The Idea of Justice*. London: Penguin.

Simpson, L. (2009) *The Private Training Market in the UK: IFLL Sector Paper 2*. Leicester: NIACE.

Sloane, P.J. *et al.* (2007) *Training, Job Satisfaction and Establishment Performance*, Skills for Business Research Report 22.

Sylva, K. *et al.* (2007) *The Effective Provision of Pre-school Education (EPPE) project: Final report*. Nottingham: DfES.

Tamkin, P. (2005) *The Contribution of Skills to Business Performance*. Brighton: Institute for Employment Studies.

The Data Service (2009) *Statistical First Release: Post-16 Education & Skills: Learner participation, outcomes and Level of Highest Qualification Held* (DS/SFR3). London: The Data Service.

The Health and Social Care Information Centre (2008) *Community Care Statistics 2008: Supported residents (adults), England*. Leeds: The Health and Social Care Information Centre.

Toynbee, P. and Walker, D. (2008) *Unjust Rewards*. London: Granta.

Tuckett, A. (2008) 'They march you up to the top of the hill, and they march you down again: Trends in adult learning in England' in Zeitschrift fur Weiterbildungsforschung 2 (2008), pp. 49–60, DVV, Bonn.

Uberoi *et al.* (eds) (2009) *Options for a New Britain*. London: Macmillan. p.57.

UKCES (2009a) *Ambition 2020: World-class skills and jobs for the UK*. London: UKCES.

UKCES (2009b) *The Employability Challenge: Full report.* London: UKCES.

UKCES (forthcoming) *The Value of Skills.* London: UKCES.

Unison (2007) *Learning and Organising in the 21st Century: The trade union role.* Evidence submitted to the Inquiry. (See www.lifelonglearninginquiry.org.uk)

Unwin, L. (2009) *Sensuality, Sustainability and Social Justice: Vocational education in changing times.* Professional Inaugural Lecture. London: Institute of Education.

Unwin, L., Felstead, A. and Fuller, A. (2008) *Learning At Work: Towards more 'expansive' opportunities.* Institute of Education, University of London; Cardiff University; University of Southampton.

Watson, D. (2009, forthcoming) *Lifelong Learning and the Future of Higher Education: IFLL Sector Paper 8.* Leicester: NIACE.

Weko, T. (2004) *New Dogs and Old Tricks: What can the UK teach the US about university education?* Oxford: HEPI.

Wilkinson, R. and Pickett, K. (2009) *The Spirit Level: Why more equal societies almost always do better.* London: Penguin.

Williams, J. and Wilson, T. (2009, forthcoming) *Work and Learning: IFLL Thematic Paper 7.* Leicester: NIACE.

Williams, R. (1990) *What I Came to Say.* London: Hutchinson Radius.

Woman Take Part Framework (2008) *'Moving On Up': the role of lifelong learning in women's journeys to active citizenship.* Evidence submitted to the Inquiry. (See www.lifelonglearninginquiry.org.uk)

Women and Work Commission (2006) *Shaping a Fairer Future.* London: Department of Trade and Industry.

Young, M. (1958) *The Rise of the Meritocracy: 1870–2033: An essay on education and equality.* London: Thames & Hudson.

Zhang Xinsheng (2009) 'The urgent need to discuss lifelong learning', *Education Alliance Quarterly,* No 3, pp.8–11.

Ziliak, S. and McCloskey, D. (2008) *The Cult of Statistical Significance.* Ann Arbor: University of Michigan Press.

Annexe A   Agenda for an intelligent system
Measures, methods and milestones

How to move from here to there? We have summarised our recommendations in the previous chapter. This Annexe sets out, quite schematically, how we might know if we are making progress towards the vision sketched out in *Chapter 1*; what is needed in order for us to build a better knowledge base; and a timetable for taking our recommendations forward.

Measuring progress

'The State of Learning'

One basic requirement for an intelligent system is to have information which is consistent over time. We propose a regular *State of Learning* report, to be published every three years. This is for use at national level, with the devolved administrations preparing their own, but using as far as possible a common template. It could also be used at local or other levels, suitably adapted, as a way of getting feedback at each level.

Developing the content of the report is itself something which should be a matter of broad public debate. The debate should focus our collective minds on what is important to measure; on what is important but cannot be measured; and on how the measurement process should itself be formative not punitive, i.e. it should enable those involved to improve rather than punishing them for failure to achieve targets.

Below is a suggested outline to kickstart that debate. Not surprisingly, we propose using our four-stage model as the basis. Clearly, there would be a large number of specific variables included within this. At the core should be a set of statistical measures, but the report should also include qualitative and evaluative information.

Individual measures

● Participation rates

Bringing together the various surveys such as the Labour Force Survey, the annual NIACE work and the National Adult Learning Survey (NALS) into a coherent form, covering a full range of individual variables (gender, ethnicity, disability etc), but also good regional and even local information.

- Qualification levels

  Detailed information on qualifications is already gathered at the different levels of the education system. We need a more grounded understanding of the relationship between supply and demand for qualifications, especially how this varies across regions and sectors. A further issue is how the system can enable experience to be adequately recognised.

- Other achievement measures

  Participation leads to achievement but not in a way that is recognised by certification. A better balanced system will bring with it appropriate means of signalling learning achievements, particularly for groups for whom motivation to learn is traditionally low.

Organisational measures: provision and expenditure

- Workplace measures

  Bringing together Investors in People (IiP) and National Employer Skills Survey (NESS) data in a more robust form, using the IiP template and strengthening the NESS data on skills and expenditure patterns. Other initiatives such as *The Learning Revolution's* pledge system also relate to organisational commitment to learning.

- Community and voluntary sector provision

  Stocktake on the state of adult and community learning and of the voluntary sector, including self-help learning organisations, such as U3As.

- Media-provided opportunities

  Broadcast and narrowcast media are a hugely important source of learning opportunities and materials. The point of departure here could be the debate around public service obligations.

- Innovation

  Descriptive and evaluative material on significant new developments. To give this shape, it could be related to specific criteria such as improving learning's contribution to equality and diversity, or to sustainable development.

- Learner voice

  Material from a cross-section of learners on their experience of the system, partly on a panel basis to give continuity.

- Capacity-building

  Report from LLUK or its successor on workforce development, including intermediaries.

- Building the knowledge base

  Update on learning-relevant research from different disciplines, with specific focus on outcomes and effects.

Using the 'State of Learning'

The *State of Learning* report should be formally prepared for and submitted to the Joint Committee/Standing Commission we recommended in Chapter 9, with the relevant government department charged with its publication. In addition, the report will speak to other government departments, and to local authorities. In England, the departments most directly concerned are Health, Work and Pensions, Justice, Communities and Local Government, and Culture, Media and Sport, for reasons we have given throughout this report.

There should be a group of committed stakeholders for whom its publication should also be an occasion for significant debate. These would include employers and trade unions; the voluntary sector; media organisations.

The Joint Committee will be responsible for promoting the results, and for drawing implications for the next triennium – in other words, it will create a rolling three-year agenda for action.

Linking to wider measures

The *State of Learning* report, and the work leading up to it, should be linked as appropriate to Public Service Agreements (PSAs) and their related indicators. Of the 30 current PSAs, lifelong learning has direct or indirect significance for around half.

It is central to PSAs 1 and 2 on productivity and skills; PSA 3 on the contribution of migration to economic growth; PSAs 10–12 on child poverty and health, through parental/family learning; PSAs 15–17, directly; PSAs 18, 19, 21, 24, 25 on Stronger Communities; and PSA 28 on a more sustainable world.

On some of these, the contribution of lifelong learning is already covered – for instance, the UKCES will be the main source on those related to productivity and employment. Where this is not the case, it should happen through new or existing channels.

International benchmarking

Some comparative information will be available anyway, from international surveys, notably from the EU, and from the OECD. The UN's Human Development Index also provides broad-brush background. A particularly relevant model is the Composite Learning Index (CLI) produced by the Canadian Council for Learning, which uses 17 broad indicators to generate widespread debate amongst policy-makers, communities and researchers on the state of learning in Canada, linking it directly to economic and social well-being (see www.ccl-cca.ca/ccl). This is also the inspiration for the emerging European Lifelong Learning Index (ELLI). A further useful source will be the OECD's Programme of International Assessment on Adult Competences (PIAAC), due to begin in 2011.

However, information needs to be shaped, interpreted and used. We need to be more proactive, in learning from other countries about how best we might carry out the measurement process; helping, in return to shape the process of comparative information collection and use; and setting up fruitful ways of actually using insights from this comparative work.

The goal must be to have a clear sense of how the information is to be used to inform progress. We recommend:

- engaging in a *benchmarking exercise*, with a small group (six to eight) of selected countries, to carry forward the ideas behind our *State of Learning* process; and
- commissioning a *review of UK strategy* on lifelong learning from the OECD.

Building intelligence

Systemic improvement entails the strengthening of the knowledge available, and constructive debate amongst practitioners, researchers and the public, as well as policy analysts. The UK has made good progress in strengthening its educational research.[1] The following are specific categories where there is more to be done.

The effects of learning: broader and longer analysis

The rationale we set out in *Chapter 2* contained evidence for the economic and social effects of learning. We need to expand and refine the way we go about estimating these, and relating them to costs. This must be done in a broad and imaginative way, assembling a range of different types of evidence, using different

---

[1] Most evidently through the ESRC's Teaching and Learning Research Programme, see www.tlrp.ac.uk

techniques but a common language. Longitudinal data and more multi-method research, within a life-course approach, will be particularly valuable.

Systematic experimentation

The increasing use of pilots to test out possible policy innovations is welcome. We propose strengthening this approach, with a greater use of experimentation, small and large, local and national. This should include randomised controlled trials, but these are certainly not the only form of experimentation. We need a clearer focus on finding out what works, in a manner that is useful for policy and practice.[2]

Voices and observations

There should be a strong learner voice on policy and practice, feeding their views into the system. This should build on the experience already gained of learner panels, and from other fields such as health. Online consultation with the learner voices can be made much more representative, and much more regular, than face-to-face, though the latter will still be valuable.

Inspection and peer review

The experience of the inspectorate is an underused source of useful knowledge, nationally and at area level. Sympathetic inspections could bridge some of the different fields of learning, for instance with community learning providers learning from workplace trainers via, and vice-versa. Similarly, peer reviews are also a useful form of systemic learning, to be encouraged within and across sectors.

Milestones

Putting the recommendations into play will take time. Here is our suggested timetable for some of the key components.

2010

- Establish Joint Committee/Standing Commission on Lifelong Learning.
- Launch debate on *State of Learning* report: content and process.
- Prepare inputs for next Comprehensive Spending Review, reflecting initial steps. to rebalancing of expenditure across the four stages.

---

[2] OECD (2007).

- Initiate (re)design of Learning Accounts and Learning Futurescard.
- Design initial set of transition entitlements.
- Initiate comparative benchmarking process with four to six countries.
- Execute latest NALS survey, and the Skills for Life survey.
- Review NESS.
- Develop a consistent approach to reporting on lifelong learning expenditure across government.

2011

- Complete format for *State of Learning* report.
- Launch Learning Accounts, with priority entitlements.
- Decide on implementation of a national credit system, with date for full implementation.
- Allocate appropriate strategic responsibility to local authorities.
- Pilot Local Learning Exchanges.
- Review the state of play on the four capabilities of the citizens' curriculum.
- Initiate review of the implications of lifelong learning for teacher and early years training.
- Commission development work on the learning needs of the fourth stage.
- Preparation of Lifelong Learning Act, covering necessary statutory requirements.
- Initiate reframing of statistical information to reflect the four-stage model, notably on defining working age as extending to 75.
- Agree common reporting for employers on training performance and expenditure, including learning leave arrangements to be published in annual accounts from 2013 to coincide with the UKCES review of entitlements to training.

2012

- Publication of first *State of Learning* report.
- Universal broadband access achieved (cf *Digital Britain*).
- OECD review of lifelong learning strategy in the UK, linked to initial comparative benchmarking results.
- Introduce minimum local guarantee on the citizens' curriculum.
- Preparation of possible legislation.
- Revision of student funding; introduction of Dearing Grants.

2013

- Move to mode-free funding for all post-compulsory education.
- First Lifelong Learning Act.
- Stocktake on progress towards rebalancing resource distribution across the four stages, and on progress on learning leave.
- Update citizens' curriculum.

2015

- Second *State of Learning* report.

2018

- Third *State of Learning* report.

2020

- Achievement of rebalancing of resources across the four stages.

Annexe B   The Inquiry Commissioners

Professor Sir David Watson, Chair of the Commission
Professor of Higher Education Management, Institute of Education,
University of London

Professor John Field
Director, Division of Academic Innovation and Continuing Education,
University of Stirling

Professor Bob Fryer CBE
Former Chief Learning Advisor, Department of Health

Leisha Fullick
Pro-Director (London), Institute of Education, University of London

Dr Helen Gilchrist CBE
Former Principal, Bury College

Clare Hannah
Head of Organisational Development, EWS Railways

Professor Teresa Rees
Pro-Vice Chancellor, Cardiff University

David Sherlock CBE
Former Chief Inspector of the Adult Learning Inspectorate

Nick Stuart CB
Chair, NIACE Company Board

Tom Wilson
Head of Organisation and Services, TUC

Annexe C   Inquiry supplementary papers

All of the Inquiry supplementary papers are available to download from the Inquiry website (www.lifelonglearninginquiry.org.uk)

Thematic

McNair, S. (2009) *Demography and Lifelong Learning: IFLL Thematic Paper 1.*

Mauger, S. (2009) *Technological Change: IFLL Thematic Paper 2.*

McNair , S. (2009) *Migration, Communities and Lifelong Learning: IFLL Thematic Paper 3.*

Field, J. (2009) *Well-being and Happiness: IFLL Thematic Paper 4.*

Schuller, T. (2009) *Crime and Lifelong Learning: IFLL Thematic Paper 5.*

Fullick, L. (2009) *Poverty Reduction and Lifelong Learning: IFLL Thematic Paper 6.*

Williams, J. and Wilson, T. (2009, forthcoming) *Work and Learning: IFLL Thematic Paper 7.*

Fryer, B. (2009, forthcoming) *Lifelong Learning, Citizenship and Belonging: IFLL Thematic Paper 8.*

Plant, H. and Ward, J. (2009, forthcoming) *Lifelong Learning and Sustainable Development: IFLL Thematic Paper 9.*

Context

Williams, J., Aldridge, F., and McNair, S. (2009, forthcoming) *Lifelong Learning Expenditure, Participation and Funding Models.*

Mountfield, H. (2009, forthcoming) *Age Discrimination and Education: A Legal Briefing Paper.*

Sector

Claxton, G. and Lucas, B. (2009) *School as a foundation for lifelong learning: The implications of a lifelong learning perspective for the re-imagining of school-age education: IFLL Sector Paper 1.*

Simpson, L. (2009) *The Private Training Market in the UK: IFLL Sector Paper 2.*

Lochrie, M. (2009) *Lifelong Learning and the Early Years: IFLL Sector Paper 3.*

Brighouse, T. (2009) *A Lifelong Learning Authority: IFLL Sector Paper 4.*

Sandbrook, I. (2009) *A Learning City Perspective: IFLL Sector Paper 5.*

Hodgson, A. and Spours, K. (2009) *Collaborative Local Learning Ecologies: Reflections on the Governance of Lifelong Learning in England: IFLL Sector Paper 6.*

Howard, U. (2009) *FE Colleges in a New Culture of Adult and Lifelong Learning: IFLL Sector Paper 7.*

Watson, D. (2009) *Lifelong Learning and the Future of Higher Education: IFLL Sector Paper 8.*

Lamb, P. and Taylor, C. (2009, forthcoming) *The Impact of Learning as a Family: A Model for the 21st Century: IFLL Sector Paper 9.*

Innocent, N. (2009, forthcoming) *How Museums, Libraries and Archives Contribute to Lifelong Learning: IFLL Sector Paper 10.*

TBC (2009, forthcoming) *Lifelong Learning and the Voluntary and Community Sector: IFLL Sector Paper 11.*

Public value

Sabates, R. (2009) *The Impact of Lifelong Learning on Poverty Reduction: IFLL Public Value Paper 1.*

Matrix Knowledge Group (2009a) *Lifelong Learning and Crime: An Analysis of the Cost-effectiveness of In-prison Educational and Vocational Interventions: IFLL Public Value Paper 2.*

Matrix Knowledge Group (2009b) *Lifelong Learning and Well-being: An Analysis of the Relationship Between Adult Learning and Subjective Well-being: IFLL Public Value Paper 3.*

Bynner, J. (2009) *Lifelong Learning and Crime: A Life-course Perspective: IFLL Public Value Paper 4.*

Jenkins, A. (2009a, forthcoming) *Mental Health and Well-being in Older Adults: IFLL Public Value Paper 5.*

Jenkins, A. (2009b, forthcoming) *Neighbourhood Skills and Children's Attainment: IFLL Public Value Paper 6.*

Further work

Clyne, P. *et al* (2009, forthcoming) *Learning from the Past.*

Gallagher, J. *et al* (2009, forthcoming) *Inquiry into the Future for Lifelong Learning: The Scotland Perspective.*

Mauger, S. (2009) *Horizon Scanning and Scenario Development: The Future of Learning Infrastructures.*

Nolan, P. *et al* (2009, forthcoming) *Inquiry into the Future for Lifelong Learning: The Northern Ireland Perspective.*

Plant, H. (2009, forthcoming) *Summary of Learner Consultations.*

Index

Page numbers in *italics* are for information in figures and tables, e.g. birth rates, teenage 40, *41*, 91

Footnotes are indicated by 'n' after the page number, e.g. time (duration), costs of 76–9, 224, 226n

Names of organisations etc. are listed by their acronyms; the full forms of names are given in a separate 'List of acronyms and abbreviations'.